DICTIONARY OF CIVICS
AND GOVERNMENT

Dictionary of Civics and Government

By

Marjorie Tallman

With an introduction by
HARRY ELMER BARNES

THE PHILOSOPHICAL LIBRARY
NEW YORK

Copyright, 1953, by
The Philosophical Library
15 East 40th Street, New York, N. Y.

PRINTED IN THE UNITED STATES OF AMERICA
BY HALLMARK-HUBNER PRESS, INC., NEW YORK

INTRODUCTION
by

Harry Elmer Barnes

Today, the world trembles or totters on the rim of the abyss as the result of conflicts and struggles between rival political systems. The so-called free nations stand opposed to those which represent various types and shades of totalitarianism.

If the free nations are to survive in this ordeal, democracy must be made more honest and efficient. To bring about any such happy and salutary result, we must have an informed electorate. The voters must have available to them an accurate and extensive body of information which touches upon and encompasses the whole broad field of political experience and its cogent borderlands. Today, we are exposed to a vast and ever-increasing mass of verbiage on public questions which reaches us through our eyes in newspapers, moving pictures and television, and through our ears over the radio. There is no dearth of material available, but it all too often lacks both technical knowledge and precision in terminology, even when there is no intent to deceive or mislead the populace.

Political education and discussion will hardly produce any decisive improvement in our democratic public life unless both the disseminators of information and their audiences actually know what they are talking about and realize its import for our welfare. Words may produce mental tyranny, as Stuart Chase has suggested, but they are likely also to create disaster if the verbiage is compounded of factual ignorance and semantic obsolescence. Precise knowledge is necessary both to enable us to detect false ideologies and erratic programs and to make it possible for us to recognize and follow sound advice.

And it is not merely a matter of mastering the terminology of politics and allied disciplines at any given moment. The problems and responsibilities are dynamic. Our culture of today, in a mechanized and electronic age, is one which changes rapidly, and political institutions and practices, though they lag behind mechanical changes, are none the less being altered and extended as never before in human experience. A man who was relatively well informed on public issues, agencies and institutions a generation ago is a babe in the semantic and functional woods today if he fails to keep up with the political procession.

Hence, there is a very real and practical need for a book which constitutes a comprehensive and reliable compendium of political, economic, sociological and educational concepts and terminology, thoroughly attuned to events and issues as they stand before us at the mid-century. Miss Marjorie Tallman has here produced such a book—a most commendable performance which gives evidence of professional industry, intellectual acumen, and precision of statement. To it the student and the alert citizen alike can turn for rapid and convenient reference about any subject which is likely to arise in the public life of our time. There is no longer any excuse for either blank ignorance or haziness of thought and information on our public issues. The book can well serve as a major item of armament in the intellectual arsenal of our democracy.

With the increasing wave of current disclosures which have alarmingly revealed the vulnerability of those democratic nations which still remain outside the iron curtains to the infiltration of foreign and undemocratic ideologies, it has become more and more apparent that extreme vigilance must be exercised to counteract such subversive activities. This requires, as we have pointed out above, wide, exact, and up-to-date information.

The student of government or the alert citizen who has already shown some concern or gained some experience on the city, state or federal level is likely to find this volume of great value and convenience. Here, he or she may gain quickly and accurately a fuller knowledge and more penetrating insight into the operation of our ever more complicated democratic processes, presented as they are in this compendium in their bare essentials and made readily available. For example, the machinery employed in the operations of our legislative bodies is admirably summed up in such items as those describing standing committees, the ranking of members of committees, the manner in which bills are handled in committees, the complicated application of the cloture rule, and the provisions dealing with the disciplining of members of Congress or state legislatures. Non-voting—the failure of the public to exercise the right of suffrage—threatens the vitality of American democracy. The problems connected with this crucial matter are illuminated by gaining familiarity with the ballot, voting qualifications, electoral laws and the like.

Political problems are inseparably linked to economic issues, and this *Dictionary* enables the student or citizen to find his way clearly through this maze. For example, the much discussed farm problem is clarified and simplified by a concise description of the "parity" program and by an outline of the tenets of and aspirations of the Farm Bloc. We can also follow with intelligence and insight the multitude of regulations to which business is subjected and comprehend better the nature and extent of the ever-increasing group of federal agencies which have the responsibility of protecting the consumer and the investor. The ever-growing burden of taxation oppresses everyone above the level of the indigent classes. The situation can be better understood by reference to the types and incidence of taxation and the laws and agencies involved in the collection of taxes.

The increasing role of labor in government is expressed in the legislation, boards and agencies which seek to adjust the interests of labor to those of the employer and the public. Full coverage is given to the extensive protection of the working population and the dependent groups through labor legislation, social security laws, and administrative agencies. The details connected with the increasingly critical and important problem of minority rights and civil liberties are set forth adequately and in illuminating fashion.

For better or worse, the United States has vastly extended its interests and responsibilities over the face of the planet until, today, international issues often seem to overshadow domestic problems. This has opened a whole new vista of contacts, agencies, and activities which receive thorough recognition and coverage in this book—one of the more novel aspects of the compendium. In no other realm of public life is there greater need for modernizing our perspective and terminology and widening our horizons.

Miss Tallman's book thus provides us with an opportunity to familiarize ourselves not only with political terminology "from A to Z," but also with all relevant details from a writ of certiorari to such broad issues and responsibilities as the National Labor Relations Board, the United Nations, and the international organizations now seeking to change the pattern of world relationships.

All who come into contact with this volume will not only be likely to extend their personal gratitude to the author but are also certain to expand the scope and precision of their information, thus becoming better and more useful citizens of our American democracy.

DICTIONARY OF CIVICS
AND GOVERNMENT

A

abjuration: Forswearing of allegiance originally by those seeking to leave one country in order to become established in another.

abolition: Doing away with something completely. The program favored by the Liberty Party in the United States in regard to slavery in the decade before the Civil War.

abrogation: Annulment by act or decree. For example the Platt Amendment to the Cuban Constitution was abrogated in 1933.

absentee voting: A practice whereby qualified voters unable to be at the polls on election day may return special ballots to the proper authorities in each state.

academic freedom: With the recent attempts to curb those advocating views held to be subversive many in responsible teaching or administrative, educational positions have begun to question how far such remedies may be an encroachment upon their much valued "academic freedom," that is their right to teach or write what they wish without any censorship. They are also concerned about the problem of the so-called "loyalty oaths" required of the teaching staff by state law, or by University Boards of Trustees. Some liberals feel that in avoiding one danger the legislator runs into another. This group would insist that every one have the freedom to speak what he pleased until he has actually committed the "overt" act which satisfies the constitutional definition of treason. Others make an equally strong case for checking the "infection" before it has time to spread, and would advocate the removal from a teaching position of any one even under suspicion of supporting "foreign ideologies."

accident insurance: A phase of workmen's compensation (q.v.)

acclamation: Loud applause usually associated with the presentation of a name at a Nominating Convention (q.v.)

1

accommodation: In the social field a means of adjustment of different national or racial groups in such a way that the identity of the groups is not lost, but possible differences are lessened by mutual acceptance, and the development of working arrangements tolerated by all and consciously worked out.

accountability: The idea that the candidate is "accountable," that is, responsible to the voters who selected him is one of the basic ideas of representative government; on the other hand the question of how far the legislator is accountable to the political party whose backing he has received is a matter that may lead in the opposite direction if the party abuses its powers. The party may under these circumstances promote democracy or if concerned only with its selfish ends limit it.

acquittal: The decision rendered in a court of law finding the accused person not guilty. An acquitted person may not be tried again for the same offense.

actuary: An expert who calculates insurance risks and premiums.

Adamson Act: An act of Congress passed in 1916 which established an eight-hour day for all railroad employees involved in interstate commerce.

adjournment: Termination of a session of a legislature. The Reorganization Act of 1946 provides that the two houses of Congress shall adjourn not later than the last day of July unless otherwise provided for by Congress.

adjusted compensation: A bonus paid by Congress to veterans of World War I in 1924 who were honorably discharged. A cash payment went to those who were to receive fifty dollars or less on the basis of a payment of one dollar a day for domestic service and one dollar and a quarter for foreign service; those entitled to more were given it in the form of paid up life insurance which in 1936 was made cashable.

adjutant: The military officer whose duties are concerned with correspondence and the keeping of records. The Adjutant-General of the Department of the Army supervises the postal service of the Army, communications with the public, the keeping of records, and the handling of matters dealing with the matters of military personnel.

administration: The management of public affairs which rests largely on carrying policy into effect and is more commonly the work of the executive agencies. The alert citizen is growing more aware of the importance and difficulties involved in carrying out the law as contrasted with the more common practice of taking an interest only in the passing of the law.

administrative law: That collection of law which includes the regulatory details of administrative agencies, their decisions, the rights of individuals involved, and also those of the public officials concerned. These laws may be on the national, state or municipal level.

administrative reorganization: The necessity for rearranging the duties or responsibilities of the various national executive departments has been especially called upon with the rising complexity of government. This search for increased efficiency and logical grouping of related functions led to many proposed reforms some of which have been carried out in the Reorganization Act of 1949. The Hoover Commission (q.v.) had presented an overwhelming quantity of valuable suggestions of enormous range. One in the process of being carried out was incorporated as the Military Unification Act. One not yet implemented has to do with the proposed creation of a Welfare Department.

admiralty jurisdiction: Authority to try cases having to do with maritime contracts, or any other matter arising out of navigation of any public waterway or the Great Lakes. These cases are tried in federal district courts.

admission of new states: Except for the original thirteen states and a few other variations such as Maine and Vermont (created out of older states by acts of Congress), all other states have been admitted to the United States after going through a stage as territories and then have had their Constitution and their requests for admission approved by Congress. *See* NORTHWEST ORDINANCE

admissions tax: A Federal excise tax of twenty percent imposed upon the price of admission to various types of amusements, such as theater, moving picture, concert or other types of entertainment.

adult education: A program of education for the mature individual. At first intended primarily to help the foreign born residents to complete the requirements of naturalization, the range of courses has become amazingly varied. The traditional courses are provided for those who have been unable to complete high school and wish to obtain such a diploma through night school courses, but many additional courses are being offered for those who want to take advantage of their increased leisure time by taking culturally beneficial courses, or those in handicraft, art, music or literary appreciation, or in vocational or professional fields.

ad valorem: Latin for according to the value. Applied to taxation it means the figuring out of duties on commodities in proportion to their value without regard to weight or quantity.

advisory opinion: The official view of a court given before the instigation of any legal proceedings as a request for information. This situation may occur in regard to an international tribunal such as the International Court of Justice, or in connection with some state court. However, the United States Supreme Court took a stand in Washington's time and has maintained it ever since that it will give no opinions on abstract law in regard to a case. All decisions must be on individual suits. *See* CONCURRING OPINIONS. DISSENTING OPINIONS.

"affected with a public interest": Originally this phrase was used to justify the federal government's regulation of public utilities because of the tremendous dependence of the public upon the type of the service rendered. Now by the more recent Supreme Court decisions it would seem that any type of business may be subject to regulation. "A state is free to adopt whatever economic policy may reasonably be deemed to promote the public welfare" is the latest view of this situation.

Affidavit: A sworn written statement, especially one made under oath before an authorized official.

affiliation: Close association with. The American Federation of Labor has over one hundred unions officially connected with it but it has over 1200 affiliated local unions.

affirmation: A statement made under conditions where an oath would normally be used, allowed to a person whose religious or moral scruples prevents his swearing. Quakers may come under this category.

agenda: A memoranda of items to be considered at a meeting or conference.

agent provocateur (labor spy): A French expression meaning one who becomes associated with a certain group, and who may by pretended sympathy lead the group to commit illegal acts. It has been used in America to refer particularly to labor spies (q.v.) who may join a union to provoke disturbances.

agrarian: Having to do with matters of land and fields of interest to the farmer. The Agrarian Crusade represents a campaign of the farmers and their supporters to obtain political and economic reforms culminating in the rise of the Populist Party (q.v.) in the 1890's and the farm bloc (q.v.) in the 1920's.

Agricultural Adjustment Act of 1933: A law passed as part of the "New Deal" Program to help overcome the depression by aiding the farmer. The "processor" of certain basic farm products, at first only wheat and pork, was to pay a tax to the federal government out of which a fund was to be set up to pay a "bonus" to those farmers who had cooperated in reducing production. By restricting production through these means the price of wheat and bacon was to rise and provide the farmer with a greater purchasing power and thus be an added stimulus to industry also. However the Act was found unconstitutional in 1936 because the measure was not for the general welfare, and was an encroachment on States' Rights (q.v.).

Agricultural Act of 1938 (Second A.A.A.): The measure was intended to serve the same purpose as the preceding act but eliminated the processing tax and had soil conservation provision and regulated the flow of agricultural commodities in interstate commerce. The law was found to be constitutional on these later points. The law establishes an "ever normal granary" (q.v.) Loans are provided for under the program of the Commodity Credit Corporation. (q.v.) by which the farmer gains parity prices (q.v.). *See also,* AIKEN ACT of 1948

agricultural credit: A continuing program to make available to farmers the essential loans their survival and the balance of our economy depends upon. Even under the Populists (q.v.)

farmers were asking for government aid for long term loans at low interest rates. By 1916 the Farm Credit Administration in the Department of Agriculture was helping out the farmer considerably in this respect. Federal Intermediate Credit Banks were established by the Agricultural Credits Act of 1923 to help by discounting paper (loans) of agricultural credit corporations, banks for cooperatives, livestock loan companies, and similar financial institutions. The New Deal provided such additional assistance especially in the Bankhead-Jones Farm Tenant Act and like measures.

agronomist: One who is a student of that branch of agriculture dealing with the theory and practice of field-crop production and soil management.

"aid and comfort to the enemy": If a person can be shown to have openly attempted to perform such an act, he is subject to indictment for treason. However there must be two witnesses to the giving of such aid to make a constitutional basis for such an accusation.

Aiken Act of 1948: Legislation supplementing the Agricultural Act of 1938 (q.v.) which extended supports, largely ranging from sixty to ninety percent of parity (q.v.), on some nineteen commodities according to a sliding scale of payments depending on abnormally large or below normal supply.

air raid warden: A volunteer worker in the Civilian Defense program who may serve in a variety of activities in preparation for an unexpected air attack.

air subsidies: The Civil Aeronautical Board administers what amounts to a subsidy by fixing the compensation to be paid to an airline for carrying mail. The liberal air mail contracts helped the struggling air transport companies in the beginning to survive and have since advanced the development of passenger service to a great extent.

Alabama Claims: An arbitration award (1871) was given to the United States of $15,500,000 because Great Britain was held to have violated her obligation as a neutral in allowing the outfitting of the confederate ship "Alabama" which did great damage to United States shipping during the Civil War.

Alaska: An incorporated terrtiory (q.v.) which the United

States bought from Russia in 1867 as a gesture of appreciation for Russian cooperation during the Civil War, and which was derisively called Seward's ice box, because its present natural resources were not at that time known. Its half million square miles make it as large as California, Texas, and Montana combined, but with a population of only 128,000 (1950) about one-third of whom are Aleuts, Eskimos, and Indians. The governor is appointed by the President of the United States, and a territorial delegate provides representation in Congress but does not have the right to vote. Congress has the seldom-exercised right to veto laws passed by the territorial legislature. Since all continental territories have become states, Alaskans have been putting forward their claims vigorously for such a chance, though Congress has been lacking in speed in its consideration.

alderman: A term used for members of a city council. The Board of Aldermen often constituted the equivalent of a lower house in a Municipal Legislature as in New York City before 1936.

alien: A non-citizen who is required by Act of Congress (1940) to register and keep the authorities constantly informed of his address and occupation. He is entitled to "equal protection of the laws" and may become naturalized (q.v.) to full citizenship status. The alien may obtain redress of grievances only through state agencies. The federal government has authority only where the general rights of citizens are violated against the safeguards of the Constitution.

Alien Property Custodian: An official authorized by Congress to seize properties that were owned and controlled by enemy countries or persons so that they might not profit from the use of property situated in the United States. The action was held to be constitutional if adequate provision was made for the return of the property in case of error in the confiscation.

Alien Registration Act of 1940: This Smith Act makes it unlawful to teach or advocate the overthrow of the government by force or to advocate insubordination or disloyalty in the armed services. The 1949 trial of the eleven top Communists resulted in their conviction under this act. It is practically a successor to the 1917 Sedition Law. Administered by the Immigration and Registration Bureau of the Department of Justice it requires all aliens over fourteen years of age to register, be finger-printed, and thereafter report address and occupation periodically to the Federal authorities.

alienation: The transfer of property by legal conveyance of ownership, or a charge made by an individual against another for lessening of affection.

alignment: The strengthening of a political party may depend upon the "lining" up of various elements of the population in opposition or support.

allegation: A statement by an individual which he undertakes to prove in court.

allegiance: The tie which binds a citizen to his state. This may be natural, that is owed by reason of birth, or acquired through naturalization, during which it becomes necessary to throw off the allegiance which one had formerly had for another country.

allocation: Assignment or proper placement of funds. In politics this term may be applied in cases of appropriations where provision is made for a single appropriation to be allocated in monthly installments in order to make sure it will not be used up too soon.

allotment: Sums of money designated for specific purposes. In the army it may constitute a portion of the soldier's pay assigned to his wife for her or the children's support.

alphabetical agencies: A term used to describe the many new agencies created especially during the early period of the New Deal in an attempt to overcome the disaster of the 1929 panic. Used also to refer to any governmental agencies when only their initials are used to refer to them as: NRA, SEC, PWA, OPA, OPM, TVA, etc.

alternate: At political conventions in addition to the regular delegates, an alternate or extra delegate is provided for in case the official delegate is not available.

ambassador: The highest diplomatic official sent by a sovereign state to represent it officially. In the United States he is appointed by the President and confirmed by the Senate.

amendment: The process by which a constitution or law may have additions made to it. An amendment to the federal constitution is first proposed by a two-thirds vote in each house of Congress and then ratified by three-quarters of the state legislatures, or in either case by equivalent conventions.

American Civil Liberties Union: An organization established in 1920 to promote and protect the civil liberty of persons in danger of having their civil rights infringed upon because of racial or other prejudice. Legal advice or bail or similar types of services are provided.

American Farm Bureau Federation: A local farm organization; when it was started about 1915 the Farm Bureau sought to obtain greater employment of agricultural agents in the counties, and favored co-operative farm activities. Later organized on a state and national basis it has attained a membership of almost one and a half million farm families whose conditions it strives to improve working particularly with the "farm bloc" in Washington. Attracting progressive farmers the organization hopes, and to a considerable extent has succeeded, in making the public appreciate the need to put the farm level of prosperity on the level with business and labor.

American Federation of Labor: A federation of national trade unions first organized in 1886. For years it represented the outstanding force for the advancement of union activities. Its concern in the field of politics was limited to the endorsement of candidates, and to the favoring of legislation regardless of the party involved. After 1936 it found both its labor and its political influence challenged by the Congress for Industrial Organization (q.v.) which generally endorsed and sponsored Democratic candidates claiming in the 1946 election partial responsibility for the election of one hundred Congressmen. *See also* "POLITICAL ACTION COMMITTEE."

American First Party: A party founded by the Rev. Gerald L. K. Smith in January 1942 of Fascist tendencies, anti-semitic, anti-Negro, and against participation in the United Nations, it blamed all America's ills on Communists and international bankers.

Americanization: The social adjustment of the immigrant to the American environment through participation in the life of the nation. With the greatly restricted immigration of the last three decades the meaning might be broadened to apply to the second generation Americans, who, though having cultural roots different from their parents have still not absorbed entirely all the American customs. Some sociologists would like to see the term applied in two directions. Not only is the newcomer involved but also the so-called native American who must accept or adjust to a more tolerant or unprejudiced view of the "foreigner."

American Labor Party: A New York affiliate of Labor's Non-Partisan League. It reached its greatest strength in 1937 in the support of Mayor La Guardia. It later split into a right wing (Liberal Party) and a left wing (Independent Citizens Committee).

"American System": A program advocated by Henry Clay by which all sections of the country were to be mutually interdependent. This was in the period immediately following the War of 1812 when Nationalism was at its highest peak. The "American System" was a dream that fell apart on the reality of Sectionalism. (q.v.)

amicus curiae: An impartial person (the expression means "friend of the court") who volunteers information in a court trial because of professional or other standing as a reputable citizen to set the record clear.

amnesty: A decree issued by Congress or the President granting a general pardon for past offenses.

amortization: Putting aside funds regularly in advance in order to liquidate a future obligation.

anarchism: A theory of society which favors the absence of governmental regulation, assuming that each individual will voluntarily act for the benefit of all. There are many variations in this philosophical view. Some of the more extreme have advocated violence as a means of getting rid of unwanted officialdom. The Syndicalists in Europe and the International Workers of the World organized in the United States represent those groups who claim to fight the inevitable tyranny and oppression that government always becomes.

ancillary restraints: Checks upon the free participation in a business may be made in some covenants such as an agreement of a retiring partner not to compete with a former partner, or of a former employee with an employer. If the restaints go too far they become illegal.

angary: The right of a belligerent nation under extreme necessity to confiscate or destroy property of a neutral state or the possessions of a citizen of such a state.

anticipation warrant: An obligation, usually short-time, issued by a government agency in anticipation of revenue not yet available.

Anti-discrimination Law of New York State: *See* Ives-Quinn Law.

Antifederalists: A group who opposed the ratification of the constitution because they considered the interests of the states had not been sufficiently safeguarded. Their support was won over partially by the addition to the Constitution of the "Bill of Rights" (q.v.). Their stress on the ideas of state sovereignity remained the foundation of the Democratic-Republican Party (q.v.) which replaced them under the leadership of Thomas Jefferson.

Antigua: An island of the West Indies leased to the United States as a naval base by the destroyer-base deal (q.v.).

antilynching bills: Laws which have been proposed to permit the federal government to punish a state officer who may permit his prisoner to be hurt, by claiming violation of the Fourteenth Amendment on the basis of punishment without due process of law. The constitutionality of such measures have been challenged.

Antimasonic Party: A party which nominated a third party candidate in the 1836 election by means of a convention and thereby established a precedent in national politics still followed today. *See* NATIONAL CONVENTION

Antipeonage Act: An act passed by the federal government in 1867 making it a federal crime to hold persons in involuntary servitude. Because of the Thirteenth Amendment courts have felt themselves prevented from compelling workers to return or remain on the job against their will. Exceptions exist as in the case of seamen who must complete a voyage to the home port.

The law does prevent a debtor from being forced to fulfill his obligation by involuntary labor.

Anti-Saloon League of America: An organization that favored temperance reform. At first their program rested upon an adequate preparation of public opinion by stressing the evils of excessive drinking. They did later favor a federal amendment to enforce prohibition, and lost prestige with the scandals of the Prohibition Era.

anti-Semitism: A hatred for or discrimination against the Jews. Various groups are attempting to curb or wipe out the effects of such feelings. Frequent proposals have been made before Congress to extend the power of the Fair Employment Practices Committee which operated during the war in connection with all work done under federal contract. The Ives-Quinn Law (q.v.) of New York State makes such discrimination subject to punishment. The National Conference of Christians and Jews is doing a note-worthy job in this respect also, as are the public school systems of the country.

Antitrust Division: This agency is a subdivision of the Department of Justice. It initiates suits against monopolistic practices. Thurman Arnold in the 1930's stimulated their activity greatly.

antitrust laws: Laws intending to prevent the creation of harmful monopolies. The original Sherman Antitrust Law (1890) did not adequately define the degree of restraint that constituted a monopoly. The Clayton Act (1914), through the so-called "Rule of Reason" listed specific harmful practices, such as pooling, rebates, and other forms of discrimination. Mere size was not to be the basis for the Attorney-General to institute a suit against an organization, but the commission of a definite unfair practice. The Federal Trade Commission was established to warn firms as part of its investigation of deceptive advertising or discriminatory prices.

appeal, the right of: The right of the accused to be tried again is not automatic, it is implied according to the Constitution which has provided means of protecting the individual's rights. If these rights have not been fully protected during the conduct of the trial, then the accused has the right to petition a higher court to set aside an adverse verdict.

appeasement: Acquiescence, or a surrender on matters of basic importance. Chamberlain's acceptance of Hitler's demands on Czechoslavakia in 1938 has been looked upon as a classic example of appeasement.

appellate jurisdiction: The power of certain courts to review a case already tried in a lower court. The United States Supreme Court exercises such jurisdiction primarily. Most of the appeals reaching it involve the constitutional validity of some state or federal statute, thus providing the court a form of "judicial review" that in effect gives the judiciary an influence over legislation passed by state legislatures, or by Congress itself.

appointment: The naming of an individual to an official position. For most federal positions the confirmation of the Senate is required though interim appointments may be made while the Senate is not in session.

apportionment: The Constitution provides that "representatives shall be apportioned among the several States according to their numbers." Most state constitutions also provide that the lower house of their legislature should be apportioned on the basis of the population. The original membership of the House of Representatives was only sixty five, requiring frequent increases to reach its present membership of 435. Newly admitted states have had members apportioned by Congress.

appraisal: Determination of value. Used particularly in regard to imported goods where the value of the item fixes the amount of duty to be paid. It is also important in regard to determining the value of real estate when about to be taken over by the government by the right of eminent domain (q.v.).

apprenticeship, Bureau of: This division returned to the Labor Department in 1945 maintains field offices in twelve regions of the United States and Hawaii to supervise the actual training program of those elected as apprentices. Employer and labor are brought together to formulate a program of apprenticeship with technical and advisory assistance in the development and actual operation of the training program.

apprenticeships, municipal: In some cities likely students study municipal affairs during their summer vacations for the valuable experience and a small salary.

appropriation: A sum of money set aside for a specific purpose. It may represent a lump-sum allocated to a department in estimating the expenses to make up a state budget, or it may be made up of a carefully detailed list of items needed to implement a bill already passed by Congress but still awaiting the action of the Committee on Appropriations to make it possible to carry out the full intentions of Congress.

arbitration: A method of settling industrial disputes whereby a third party is chosen to render a decision on the merits and facts of the case. A method of settling difficulties between nations. One of the most interesting cases of arbitration concerning the United States was that of the "Alabama Claims" (q.v.).

archives: A depository for public records and documents.

area of the United States: The continental area of the United States is equal to about three million square miles. With Alaska adding another 590,000 and all our island possessions another 138,000 the total area of the United States approximates 3,628,000 square miles.

armed neutrality: The position assumed by a neutral power when it declares that it will protect its neutrality by force if it becomes necessary. Both President Wilson and President F. D. Roosevelt allowed arming of our merchant fleets in peace time when our neutral rights were being violated by Germany just before World War I and also before World War II.

Armed Services of the United States: By the National Defense Act of 1920 and many subsequent modifications the following include the recognized military units of the United States: Regular Army, National Guard, Organized Reserve Corps, Naval Reserve, Marine Corps, Air Force, and the Women's Army Corps.

armistice: A temporary halt in fighting by agreement between opposing commanders. After World War I November 11, 1918 was celebrated as Armistice Day.

arms, right to bear or keep arms: Though the "bearing of arms" is a right not to be infringed upon according to the Second Amendment, the arms referred to are those of a soldier, but under its "police power" (q.v.) both state and federal governments may regulate and restrict the carrying of concealed weapons by private individuals, and forbid the sale of or possession of sawed-off shot guns and other weapons habitually used by criminals.

Army, Department of the: A newly organized department replacing the former War Department now in the Department of Defense. It handles all matters connected with the organizing, training and maintaining of an army.

arraignment: The requirement that an individual appear before a court of law to be identified and answer to an indictment after which he may make a plea of guilty or not guilty.

arrest: The legal detention of a person by an authorized agent of the government. If the cause of the arrest is not found to be sufficient the prisoner may obtain release by means of a writ of habeas corpus. (q.v.)

arsenal: A state owned establishment for the manufacture and storage of munitions of war and military and naval equipment.

arson: The crime of setting fire to building or property with malicious intent, or with interest to defraud fire-insurance companies.

Articles of Confederation: A plan for declaring the colonies free and independent states and for governing them was prepared in 1777 but was not ratified until 1781. The delay was occasioned by the need to settle a dispute in regard to the ownership of western land to which several states had conflicting claims. By refusing to sign until the states agreed to cede their western lands to the federal government, Maryland won an advantageous settlement for the United States. The Articles, on the other hand stressed state sovereignty. A Congress of very limited power was created. So limited was this power that eventually the lack of an executive, of a judiciary, and of control over interstate commerce led to the calling of the Philadelphia Constitutional Convention. Many valuable lessons had been learned from the very weaknesses of the Articles which resulted in their replacement in 1789 by our present Constitution.

Articles of War: A code of rules enacted by Congress for the government and disciplinary control of the military forces. They were taken over from a similar book of British rules in use at the start of our government. They were revised in 1824 and have had some additions since especially in regards to the conduct of courts martial.

Article X: A provision which Mr. Wilson called the "heart of the League of Nations" because nations joining the League agreed "to respect and preserve as against external aggression the territorial integrity and existing political independence of all members."

assembly, right of: A privilege accorded by the First Amendment (q.v.) to the Constitution, and supplemented by state constitutions which limit their legislatures from interfering with public gatherings. This is not an absolute right since under certain circumstances a public meeting may be harmful because of considerations of health, morals or fear of riot.

assessment, special: A tax levied upon property owners in proportion to the extent benefited by some public improvement which would increase the value of their property. If streets are paved or a sewer constructed those nearest the improvement must pay the largest amount, those farther away, less.

assessor: An official who determines the value of property for taxation purposes. The total assessed valuation of a community's property and the amount to be raised would determine the tax rate for some specific period.

assimilation: The absorbing of a different national or racial group into the culture of the country by a complete and unconscious process that goes deeper than mere surface accommodation of language or clothing to full spiritual and intellectual fusion of attitudes and habits.

Associated Press: An organization that was the forerunner of this newsgathering agency existed before the Civil War but became a general organization in 1892 for the pooling of resources in the fast and efficient assembling of news. The revenue of the association is collected from the members by weekly assessments pro-rated among them according to the cost or value of the service provided. Information is speeded on its way over a leased wire system exceeding 50,000 miles to a membership which in 1950 had over 860 subscribers.

asylum, right of: A place exempt from the territorial jurisdiction of a state within which it is, within which refugees may seek safety and not be followed. It resembles in a sense the practice of extraterritoriality.

Atlantic Charter: A joint declaration by President Roosevelt and Winston Churchill prepared while on board ship in the North Atlantic in August 1941. The points covered later served as an avowal of war aims on the part of the United Nations and also as a goal for post-war recovery plans. The points covered were as follows: no territorial aggrandizement to be undertaken, no territorial changes without the approval of the people concerned, the right of people to choose their own governments, equal access to raw materials for all peoples, collaboration for economic and social betterment, peace that would assure all men of freedom from want and fear, abandonment of the use of force and the reduction of armaments.

at large (congressman at large): A term used to refer to a candidate selected from the whole state rather than a specific district. When redistricting of the state occurs after the census returns have indicated the amount of increase in the population this position will usually disappear.

Atomic Energy Commission (United Nations): This commission made up of the Security Council of the United Nations and Canada has had to face the greatest difficulties in attempting to arrange for international control of atomic energy plants. The Baruch Plan provided for international inspection, and the Russian proposals advocated national responsibility for the manufacture and development of atomic power. So far a deadlock has resulted in no action in the international field.

Atomic Energy Commission (United States): An agency created by the Atomic Energy Act of 1946 (McMahon Act) consisting of five members whose primary work is to encourage public and private research in nuclear fission, and to advance the production of uranium, and to control atomic weapons, and finally to push the application of atomic energy to industrial purposes.

attainder: Extinction of civil rights of a person accused of treason and carried out on his heirs also. *See* BILL OF ATTAINDER.

Attorney-General: Executive head of the United States Department of Justice, who in addition renders opinions on legal questions put to him by the President or other cabinet heads.

auditor: An elected or appointed official who checks up on government expenditures or upon state treasurers. This may be accomplished by a before-hand certification of a payment or claim so as to prove that it is for an object representing a legitimate and necessary purpose, and by inspection of all the accounts of various government agencies at subsequent intervals.

Australian ballot: This is a secret ballot printed by official authority and at public expense. It was first used in Victoria in 1856 and first copied in America by Kentucky in 1888 for local elections. American practice has been to include party designations, though British practice was to list candidates by name only.

autarchy: Economic self-sufficiency is a condition usually connected with a phase of super-nationalism. This was exemplified particularly in Nazi Germany which through protective tariffs, subsidized research and subsidies to manufactures attempted for a time to be free from any interdependence on other countries.

authoritarian: Favoring the principle of obedience to a supreme authority or "leader" and subordinating the rights of the individual by a restrictive program usually assumed without legal responsibility.

autonomous planning: Many subdivisions of governmental bureaus or agencies may be given authority to act without constant approval or supervision by a higher agency. This degree of self-government would, of course, be limited by the basic law which created the parent organization.

autonomy: Loosely a degree of self-government. Practical independence under nominal control of another country. This situation might arise in some European countries but is incompatible with ideas in this country where a very definite separation of powers exist as between state and nation, and state and local unit.

"availability": The lucky combination of circumstances that calls a person to the public's attention and to that of the party at just the right time to be considered for high office. Among the attributes making for availability in the American political scene are; geographical residence, Protestant, "good American stock," and some conspicuous accomplishment. When F. D. Roosevelt won over a number of up-state New York strong-holds in the gubernatorial election in 1930, when Taft swung a Republican majority in his favor in the 1939 election for Senator, when Coolidge broke the police strike in Boston, they all made themselves "available for future advancement."

avocational interests: Those interests which an individual has outside of his professional concerns or his job. Modern communities are attempting to provide for more such interests by setting up municipal golf courses, swimming pools, or providing for courses in such hobbies as jewelry making and various other forms of art work.

ax to grind: Campaigning or speech making by a candidate for a secret or selfish reason.

aye and no vote: A special vote taken in a legislative body by which the decision is determined by the volume of sound. If this is not clearly distinguishable, recourse must be had to a rising vote.

B

bail: The money or equivalent thereof which an accused person must deposit with the proper court to insure his appearance there when his trial is finally ready to begin. To "jump bail" is to forfeit the amount posted by fleeing from the jurisdiction of the court. Excessive bail may not be required according to the Eighth Amendment of the United States Constitution.

bailiff: A sheriff's deputy who enforces writs issued by court officials.

balance of trade: A condition determined by the number and value of the exports as compared with the imports of a country. An excess of exports was usually considered "favorable." However "invisible" items such as insurance payments abroad, family remittances overseas may upset the "simple balance" once felt to be so beneficial in foreign trade.

ballot: An official paper containing names of candidates. The usual practices is to have party designations attached.

ballot box stuffing: The wholesale voting of names on the register by the election officials without an attempt to have an individual actually cast a vote.

ballyhoo: The sum of all activities by which an attempt is made to stir up interest in public affairs among the voters has been called "ballyhoo" by those who feel that some of the performances are definitely not dignified. Unfortunately much of this "interest" is of a highly emotional nature, some even of a sensational character more appropriate to a circus than to a campaign, or investigation.

band wagon, to get on: To throw one's support to the candidate that seems to be winning, without serious consideration of the advantages or disadvantages involved.

bank deposit insurance: *See* FEDERAL DEPOSIT INSURANCE CORPORATION.

bank holiday: Any period during which a bank is closed but usually referring to the interval in March 1933 when President Roosevelt closed all banks for over a week to prevent the spread of panic withdrawal of funds from sound banks, which were allowed to open promptly.

bank note: A form of paper currency carrying a bank's promise to pay to bearer a specific sum of money. National bank notes were issued by National Banks, private enterprises chartered by the National Government which were permitted by an Act of Congress in 1863 to issue notes upon purchase of government bonds which were used as security for the notes. Since 1935 this type of bond has not been issued, therefore such notes are no longer in circulation.

bank tax: The states generally tax the capital of banks either under the general corporation tax or by a special tax. In New York it is one percent of the value of the shares of stock in the bank. In California there is no tax at all. The Federal Government taxes the bank note circulation of national banks at one-half of a percent, but taxes note circulation of state banks at a ten percent rate, thus effectively preventing state bank notes from circulating.

Bankhead Jones Farm Tenant Act: An act passed by Congress in 1937 to reduce the number of farm tenants or share croppers by arranging for long-term, low-interest loans to approved tenant farmers and farm workers to permit them to buy land and farm equipment. It is hoped that this program will result in more diversified farming and greater consideration of soil conservation, and the raising of the standard of living of one of the most depressed groups of the whole population. The former process of share cropping resulted in many cases in the production of a "money crop" on a large scale with consequent depletion of the soil and low prices when surplus crops were produced. Under the new program the farmer can afford to put in a vegetable garden to improve his badly neglected nutritional needs and to produce crops in products less likely to lead to overproduction.

bankruptcy laws: Legislation dealing with persons whose business enterprises are in an insolvent condition. The federal courts must act not only to recognize a bankruptcy, whether voluntary, that is, declared upon the individual's own initiative, or involuntary, upon the petition of creditors, but also, must supervise all the subsequent steps in the proceedings. This may include paying out the individual's assets, or in appointing receivers to reorganize the corporate structure, or in carrying out other complicated tasks to put the business on its feet again.

"basing point system": A method of charging uniform delivered prices for commodities. For example prices for steel, no matter where produced or how delivered were fixed as the sum of a Pittsburgh "base point" and the rail freight charge to the point of delivery. This form of geographical discrimination was finally found a violation of the Clayton Antitrust Law since payment was being exacted for a mythical freight rate for those concerns fabricating and buying steel in the West.

Baumes Law: A New York law (1926) which requires that a habitual criminal (one convicted of four felonies) be sentenced with life imprisonment.

belligerency: A state of armed and legally recognized hostility. To acknowledge the belligerency of a party not a state gives to that area all the rights of war of an established state. Though the Confederacy had been recognized as a belligerent in regard to treatment of prisoners of war and other conditions establishing her "independence," Lincoln in order to quicken reconstruction chose to consider that the states had never seceded and proposed a very generous treatment in his "Ten percent Plan," which provided for full restoration to the Union if merely ten percent of the population of the people voted loyalty to the United States. If the belligerency of the Confederacy had been fully insisted upon, this action would not have been possible. Lincoln had assumed that as Chief Executive he had the right to grant amnesty to a rebellious group.

benefit of counsel, right to: The Sixth Amendment provides: "In all criminal prosecutions the accused shall enjoy the right to be informed of the nature of the accusation . . . and to have the assistance of counsel for his defense." The United States Supreme Court has upheld this point in any case where the death penalty is involved, but it does not necessarily prevail in non-criminal cases.

bicameral: A law making body having two houses. The Nebraska legislature is the only one house law making body in the United States.

"Big Business": A term used to indicate business enterprise on a large scale, nation wide in scope, involving a large amount of capitalization and often associated with some outstanding industrial figure. Such usage began about the 1880's when the big oil, and steel, and railroad companies were being created.

"Big Inch": A pipe line originally constructed to transport gasoline from the Southwest to the Northeast. After World War II it was sold to a private company for the transportation of natural gas under the supervision of the Federal Power Commission (q.v.).

Big Labor: An expression used in contrast to that of "Big Business" to indicate the growing strength of organized labor as shown especially in the big industrial unions after 1936 in regard to the numbers likely to follow a concerted policy, or in the large funds accumulating in the union treasuries.

bigotry: Excessive devotion to one's church, party or opinion, usually with the implication of a lack of toleration for the position of others.

"Big Stick": A policy associated with Theodore Roosevelt, who is quoted as saying "tread softly but carry a big stick." This applied at the time, in the early 1900's, to his advocacy of a big navy, but might have been equally well applicable to his defense of the Monroe Doctrine and to his trust-busting program.

bilateral: Affecting both sides. Used in regard to a treaty which is binding upon the two signatories. If more countries sign it is called a multilateral treaty.

Bilboism: A term created because of the record of Senator T. G. Bilbo of Mississippi which indicates primarily the practice of illegally maintaining "white supremacy" in the South and carries also the overtones of implying willingness to accept financial rewards for favors rendered. In the eyes of some reformers the trend toward Bilboism shows clearly how the attempt to harm or discriminate against a minority hurts the morals of those involved, and in this example was particularly hurting our prestige abroad. Investigation showed ample evidence of terroristic tactics against Negro voters uncovered in considering Bilbo's acceptance by the Senate; but a report which exonerated him, blamed the small vote on lack of interest. Evidence was also piling up that he had benefited from "gifts" from war contractors, but his death in 1947 was followed only by eulogies.

bill: The first draft of a law until it is signed into law is known as a bill. A bill introduced into Congress must have three readings in each house and be signed by the president in order to become a law. After it is introduced it is sent to the appropriate committee for careful consideration. Later it is discussed in detail in the house in which it originated and then goes through a similar procedure in the other house.

"Bill drafting services": The correct wording of a law is a matter of vital importance and many states have made special provision for such supplementary services though it is not an easy matter to find the trained personnel for such exacting work. Law schools do not yet teach the subject of legislative drafting, so that merely selecting lawyers for the job is not the whole solution. Congress also has such an office to provide a somewhat similar service—the Legislative Reference Service—which by the Reorganization Act of 1946 receives now a much larger, appropriation than before in order to make available far more expert service.

bill of attainder: The taking away of a person's civil rights when he has been declared an outlaw or sentenced to death. It is specifically prohibited by the Constitution of the United States.

Bill of Rights: Measures to protect the individual's rights included in all the original state constitutions. It is also an expression used to designate the first ten amendments of the United States Constitution which were added as a group in 1791 in response to popular demand that such safeguards be repeated on a national level. The term is also used for the results of the English Revolution in 1688 by which measures were passed to limit the power of the king and protect the rights of the individual through the same basic provisions, such as freedom of speech, and trial by jury. *See* FIRST AMENDMENT, SECOND AMENDMENT &.

bimetallism: The practice whereby two metals, usually gold and silver may serve as the standard of value for money with an attempt to keep them at some legally determined ratio. A great political campaign was fought on this issue in 1896 when the Populists favored bimetallism. The program was disastrously weakened by their defeat, and by the passage of the Gold Standard Act of 1900 providing for a single standard.

bipartisan: Involving two parties. Congress during World War II was especially concerned that foreign affairs be carried out on a bipartisan basis. This was undertaken by appointing prominent Republicans to all important conferences and committees concerned with such matters.

blacklist: The preparation of a list of persons or organizations to be discriminated against. It has been claimed that some employers used such a list in retaliation against labor organizers, agitators or other malcontents. If an individual claims his dismissal from his job was for activities in behalf of union organization alone he may bring suit against the employer for unfair labor practices under the National Labor Relations Act.

"blackmailing legislation": Bills proposed for the purpose of extorting money from corporations by the threat of putting through measures to their disadvantage: or in other ways using political influence for unfair benefits.

black market: A practice of selling goods in violation of rationing or other types of price-fixing, or regulatory measures.

blighted district: An area in which the large majority of buildings whether commercial, industrial, or residential, are old and on which fundamental repairs are no longer being made. As soon as conditions become unsanitary and otherwise injurious to health of the occupant, it rates the designation of a slum.

blind pensions: Under the Social Security Act of 1936 the federal government contributes a sum equal to a half of that raised by state governments for the pensions to be paid to the blind in that state, if there has been legislation passed meeting the federal standards. By 1950 over 92,000 persons were receiving pensions of this type averaging about $646 per person.

bloc: A group of legislators working toward the same common goal, though not necessarily of the same party, as "farm block" (q.v.), or silver bloc.

blockade runner: A ship attempting to bring in or take out goods while a blockade is in effect. Many Southerners during the Civil War tried fairly successfully to "run" the North's blockade of the Southern ports.

blocked currency: Currency is held to be blocked when it is not allowed to circulate freely, but is subject to restriction when used in foreign exchange.

bloody shirt, waving of: The practice of many Republican politicians to stress the fact that Republican candidates had been officers in the Union Army, and to emphasize the contrast with reference to the facts that many Democrats had avoided an active support of the Civil War. *See* COPPERHEADS.

Blue Eagle: Symbol of the National Recovery Act (1933). It was first used as a reward of merit to be displayed by a firm obeying the codes of fair competition agreed upon by all the major industries.

"Blue Laws": State or country laws of a restrictive type interfering with an individual's freedom in regard to Sunday activities. Some communities require the closing of movies, race tracks and of most stores on that day.

"blue-ribbon jury": A special jury composed of persons who have had to meet additional tests or qualifications for fitness beyond those used for the selection of ordinary jurymen. This type of jury has been in use in certain states for sometime, for example, in New York since 1901. A judge may use such a jury where the intricacy of the case, or a large degree of publicity, or other special need has made the necessity for an impartial view especially important.

"blue-sky" laws: State regulations to protect investors from buying stocks that have inadequate backing or security.

Board of Estimate: One of the two bodies forming the law-making agency of New York City. Besides its function as the equivalent of an upper house this group of men handle all the financial matters of the city especially those having to do with the making of the budget and the issuance of franchises and like matters. The Mayor, the Comptroller and the President of the City Council and the five borough Presidents form the membership.

Board of Tax Review or Tax Appeal: An agency of a town government which receives appeals (complaints) from those owners who think their holdings have had too high a value placed upon them by the assessors.

bolter: A voter who deserts his party—usually at the last moment in the election.

bondsman: One who provides bond or surety to guarantee another person's return for trial.

boodle: A slang expression for a campaign fund, now used also to designate money stolen from the public treasury or received in bribes.

boondoggling: A term used during the "New Deal" in regard to some of the projects carried out under the Works Progress Administration and held to be of doubtful value or just a wasteful expenditure of federal funds.

bootlegging: Making and selling an object secretly, usually liquor, but extended to any product forbidden legally, or rationed or heavily taxed.

"boring from within": A practice much credited to Communist organizations, by which an individual or small group joins an organization to which they are hostile and then attempts to mould their program so as to follow their own secret plans.

borough plan: A variation of municipal administration. Usually the centralized policy of a municipal unit is determined by a common council, but decentralized administration is obtained by dividing certain supervisory practices between the central authority and the government of territorial districts or areas sometimes called boroughs as in New York City.

bossism: American slang to describe the rule of a political boss, a word that has come to mean a professional politician who controls a large number of votes, dictates policy and names candidates for office in his particular district.

bounty: A direct grant of money to private enterprise by a government agency. At one time the Federal Government paid a bounty on sugar at the rate of one and a quarter cents a pound until nearly $36 million had been paid out. The states have paid bounties to railroad companies and for irrigation projects, and also to encourage the extermination of coyotes, wolves and mountain lions.

bourgeoisie: A French term that has general acceptance as referring to the middle class, small property owner or business man or shop keeper as a contrast to the other two extremes, the very rich, or in the other direction, the proletariat or working man.

boycott: An agreed upon action by one group to refrain from doing any business with another in order to force a favorable decision or as a punishment. If, as in a labor dispute, the group with a grievance brings pressure upon third parties to assist them, the situation becomes a secondary boycott (q.v.).

Boys' Clubs of America Incorporated: An organization to combat juvenile delinquency by providing a vital and varied program of activities for boys of eight to twenty. There are centers in over 300 cities with over a quarter of a million members. Trained leadership, low membership dues and community cooperation have encouraged enrollment.

"Brain Trust": A term used to describe F. D. Roosevelt's advisors other than his cabinet during his first term in office including such figures as Raymond Moley, Rexford Tugwell, Benjamin Cohen, Thomas Corcoran and others.

Brannan Plan: Because of growing dissatisfaction with various phases of the Department of Agriculture's activities, especially the effect of rising food prices on the cost of living in the cities, Secretary of Agriculture Brannan, with President Truman's approval in 1950 suggested that the entire program of support prices be dropped. All farm products would be dumped on the open market. Prices would rise or fall according to normal supply and demand. By careful calculation a "parity," or fair price would be ascertained for every product, and the farmer would receive from the federal government compensation in full for their losses. The opposition to this plan claims that whatever the individual might gain from the lower prices of food products would be taken from him in taxes to finance the unpredictable but heavy costs of operating the scheme.

Bryan-Chamorro Treaty: A treaty signed by Nicaragua and the United States in 1914 granting the United States permission to build a canal, in the southern part of Nicaragua from the Atlantic to the Pacific, at any time. Coaling stations and possible naval bases were also leased in Fonseca Bay.

brown derby: The personal symbol of Alfred E. Smith, well beloved governor of New York and Democratic candidate for president in 1928 defeated by Herbert Hoover.

budget: A balanced estimate of expected income as contrasted with expected expenditures. A complicated procedure for determining the final budget is characteristic of municipal, state and national government. When expenditures have been agreed upon it then becomes necessary to match the outgo with provisions for adequate income or an unbalanced budget results with other serious consequences.

Budget, Bureau of: An agency of the Department of Treasury, but since 1939 a part of the Executive Office of the President. The specialists of the Division on Administrative Management play a significant role in assisting the President in carrying out his constitutional responsibility of supervising the many administrative agencies of the national government. Other divisions indicate the further important functions of this vital bureau: Division of Estimate, Division of Fiscal Analysis, Division of Legislative Reference, Division of Statistical Standards. After a tremendous amount of work on the part of a host of experts, by the first week in January a document has been printed for the president to present to Congress often amounting to more than a thousand pages. The Bureau of the Budget continues its supervisory duties once the budget preparation has been completed.

Building Code: A collection of ordinances passed by a municipal legislature providing detailed regulations for the construction of buildings within the city limits. Usually a permit must be issued to provide for the final occupancy. Revision of these codes are being strenuously urged in many areas to make allowance for new technological improvements in methods and materials of construction.

"Bull Moose Party": The name given to the Progressive Party (q.v.) during the campaign of 1912 when Theodore Roosevelt assumed leadership of it in opposition to Taft. He is supposed to have selected the moose as a symbol because he felt "as strong as a bull moose."

buncombe: Bombastic speech-making, or another specious utterance for political effect.

"bureaucracy": Literally the expression means the running of the government by means of a number of administrative agencies. The implications follow that there is a slavish devotion to a rigid body of laws and that there is little thought of the individual or of improvements for the general welfare.

business affected with a public interest: Any business, especially a public utility which may enjoy a virtual monopoly due to the nature of the business, and because of its importance in connection with the general welfare may be subject to special regulation at the state or federal level.

business agent: The paid representative of a local trade union whose function it is to look after the interests of the members of the union. He may inspect the premises where work is being done to check upon the introduction of labor-saving machines or oversee any such related matters. Also called a "walking delegate."

business cycle: An attempt to describe the rhythmic fluctuations through which modern business seems regularly to pass has been expressed through the business cycle. After a panic, a depression, then recovery and with prosperity a boom that leads to the circle starting over again in depression etc.

"business unionism": The activity of the early craft unions was concentrated on the practice of "business unionism," that is on the improvement of their own wages, hours, and working conditions, with only incidental interest in wider reform or in general political action. The depression of 1873 rendered such a program of no avail and working class interest shifted to the Knights of Labor (q.v.), and later to the A. F. of L. (q.v.) where Gompers revived the program of "business unionism" but with some political effort on a non-partisan basis of "rewarding its friends and punishing its enemies."

by-election: A special election to fill a vacancy in a legislature due to the death or resignation of a member.

bylaw: A regulation adopted by a corporation for the management of its affairs.

C

cabinet: An advisory group selected by an executive to assist him. President Washington started the precedent with four advisors in his first cabinet. Three of whom were heads of department, secretary of state, secretary of the treasury, and secretary of war, and one of whom gave him his legal advice without the assistance of a department—the attorney-general. By 1913 there were ten cabinet positions, but with the consolidation of War and Navy we now have a Department of Defense and only nine official cabinet positions as follows: State, Treasury, Defense, Justice, Post Office, Interior, Agriculture, Commerce and Labor. The Vice-President may be invited to attend cabinet meetings. No matter what opposition may develop among the members the President's view is final for he is held directly responsible for the executive departments.

Cable Act: The original act in 1922 authorized women of a race eligible for naturalization who married American citizens to obtain citizenship after one year. Modifications provided for in the Nationality Act of 1940 allow any alien (male or female) who marries an American citizen to become an American citizen within one to three years.

calamity howler: A deprecatory term for a member of the opposition who fears a financial panic will result from measures being proposed by the administration.

calendar: A list of cases to be heard in a court of justice.

calendar of bills: This term refers to a list which contains the names of bills to be taken under consideration before a legislature. When a bill has been approved by one of the standing committees of the House of Representatives it may be assigned to one of three possible calendars: the "Union" Calendar for the Committee of the Whole House on the state of the Union, for appropriations or matters dealing with public property, or the "House" Calendar for other public bills, or a third calendar for the Committee-of-the-whole-House. Bills remain on these calendars until adjournment when the two-year life of the House has expired, unless they are removed for consideration. The Steering Committee (q.v.) makes the selection as to what bills will be called up. Others may be reintroduced at the next session and again wait their turn for consideration.

call of the House: This is a motion put through in the House when a majority necessary to do business is not present. Warrants may be issued to the sergeant-at-arms to arrest members and force them to be on hand for the voting.

campaign fund: Money used to win a nomination or election. Corrupt practices acts (q.v.) regulate the amounts that may be spent in campaigning.

candidate: A person more or less actively seeking to attain public office.

cannonism: The excessive control of the House exercised by the Speaker who found his privileged position curbed by an "insurgent revolution" in 1910. The Speaker could no longer appoint the members to the various committees and designate their chairmen. The Rules Committee (q.v.) took over his formerly powerful position.

canvassing boards: These boards are usually made up of the county boards of supervisors, or county boards of election which supervise the local election count and then send the returns to the higher authorities.

capital: The city in which the seat of the government of a state is located, or for the nation—Washington, D. C. Also means wealth saved from income and used in the production of goods and services.

capital gains tax: The Supreme Court has held that a capital gain is a profit on a business transaction involving the sale of a capital asset such as securities or real estate, and as such taxable. Losses made during such a transaction are deductible and may result in the government actually obtaining little revenue through this means. Considerable dispute has arisen on the point as to whether such gains really constitute income.

capital levy: A tax which appropriates part of the capital of a taxpayer, as distinguished from a tax on income. This is a program advocated by those desirous of a more rapid redistribution of a nation's wealth.

capital punishment: The death penalty. This is imposed under national law for murder in the first degree, rape and kidnapping.

capitalism: An economic system based on the provision for private ownership of property, and the right of the individual to engage freely in any business for profit. Regulations may still be required for the safeguarding of the individuals employed and for the purchasers of the goods produced, but still the individual makes the final decision as to whether he will or not go into business and the type of product or amount of goods to be produced.

captain of industry: A term much used with the start of the twentieth century to indicate a conspicuous leader in some outstanding field of private enterprise involved in a large scale or country-wide operation.

card-stacking: A propaganda device which includes improper emphasis so as to produce a distorted picture. Irrelevant material will be introduced into the argument to confuse. Tricks in logic will be employed for the same purpose.

career diplomat: A member of the foreign service of the United States who has won his employment on the basis of tested fitness, wins promotion according to merit, and has tenure security. The highest diplomatic representative is an ambassador or a minister selected by the president from his own party and usually in repayment of a political debt. This is in marked contrast to the "career service" but more and more there is a tendency to select men who have worked themselves up from rung to rung of the service.

carpetbagger: Northern politicians who obtained positions in the South during the period of Reconstruction 1865-1875, largely through the protection of federal troops and Republican support, and who acted in very irresponsible and corrupt ways.

cartel: A voluntary combination of private business enterprises usually international in their activities whose purpose include price fixing, limiting output, sharing profits, assigning marketing areas, and other monopolistic undertakings. Nazi Germany encouraged such groups most successfully and the revival of such combinations has been looked upon with disfavor in the post-war period.

Casablanca Conference: A meeting in Morocco in January 1943 between F. D. Roosevelt and Winston Churchill in which the United Nations agreed to demand unconditional surrender of the Axis ultimately, but arranged more immediately for the crossing into Italy from North Africa.

cash-and-carry principle: This policy was provided for in the Neutrality Law of 1937 as an attempt to keep the United States from being drawn into any world conflict. The President had the power to issue a proclamation requiring belligerents trading with the United States to pay for goods in American ports and to transport them in their own ships.

caucus: A meeting of party leaders. Especially a group of Congressmen of the same party. In 1796 such a group began the practice of nominating party candidates for president and vice president. This practice continued until Jackson's time when the use of Nominating Conventions (q.v.) began. A caucus is still used for the ordinary meetings of party members in Congress to determine policy. The House caucus strives for stricter discipline of its members than the Senate caucus.

caveat emptor: "Let the buyer beware." In the 19th century there was felt to be no necessity for legislation to protect the consumer. He was expected to look out for his own interests. For a modern contrast see Federal Trade Commission, or Foods and Drugs Administration.

cease-fire: A temporary cessation of hostilities pending further efforts to determine a lasting peace. The term was applied particularly to the Korean situation in 1952.

cease and desist order: An order issued by an administrative agency requiring an individual or corporation to stop a particular action. For example the Federal Trade Commission may order a certain type of advertising claim to be discontinued.

ceiling price: Control of prices established during 1943-1945 and revived in 1951 so that prices would not rise above a certain level predetermined by either the Office of Price Administration or of Price Stabilization.

censure: An official announcement made as a resolution by a legislative or administrative body showing dissatisfaction with a public official.

census: A decennial enumeration first taken in the United States in 1790 in accordance with the provisions of the Constitution which directs that direct taxes and representatives must be apportioned according to their respective numbers. The state governments have a similar system of counting the population, but authorize them in the years half-way between the Federal census years in twenty-four of the states.

center of population: An arbitrarily selected location in the United States where the number of persons in the population are exactly balanced in either direction on a straight line drawn from east to west across the nation. This point has been moving westward steadily until Illinois was reached in 1951.

Central Intelligence Agency: This agency was established by the National Security Act of 1947 to provide for a single integrated agency with adequate resources. It advises the National Security Council on matters related to intelligence activities of the various departments of the government, and coordinates the intelligence activities of various federal agencies, and collects information of interest to the United States by analysis of special reports and available information.

centralized purchasing on a state level: An important method used by the states to promote efficiency in the obtaining of necessary state supplies by a large scale coordinated buying that helped reduce the increasingly large state budgets. This program arranges for the central purchase of materials, supplies and equipment for all state departments and institutions with savings accomplished by maintenance of a state warehouse and stores to handle large orders, and provision for a permanent inventory of supplies, and, also, for the purchase of insurance. The advantages include overall supervision, more competitive bidding and lower prices for quantity buying with more definite specifications and standardization.

certification: An official order stating that a union is free from employer domination, and is authorized to act as a bargaining agent. National or state Labor Relations Boards issue them. An act of a civil service commission indicating to an appointing authority the names of those eligible for appointment.

certiorari: A writ or order from a superior court directing a lower court to send up the full record and proceedings in a case before verdict for review or retrial.

cession: Legal transfer of territory from one nation to another as in the case of the Mexican Cession of 1848 which resulted in the United States acquiring parts of the future states of Nevada, Vermont, Arizona, Colorado and New Mexico.

Chain store anti-discrimination law: See ROBINSON-PATMAN LAW.

chain-store tax: A tax levied by many states on retail stores when the number of stores under a single management is in excess of a specified maximum. The rate of tax usually increases fairly steeply as the base amount taxed increases.

challenge: In the political field this is an allegation that a vote is invalid. In judicial matters it represents an objection to the acceptance of a particular individual as a member of a jury about to be formed.

Chamber of Commerce of United States: Business and industry have an alert watch dog in Washington, D. C. in this chamber concerned with a host of government agencies and eager to build up a favorable attitude on the part of Congress, the public, and the government administrators toward business. The Chamber of Commerce relies on the activities of three thousand or more local units, and trade associations (q.v.) with some twenty thousand firms and corporations as members.

Chandler Act of 1938: Because so many municipalities suffered from tax delinquencies, in January 1934, 2,000 units were known to be in default over a billion dollars, this law was passed by Congress to permit such state sub-divisions to reorganize their indebtedness under the Federal bankruptcy laws. This had been considered unconstitutional under an earlier Supreme Court decision as interference with States' Rights.

Chapultepec, Act of: A measure ratified in 1945 as the symbol of the unity among the Latin American countries attending the Mexico City Conference on the Problems of Peace and War. It provided that sanctions could be employed, but only in the case of a threat to the peace, or as the result of an actual aggression, and this action could not be undertaken unilaterally. The United Nations charter upheld such "regional agreements" though some delegates deplored the possibility of the world being divided into a number of armed camps.

charge: The statement of a judge at the conclusion of a trial informing the jury of the law governing the case.

charter: A formal document granted by a government giving certain rights or privileges. It may be private, as one issued to a corporation, or public, as one issued by a state to a city. A charter may also be the basic statute of an international organization like the United Nations.

Chatauqua movement: A program, the idea for which had been originated at Chatauqua, New York in 1873 which combined a vacation with an education. Financed by fees paid by those attending; the idea spread over the country where auditoriums, and lecture halls were crowded by those seeking to hear eminent speakers on a host of subjects. Music, discussion of current events, dramatic presentations, provided a varied program to which many subscribed for the season.

chattel mortgage: An arrangement by which a creditor may take possession of almost any kind of personal property that has been pledged as security if the debtor should fail to meet the terms of his agreement.

"cheap money": When prices are high and the purchasing power of the dollar is low, money is said to be "cheap" for it will buy less. If a large amount of money without adequate backing (fiat money) is put into circulation it will produce "cheap money." This situation is usually favored by the debtor class because it is easier to pay off an obligation. For political parties favoring this policy, *see* GREENBACK PARTY OR POPULISTS.

Check and Balance System: A system provided for within the framework of the three divisions of our government whereby one division seeks to protect itself against the other by requiring approval by one department of the acts of another. Typical examples include; the executive department (cabinet) must be approved by the legislative body (Senate); The house originates a money bill, but the Senate must approve also; the Supreme Court (judiciary department) judges who may be impeached by the House of Representatives (legislative department).

check-off system: The system by which the employer deducts union dues from a worker's paycheck when the individual gives written consent. There might also be deductions for union welfare funds if provided for in the union contract and administered by both labor and management.

cheeseparing: A term derisively applied to attempts to make savings by reducing the budget or similar practices by insignificant amounts and without much foresight.

chemurgy: The application of chemistry to the industrial utilization of farm grown products of organic nature. Corn sugar is being turned into glycerine, corn protein into vicara an excellent wool substitute, soy beans into a coating for paper, kenaf into jute. The prospect is excellent for replacing dwindling metal supplies by satisfactory plastic materials helpful to both the farmer and the industrial worker.

chief justice: The head of the Supreme Court is merely the titular head for convenience of administration. He earns only $500 more than the $25,000 each for the eight associate justices. He presides at conferences and assigns each case to one of the justices or to himself in appropriate rotation.

chiefs of mission: Positions held by the top diplomats in our Foreign Service. They include the positions of minister, counselor, and first, second and third secretary.

Child Labor Laws: Laws limiting the gainful employment of children by others than their parents would ordinarily be provided for by state regulation. Early attempts to do so by the federal government were felt to be necessary because some states had failed to do the job as many reformers considered it should be done. This federal control was undertaken through the power of Congress to regulate interstate commerce and an attempt was made to exclude goods made by child labor from interstate commerce. These laws, however, were found unconstitutional as regulation of manufacturing, not within the power of Congress to control, rather than of interstate commerce within its control. A federal Child Labor amendment has been prepared to give Congress the power to regulate such employment. It has not yet been ratified by the required thirty-six state legislatures. On the other hand much the same effect has been obtained through the Fair Labor Standards Act of 1938, which restricts the handling in interstate commerce of goods produced under "oppressive child labor," and through the provisions for minimum wage and hour requirements which makes the less efficient child labor uneconomically at the higher rates now required. *See* KEATING-OWENS ACT of 1916.

Children's Bureau: In 1946 this top ranking agency became part of the Federal Security Agency. It has been one of the most efficiently operated of all the national administrative units making valuable contributions to American life by the preparation and publication of millions of copies of an extensive booklet dealing with the care of small children and giving in understandable terminology scientific information about children's diseases, correct feeding, proper clothing and giving rural areas the best available information formerly more easily accessible to city mothers.

Circuit Court of Appeals: In 1789 Congress had created both district courts and circuit courts but the latter were abolished in 1911. However, in order to relieve the overburdened Supreme Court a new series of courts of appeals were established having no original jurisdiction but trying cases only on appeal. Since the Supreme Court has limited itself to hearing appeals in only five types of cases these courts may on occasion be the last court of appeal. If, however, a particularly significant case arises in one of the ten such courts, the Supreme Court may claim jurisdiction on a writ of certiorari (q.v.). There are from three to nine judges assigned to each court and a presiding judge is one of the associate judges of the Supreme Court who go on "circuit" for this purpose, one assigned to each of six districts, and two judges being assigned two districts, with a total of 65 judges.

citizen: Any person born or naturalized in the United States or subject to the jurisdiction thereof is a citizen according to the Fourteenth amendment. However according to "jus sanguinis" a child claims the citizenship to which his father owes allegiance, though if born in this country he at maturity may make claims for American citizenship under certain arrangements.

Citizens Union: An organization founded in 1897 to advance political reform while remaining carefully non-partisan. The association publishes a Voters Directory each year giving its recommendations in regard to local candidates in the following elections in New York City.

citizenship: Citizenship is membership in a political society and implies a duty of allegiance on the part of the members and a duty of protection on the part of society. Citizenship is acquired by birth or naturalization (q.v.) as provided for in the Fourteenth Amendment to the Constitution of the United States (q.v.).

city charter: A plan of government authorized by a state legislature for a city. It may provide for home rule (q.v.). *See* MUNICIPAL GOVERNMENT.

city-manager: An official employed by the city commission of a particular community as a non-political administrator (for no fixed term) and serving as its agent to supervise and control the city's activities and services. A city managership has grown to be a position of professional standing providing a supply of experienced, efficient, supervisors outside of political interference. The plan originated in Staunton, Virginia in 1908. Now over nine hundred cities in the United States have city-managers.

City Planning: A policy of integrating all the varied functions of a large city into a master plan for improvement and development that results in a well balanced program. New York City under its new charter created a City Planning Commission with authority to carry out such a program for the city and required that the membership include the chief engineer of the Board of Estimate and six other members appointed by the mayor.

City Record: A daily publication in New York City giving notice of every type of public hearing to be held that day, and announcing all changes for improvement in the master plan of the city, after approval by the City Planning Commission.

city-state: A unit in the development of government where a local community has complete independence particularly associated with the Greek city-state of the fifth or sixth century before Christ; such as Athens, Sparta or Corinth. Some Near East cities of ancient times also were independent units at some period as Babylon, Sumer, Tyre and Sidon.

Civil Aeronautics Administration: This agency enforces the safety regulations ordered by the Civil Aeronautics Board (q.v.) and administers the Federal Aid Airport Program through a $500 million appropriation from the National Treasury to assist local governments to develop airports, and provide navigation facilities with over 57,000 miles equipped for day and night contact and instrument flying over the United States and to Alaska.

Civil Aeronautics Board: The Board consists of five members appointed by the President with the consent of the Senate. Under the Reorganization Act of 1939 it regulates the economic side of civil aviation, prescribes safety standards, investigates accidents, and tries to develop international routes. To carry out the preceding program the Board licenses aviation companies, fixes rates, determines compensation for carrying the mails providing subsidies as needed.

civil case: A judicial proceeding in which an individual, not the state, acts as accuser. It includes such matters as a breach of contract, or a question of property rights or some personal wrong for which money damage is sought. The other type of court case is the criminal (q.v.).

Civil Liberties Union (American): An organization established during World War I to provide legal aid for persons whose liberties had been threatened. It is now particularly concerned about minorities and has attempted to preserve their constitutional rights to teach, print, speak, petition, assemble and worship without interference. Sometimes the causes they protect are not popular, but they have defended even those accused of being subversive if they feel that their individual rights are involved.

Civil Rights: They are those rights of an individual guaranteed in the federal Constitution, and by the states in local affairs which include personal freedom, religious liberty, freedom of speech and press and assembly, and of fair trial and also extend to the protection of property interests as well.

Civil Service: All the employees of a government, federal, state, county or municipal, other than the military are Civil Service workers, some of whom are appointed on the basis of examinations (merit system) and have established procedures for promotions, salary standards and pensions. The "unclassified" service includes those appointed without competitive examination. It is estimated that there are over two million civilian employees of the Federal government in 1950, and over six million in some type of civil service job, including state or municipal employment.

Civil Service Reform: Reform had been proposed as early as 1872 in the Civil Service, particularly by the Liberal Republicans, but got no where until after the death of President Garfield at the hands of a disappointed office seeker. Public indignation reached a high pitch and provided the weapon for the enactment of the Pendleton Act in 1883. A Civil Service Commission was established to administer open competitive examinations. Discrimination for political reasons was forbidden. Succeeding Presidents added to the list of those positions which were to be filled by the "Merit system" until the classified list (q.v.) covered up to 70% of those in government service in contrast to the 10% at the start.

classification of cities: A practice used by some state governments of grouping cities according to population for the purpose of granting charters. *See* MUNICIPAL GOVERNMENT.

classified material: This constitutes statistics and information not at the time available for publication for security reasons.

classified service: Those government employees whose jobs have been "covered" by Civil Service requirements resulting in their appointments through the passing of a series of written and oral examinations, are part of the "classified service." Heads of departments may select candidates from the top three of the eligible list. Veterans and widows of veterans are assigned additional scoring to bring them at the top of a list sooner. Removals may only occur after adequate hearings for such cause as will advance the good of the service. By designation into special categories as to type of work involved, equal pay for equal ratings have been worked out for the whole country. With tenure of office and reasonable pensions provided government service for the middle class group has grown more attractive.

Clayton Antitrust Law: Because the Sherman Antitrust Law (q.v.) was not found to be sufficiently definite in regard to what constituted monopolistic practices the Clayton Act of 1914 was passed. This act listed the specific discriminatory acts which were forbidden. Labor unions and farmer's organizations were exempt from its regulation, as later were export businesses.

clean sweep: The removal of all appointed officials when a new executive has been elected, and their replacement by members of new party.

"Clear and present danger" rule: An interpretation of the Constitution that permits restriction on certain individual rights as covered by the first ten amendments if conditions are sufficient to justify such a danger. This rule has been particularly used in sedition cases.

clemency: Mercy or pardon. Use of executive clemency in regard to the overlooking of misconduct on the part of presidential appointees.

"closed session of Congress": A secret or executive meeting of Congress called to consider treaties or appointments. Members may reveal how they voted in such a session, but not what was discussed.

closed shop: A shop or factory in which only union workers may be employed. The Taft-Hartley Law makes a distinction between a closed and a union shop prohibiting the former. The closed shop does not hire non-union labor. The union shop may hire a non-union man but he must become a union member and remain in good standing with the union during the period the labor contract under which he is working is in effect.

clôture rule (or closure): Because of many cases of filibustering (q.v.) the Senate decided in 1917 on a rule which might provide some limitation on their jealously guarded right of unrestricted debate. The rule stated that if sixteen senators signed a petition which was accepted by the rest of the house, two days later a vote could be held on the question of closing the debate, and if two-thirds of the senators agreed then debate would be limited to one hour for each senator and no dilatory motions could be introduced. This procedure has been seldom carried out probably because each senator is afraid that if he should vote cutting off debate for one man or one issue he might be the one restricted the next time.

Coast Guard: An agency in the Treasury Department in peace time and under the Navy in war time, charged primarily with the policing of United States coastal waters, and with the prevention of smuggling, dope running and other illegal practices. It also performs many functions connected with transportation, such as various aids to navigation and life-saving facilities on the ocean shore as well as on navigable waters within the United States, and enforcing safety regulations on board ship, and the investigation of accidents at sea.

coasting trade: Coast wise shipping that passes from city to city within American jurisdiction and is reserved exclusively for ships of American registry. Foreign ships engaged in such coastwise shipping may refuel or unload passengers or freight but may not compete with American business.

"coattail theory": This is the theory that in a presidential election year a sizeable number of congressional candidates are swept into office in part because of the strong enthusiasm aroused by the campaign itself, and in part by the prestige and program of the presidential candidate. Much evidence is offered by opponents of this theory that its influence is greatly exaggerated. They show incidents where Congressional candidates have drawn more votes than the president in the same district, in the same election.

code: An orderly arrangement of laws and regulations concerning various fields such as building code, criminal code or civil code.

Coin's Financial School: This imaginary institution served as the basis of a series of newspaper articles in the 1896 campaign by means of which the Populists supporting Bryan tried to show the advantages of his claims for a bimetallic standard. Thru a program of questions and answers "Silver Dick" makes clear to the public the virtues of having money backed by silver at a fixed ratio with gold. The style was very clever though the poor economics could be easily refuted.

"cold war": A term created to describe the antagonism aroused between the United States and the Soviet Union over their interests in the western and eastern zones of Germany. The expression has broadened with the start of the Korean War to imply any strained relation with the Soviet Union short of war.

collective agreements: As the result of "collective bargaining" of organized workers with management, negotiations may produce specific terms which all agree upon and which are known as "collective agreements." They may be on a local, craft, or even regional basis. Though there may be differences in detail they usually cover such items as definition of policy, relationship between union and management, job priority provisions, wage and hour arrangements, and administrative provisions for enforcement.

collective bargaining: The practice by which discussion between employer and employee regarding labor policy or wages is carried out between the employer and a recognized bargaining agent, the union, for the group rather than on the basis of individual demands. This practice was first established nationally by the famous section 7a of the NRA Codes. When the National Recovery Act was found unconstitutional this provision was repeated in the Wagner Act of 1935.

collective security: A method of avoiding attack by an aggressor because of the protection afforded by the joint action of a group of nations pledged to come to one another's aid. This action was supposedly provided for under "sanctions" in the Covenant of the League of Nations (q.v.) but the full support of all the member nations was not obtained. Under the North Atlantic Treaty Organization (q.v.) it is hoped that the idea of collective security may again have a chance for the fourteen nations cooperating.

collectivism: This is a term used to express the economic theory of the ownership by the community of those agents of production, land and capital, which under private control might be used to endanger society. The term is often used synonomously with, and as a substitute for socialism.

collusion: A secret agreement and cooperation for a fraudulent or deceit purpose, as to obtain a divorce.

collusive bidding: Bidding for public contracts where all those offering bids have agreed secretly before hand on what they will offer in an effort to prevent competition which might result in lower offers and less profit to the contractor selected.

combinations in restraint of trade: If a group of industries organized so as to control the production of specific goods or services and thus constituted a monopoly they could be found to be combinations in restraint of trade and could be prosecuted under the Sherman Antitrust Law (q.v.).

Cominform: This Communist Information Bureau consists of two delegates from each of nine countries which held its first session in 1947 in Poland "to organize and exchange experience and, in case of necessity co-ordinate the activities of Communist Parties on a foundation of mutual agreement." This organization would seem to be a substitute for the Comintern (Third International) which had been abolished in 1943 by the Soviet Union presumably to win more United Nations support during the war.

comity: Literally this means courtesy, but as between nation and nation, or of federal government and state it may mean the recognition of the authority of each, in regard to one another's laws, as in the rendering up of fugitives of justice, or in other ways observing treaty provisions. As between states in the United States the observation of the "full faith and credit clause" (q.v.) is sometimes called the observation of the comity clause.

commerce: The exchange of goods. Commerce has been interpreted under the Constitution of the United States as including navigation, but not manufacturing. Congress has the power to control commerce between the states and with foreign countries. The states retain control over exclusively intrastate commerce (within their own borders). The inability to regulate commerce under the Articles of Confederation was a primary factor in the calling of the Philadelphia Convention and the establishment of our present government.

Commerce Department: Originally created as the department of Commerce and Labor in 1903 it was found wiser to separate the two into separate units in 1913. Some of its functions are indicated by the following agencies, Census Bureau, the Bureau of Standards, the Patent Office and the Coast and Geodetic Survey. The Department supplements the diplomatic and consular offices in foreign countries through its officials of the Office of International Trade helping American business to obtain markets abroad and assisting recently in the operation of the European Recovery Program (q.v.).

commercial bank: A bank whose principal function is to receive deposits for short term intervals by business firms drawing against them promptly for purchase of raw materials or wages and then redepositing funds from retail or wholesale transactions, or to make short-term loans also for immediate business needs. All national banks are commercial banks and some state banks. They have much broader functions than savings banks. Interest may be paid for time deposits. Cash reserves and investment opportunities are closely supervised by state or federal authorities.

commercial paper: Any written document constituting evidence of debt, which may be transferred by endorsement such as checks, drafts, and bills of exchange. Such commercial paper provides the flexible element in the circulation of United States Federal Reserve Notes which are secured by a certain percent of gold and the balance of "commercial paper."

commissary: A general store or depot attached to a business, government agency, or military establishment, usually on a military post concerned with the procurement of supplies for troops. In the United States this service is performed by the Quartermaster Corps.

commission plan of city government: This plan originated in Galveston, Texas, in 1901 as a result of a flood which demoralized the old city government. There are three to nine commissioners elected by the people and each serves as a head of a department. Administrative and legislative functions are blended. Typical departments might be, public safety, public health, public welfare, public works and public finance. There is no one head of the government. The chief criticism has been based on the lack of an executive, the mixture of policy making and administrative duties, and the tendency toward administration by amateurs.

commitment: An order to imprison a person. Reference of a bill to a legislative committee. Pledge by a state that it will follow a certain line of policy.

committee of the whole: A legislative body reorganized for special discussion. On the national level the House of Representatives resolves itself into a committee of the whole House on the state of the union for considering either private or public bills. A quorum (q.v.) then is only 100 members. Debate is informal allowing only five minutes at a time to a member. After dissolution of the committee the measure must be approved by the House in formal session.

Committee on Credentials: An important committee in the National Convention (q.v.) settling the question of the admission of the official delegates assembled for the purpose of nominating a president and vice-president. Refusal of admission to certain delegates may have important consequences as was shown in the Republican Nominating Convention in 1912 when the supporters of Theodore Roosevelt found their credentials rejected in many cases and following the renomination of Mr. Taft proceeded to call a special convention at which they nominated T.R. anyway. Some consider that this split in the Republican vote was sufficient to throw the election to Woodrow Wilson.

Committee on Fair Employment Practices: This organization was established in 1941 to promote the best possible production efforts in order to carry on the war successfully and to eliminate discriminatory practices due to race, creed, color or national origin. It was largely effective because of the requirement that such conditions be met in accord with federal contracts. Though the agency went out of existence in 1946 there has been much agitation for the creation of a permanent national organization to do the same work.

Committees of Congress: *See* STANDING COMMITTEES.

Commodity Credit Corporation: An agency chartered under the laws of Delaware in 1933 but rechartered by the United States Government in 1948, it is empowered to buy and sell agricultural commodities. It has had over $4½ millions in outstanding obligations fully guaranteed by the government. Its major program since the war has been that of price support of agricultural products, and it has been buying goods in short supply in the United States from abroad such as sugar, rice, copra and fish. For complying with the requirements under the Agricultural Adjustments Law of 1938 (q.v.) the farmers receive their parity payments by mortgaging their crop to the CCC to be paid in dollars that have a purchasing power equal to the base year 1904-1914. If the market price later falls below that of the time at which the goods were placed with the CCC it must take the loss in the interests of price stability.

common law: Common law is the basic law of Anglo-Saxon derivation developed by customary practice and precedent. It was brought to this country during the colonial period and has developed with slight variations in every state. Federal courts have tried to reconcile conflicting deviations when suits have arisen involving more than one state, but that Supreme Court has ruled that the common law of the state in which the act complained about took place must be followed. This accumulation of experiences which the common law represents has been broadened by usage in application to cases having slight variations. It may be repealed by state laws or still further developed by subsequent decisions.

commonwealth: A term used to designate a body of people politically organized into a state, as the Commonwealth of Australia, or of a subdivision such as the Commonwealths of Virginia or Massachusetts.

Communism: This term is used in so many connections, and has such an emotional context that a meaningful definition is difficult to make. To many it means anything objectionable. Historically it means a program by which, through revolution if necessary, a people take over virtually all property in the name of the people. Government would then "wither away" and life would be a heaven on earth with everything needed provided out of the common store and all human beings so socially responsible that there would be no need for laws, police or controls. As the U.S.S.R. is the only country that has been applying these views to a large extent one can only wonder how long before the "withering away" begins in the light of the extreme control now exercised.

Communist Party (U.S.A.): A combination of the Communist and the Communist Labor Party was brought about in 1919 practically as a branch of the Communist International. It suffered many schisms, and reversed its policies obediently upon orders from Moscow. Though opposing the Socialist's position because of their willingness to use parliamentarian means to gain their aims on government ownership, the Communist Party has actually in its announced policy become less radical. This may have been partially due to the Voorhis Act which forced the party to sever its formal allegiance with the Third International in 1940.

community: A group of people who live together in the same locality, originating as a family group or a tribal village, customs and rules were enforced which finally resulted in the organization of a formal government. Also, simple agricultural division of labor finally resulted in the varied occupational divisions that now make the working together of all so important in a modern community, whose divisions may be predominantly, rural, suburban or urban, depending on the degree of concentration of the population and the extent of industrialization.

Community chest: A program supposed to have started in Cleveland, Ohio, to raise money to support social and recreational agencies which provide benefits for the community not adequately provided for by governmental means. Through this device a concerted drive is made to assist all needed activities at one time with all groups cooperating rather than sporadic drives undertaken by numerous organizations duplicating one another's efforts.

"community of interest": When trusts (q.v.) were found illegal under the Sherman Antitrust Law big business interests sought another form of organization which would serve the same purpose. They found this in the "community of interest" program which permitted one company to buy a sufficient quantity of another's stock to make its influence felt, and which could have representatives of one company on another's board, despite the Clayton Acts forbidding interlocking directorates under some circumstances. If no "unfair practices" are committed this "cooperation" of a number of related businesses is able to continue.

Community Planning Councils: Groups of individuals living in a local neighborhood interested in civic betterment, who know what improvements are needed and who participate in the actual planning and the securing of community support.

Community property system: A principle accepted in over a dozen states; a heritage from Spanish law, that a husband and wife may create a community estate of the property owned by each, and have an equal interest in it during their marriage. In 1948 a revision in the federal income tax provisions allowed this principle to operate, so that the husband and wife may split their joint income in two and each pay half the tax and thus take advantage of a possibly lower income tax rate.

community theatre: An amateur or semi-professional acting group which originated in New York City in 1915 through the activities of the Washington Square Players who later became the Theatre Guild.

Community Trusts: Because there was the possibility that a number of persons who desired to donate funds for charitable purposes might provide for a great many scattered contributions to very limited activities, the Cleveland Trust Company initiated a plan where an accumulation of funds could be assembled and a group of trustees decide for what worthy purpose this should be used. This practice has been extended greatly in recent years, operating in many cities and administering larger and larger sums without waste or inefficiency, and within the needs of the community welfare.

commutation: The reduction in a penalty or a punishment to a lesser degree. The power to commute a sentence rests only with the chief executive of the state for state offenses, and with the President of the United States for federal offenses and is in line with the pardoning power of these officials.

Compact Theory: A theory from which the States' Right Theory was derived based on the premise that the states were sovereign and that they had agreed to a "compact" with one another to create the federal government. This idea was revived by Calhoun in his "Exposition and Protest" giving the viewpoint of the South in opposition to the Tariff of 1828. Later it was stated that because of the compact theory the state of South Carolina was justified in declaring the Tariff of 1832 null. Finally in the 1860's this theory was carried to its ultimate false reasoning —that of the right of South Carolina to secede.

company union: A labor union whose membership is made up exclusively of members employed by one company and which is usually not connected with a labor union. Because of expected domination by management they were found illegal by the National Labor Relations Board in 1935. However they were later recognized if sufficiently independent.

compensated dollar: A suggestion for attempting to eliminate the evils of the business cycle with its recurrent rising and falling prices has been proposed in this idea for backing up the dollar with a varying gold content that should keep the price level on an even keel. When prices are rising too steeply the gold content would be increased thus fewer dollars would be in circulation and the prices would fall. When prices were falling too fast the gold content would be lessened, as was done in 1933, and with more money in circulation prices would start rising again. This is what it is expected would happen with such a dollar in circulation, all other conditions being equal, no artificial shortages, or no war hysteria. Some economists, however look upon the cure as worse than the disease, mistrusting any sort of "managed currency" that acts contrary to the economic laws of supply and demand.

competition: A condition that exists when there are a large number of individuals or corporations offering similar products no one of whom could offer enough to materially affect the price. Competition has been considered the greatest stimulus to the existence of a capitalistic society in the introduction of new, and improved products and services. On the other hand it is the situation most attacked by the socialists for its duplication and waste.

complemental motion: In correct parliamentary procedure such a motion is one intended to fill some gap in the main motion, such as the insertion of a date or other detail.

complimentary vote: The casting of votes for certain individuals at a Convention in order to show respect to a former official, or any popular local individual whom they have no real intention of nominating or electing.

Comptroller General of the United States: This financial official is head of the General Accounting Office and is appointed by the President of the United States for a period of fifteen years and may only be removed by joint resolution of Congress or by impeachment proceedings. Because of this position of comparative autonomy the Comptroller General has been one of the controversial figures of recent times. Recommendations have been made that the office be put under executive supervision, since his chief function is to prevent any disbursements not authorized by Congress.

compulsory arbitration: This situation exists where there is a legal requirement that all disputes must be submitted to a tribunal and the decision must be binding on both sides, or in some cases the acceptance of the decision may be voluntary. Representatives of both labor and management are much in agreement in that both are opposed to any form of compulsion.

compulsory education: The states of the United States require that children remain in school up to a certain age which varies in the different states though ranging from 14-17. Funds for the public schools are raised in different fashions also. The state may contribute from the general taxation or designate a portion of a sales tax, or income tax for that purpose, or may assign all taxes on public utilities or railroads to be turned over for that purpose.

conciliation: An attempt to reconcile two parties to a dispute by suggestions and advice, but with no authority to compel a settlement.

concurrent majority: A majority gained by the concurrence of legislators who have agreed on a particular issue but still remain divided on other issues. These majorities are common in the American political scene because of the diverse economic and regional interests that often cut across partisan lines.

concurrent powers: The powers that rest with both the federal government and the state government so that the two governments may act jointly or independently. The power to tax, and at one time, the power to limit the sale of intoxicating liquor, and the exercise of "police powers" (q.v.) are examples of this power.

concurrent resolution: A special type of measure employed by

Congress which does not require approval by the President for matters peculiarly within the scope of Congress alone. Examples-creation of joint committees and publication of documents.

concurring opinion: An opinion expressed by one of the judges in a court decision which agrees with the verdict of the majority but is based upon different reasons which are usually presented in a separate report.

condemnation: A judicial proceeding by which private property is taken under the rights of eminent domain (q.v.).

Confederacy (Confederate States of America): The eleven states of the South, having announced their secession in 1861, remained independent until forced to surrender in 1865 and underwent a process of reconstruction until all were readmitted to the Union.

confederation: A union of sovereign states which may have a central administrative body but have the greatest authority remaining with the states. Usually contrasted with a federation such as the present government of the United States represents with much needed delegation of authority to Congress and the President. *See* ARTICLES OF CONFEDERATION.

Conference Committee of Congress: After a bill on the same topic has been passed by both houses of Congress and the provisions are not identical an "ironing out" process must be undertaken. For this purpose a special committee is created containing an equal number of members chosen from each house, usually about three, who attempt to compromise the differences and obtain a majority vote. This compromise measure then goes back to each house where it is customary for it to be accepted.

confirmation: Approval of appointments to executive positions made by legislative bodies. The United States Senate must confirm most United States diplomatic and administrative positions not covered by Civil Service examinations.

confiscation: Seizure of private property by the government without compensation as a result of the commission of a crime or similar action.

conformity: Compliance, regimentation. A situation which may easily lead an individual to accept fascist tendencies in extreme cases or at least to be an easy prey for unscrupulous politicians. Not to be confused with a sense of community solidarity.

Congressional Campaign Committee: In the period between presidential elections each major party has a National Committee (q.v.) to keep the basic organization intact. However this activity was not held to be sufficient by the members of Congress whose critical election period falls in the off years, and who wanted to keep the campaign machinery from disintegrating. The Republicans maintain a Congressional Campaign Committee made up of one Congressman from each state having Republican representation. They are designated by each state's party members in the House of Representatives and are formally elected by a caucus of Republican Senators and Representatives. The Democrats have a like organization but permit each state whether represented in the House or not to have a seat on the Committee. Each committee undertakes to help out in the nomination and election of members of the House. The Senate has similar committees.

Congressional Directory: An annual handbook which includes much pertinent information regarding committees, committee members, brief sketches of the lives of Senators and Representatives.

Congressional Record: The Record purports to give an exact stenographic reproduction of everything said on the floor of the two houses of Congress. However members may edit their remarks and speeches are frequently printed under special leave ("extension of remarks") which were not actually delivered. The Record has been published since 1873. It replaced the "Congressional Globe" which had done a similar job between 1823 and 1873.

Congress of Industrial Organization: Recognizing the trend toward larger and larger business consolidation a group within the American Federation of Labor started to promote a similar idea for labor by setting up a Committee for Industrial Organization. Unable to overcome the A. F. of L.'s basic belief in the craft or horizontal union the sponsoring group broke away and set up a new confederation, the Congress of Industrial Organization in 1938, made up of a number of industrial unions (q.v.) or vertical unions composed of all the workers in a particular union whether consisting of skilled workers or not. The automobile, rubber and steel industries provided a large membership. John L. Lewis was the first president of the C.I.O. but the United Mine Workers Union later withdrew and Philip Murray became and has remained president.

conscience money: Funds paid into any government treasury by those who have defrauded that government and whose conscience bothers them.

conscientious objector: One who for religious or philosophical reasons refuses to support a policy of war, or take part in combat duty. Under the Selective Service Act of 1940 those able to prove their claims were allowed to take part in activities of "national importance" such as conservation programs, or varied duties in hospital or mental institutions.

conscription: The compulsory selection of a man for service in the armed forces of his country. In the Selective Service Acts of 1917 and 1940 there were no provisions for hiring substitutes or for paying bounties as in the Civil War draft laws. In American policy it was not considered suitable to have a draft in "peace time" but so critical were conditions in the world in October of 1940, Congress passed its first peace time draft as it was forced to do again in 1950 as the result of tensions in the Far East.

conservation: A program of preservation of natural resources, land, forests, minerals, actively participated in by the federal government. Theodore Roosevelt was especially active in this field in the early 1900's. Franklin D. Roosevelt also furthered the program greatly particularly in his support of Tennessee Valley Authority (q.v.).

conservative: In politics a conservative is usually one who is content with conditions as they are and feels that far-reaching changes in political and economics situations are not wise.

consolidated schools: Modern replacements of the "one room school" are now common as the result of the effort of several communities to band together to form a single school district. One efficient well equipped school building is constructed with the cost apportioned among the towns in relationship to the size of the community or the number of pupils from each district.

conscription of labor: The issue of whether a person may be forced to work for the government, or for a private concern has not been definitely settled by a decision of the Supreme Court. This will have to be done in the light of the Thirteenth Amendment which forbids involuntary servitude unless the person has been duly convicted of a crime. During World War II Congress was considering the necessity of drafting labor and thus forcing civilians to work for private persons who might have made a profit from their labor. A general labor draft failed of enactment but severe restrictions were placed on the mobility of labor, the penalties being inabilities to get other jobs, or the threat of reclassification and draft into the military service.

constable: A policeman, or an officer of the peace. A high military figure originally (count of the stable).

constitution: The basic or fundamental principles upon which a government is established.

Constitution Day: A day to commemorate the completion of the writing of the federal constitution by the Constitutional Convention on September 17, 1787. The session had begun the preceding May with delegates from all the colonies concerned about the critical task of establishing a new government to overcome all the weaknesses that had developed under the Articles of Confederation (q.v.).

constitution, state: As war with Britain started in 1775 the colonies or states as they now called themselves, formed or adopted fundamental laws for their governance. Massachusetts and New Hampshire were two of the earliest to have constitutions ratified by the people, both before 1784. Some states retained these early constitutions for fifty years or more. Massachusetts did not revise hers until 1918. All newly admitted states had to have Congressional approval of theirs.

Constitution, United States: The document prepared by the Constitutional Convention in 1787 which after ratification went into effect on March 4, 1789. It lists the powers of Congress, of the president and the qualifications and duties of all such officials; creates a judiciary branch while also guaranteeing the states certain rights, limits them in others. The first ten amendments (Bill of Rights q.v.) safeguard the rights of individuals. Custom, judicial interpretation, usage, and formal amendment have modified the original constitution in some respects making it a living, flexible document, particularly in the trend toward extending the power of the national government but the basic safeguards remain effective in a nice balance of "loose" and "strict" interpretation (q.v.).

Constitutional Commissions: These commissions are created by the legislatures of the states to advise on the matter of the revision of the state constitutions since the legislators have neither the time nor the special knowledge for this critical and important job. The result may be the submitting of a whole new constitution to the voters for approval, and rejection as sometimes happens, or the introduction through the appropriate machinery of a number of constitutional amendments expertly prepared.

consul: Officials sent by one state to another to assist its nationals and advance its commercial relations.

Consular jurisdiction: The Consul of the United States in a foreign post has authority over the internal economy of American vessels, he settles disputes between masters, officers and men. He also assists in excluding prohibited classes of immigrants from sailing on any vessels. He issues a bill of health after sanitary inspection. Shipwrecked American sailors and mutineers are sent home, and visas are issued to foreign travelers desirous of visiting the United States.

containment: A policy of preventing overt Communist aggression against states not now under Communist domination. This program was implemented by the Truman (q.v.) Doctrine and the proposed extension of the North Atlantic Pact was in the same direction.

contempt of Congress: Either house of Congress, or any duly authorized investigating committee has the authority to issue orders requiring witnesses to appear and give testimony, but also have authority to impose punishment when orders are not obeyed, or Congress may leave to the courts the duty of applying the criminal statute to disobedient individuals.

contempt of court: Wilful disobedience of a court committed in its presence or near enough to weaken its authority. It may be criminal contempt, or in a failure to carry out a court order in a civil suit, be civil contempt, but both are punishable after trial by jury, by fine and imprisonment.

contested elections: Each house of Congress is the sole judge of election returns and the qualifications of its members and may create an investigating committee to look into any questionable returns.

Continental Congress: The First Continental Congress met in Philadelphia in 1774 bringing together irregularly chosen delegates from every colony except Georgia. The Second met in 1775 and was faced with the job of carrying on the Revolution. It served as the sole organ of national authority until March 1781.

Continentalism: The name given to the policy of political self-containment advocated for the United States in regard to its continental homeland. It was warmly recommended by Washington when he found Europe had a "set of primary interests" of little concern to Americans. The term has become practically equivalent to isolationism (q.v.) today.

contingent expense: An incidental or unforeseen expenditure usually met from some reserves designated for petty accounts.

contraband: Those items which a neutral may not supply to a belligerent. Difficulties of interpretation as to what constituted these items became particularly critical in the early years of World War I because oil and cellulose products and even food stuffs were felt to be important factors in the winning of modern wars.

contract clause in the Constitution: This clause Article 1, section 10, stipulates that no state may pass any law "impairing the obligation of contract." Clear as this statement seems many legal complications have arisen. Charters issued by state legislatures are not considered contracts.

contract labor: A situation where a worker, especially an immigrant assumes a specific obligation, such as paying for his transportation. This practice is forbidden in the United States.

contractors: Because there are so many jobs which a city administration may award to contractors it is not surprising that they represent a large element in the municipal pressure groups. Some have tried to get contracts by means of eliminating competition, or to make sure of approval of their work by having friends appointed inspectors in the field in which they are engaged. Some may also be able to take advantage of the "honest graft" with which a city administration abounds, such as previous knowledge of sites to be bought up in advance of the city for playgrounds or schools.

cooling-off periods: A method available under the Taft-Hartley Law to try to prevent strikes by requiring that a party to a labor contract may negotiate a change in the contract only by giving sixty days advance notice or until the contract expires or for the time limit set no strike may be undertaken.

cooperatives: Consumer cooperatives are types of business organizations patterned after the Rochdale stores first established in England in 1844. The individual may buy stock in these enterprises but is limited to one vote despite the number of shares he may possess. Profits are divided among the share holders in proportion to the amount of individual purchases made. The Capper Volstead Act of 1922 states that producers of agricultural products who form cooperative organizations are free from possible regulation under the Anti-Trust Acts.

Copperheads: Those in the North who favored the Southern cause in the Civil War. It was suspected that many of those supporting Democratic candidates were Copperheads. *See* "Bloody shirt, waving of."

copyright: The special right enjoyed by an author to publish and sell his literary works. The Library of Congress receives applications which when granted gives the writer, composer, artist or cartoonist exclusive control for twenty-eight years with a possible renewal for an equal period.

coroner: A local official who is required to preside over an inquest which must be held for every person who dies a violent death.

Corporate Revolution: Vast increases in the size of business units offering better opportunity to use technical processes and new machinery to attain the economics of specialization and division of labor constitute the "corporate revolution." All this activity of the 1880's was speeded up in the following twenty years with mergers and consolidations succeeding one another in rapid development.

corporation: A group of persons joined together under the specific requirements established in the state in which the proceedings were initiated. The corporation is considered as an artificial person which as a legal entity may sue and be sued, and benefit from all the safeguards established in the Fourteenth Amendment (q.v.) to the United States Constitution for a real person. The federal government also may permit incorporation of independent agencies such as the Federal Deposit Insurance Corporation or the Reconstruction Corporation.

corporation income tax: A federal tax providing an important source of federal funds. The rate was felt to have been so high during World War II that few firms had sufficient surplus funds available to make conversion plans, and in 1945 the rate was lowered somewhat, however sharp increases were felt necessary in 1950 and afterwards. In 1947 the corporation income tax netted the federal government over $10 billion.

corrupt practices acts: These are laws that prevent corruption in connection with elections that might arise because of the fiscal activities of parties and candidates. The Hatch Acts (q.v.) fixed maximum expenditures for individuals and the national committees. The Taft-Hartley Act restricts a union's direct contributions to political parties. Other federal laws have attempted to limit the amount candidates for Congress may spend to $25,000 for Senators, and $5,000 for Representatives. Not too great success has followed from the attempt to apply these laws.

cost-of-living escalator: An arrangement included in some union-employer contracts by which wages increase when the Bureau of Labor Statistics announces a rise in the consumer price index, or go down when it falls.

cost-plus contract: An arrangement made with the government which provides that the contractor will be paid for his work in accord with the cost of materials and of labor plus a fixed percentage fee.

council-manager plan: This type of city government is also the city-manager plan and was originated in Staunton, Virginia in 1908 though the first of the large cities to adopt it was Toledo,

Ohio in 1914 where its success attracted much attention. Its greatest asset is centralized responsibility which has caused it to grow more and more popular in its appeal to those wanting efficient and economical city government. The council appoints or "hires" its city-manager to direct the affairs of the city in all respects except the field of education and holds him directly responsible for all inadequacies. He is not supposed to be a politician but an expert administrator. The council formulates the policy and he must carry it out.

Council of Economic Advisors: Fearful of any recession in the necessary economic readjustments following the end of the war Congress provided in the Employment Act of 1946 that a Council be established called the Council of Economic Advisors to be appointed by the president and to consist of three prominent economists. These officials were to be part of the Presidents Executive Office and after study of the trends of employment, prices, taxes and related matters were to prepare an annual report whose aim would be to maintain economic stability by trying to foresee the economic road the country was following.

Council of State Governments: This organization with its headquarters in Chicago is a part of the Public Administration Clearing House, and is supported by the State governments. It acts as a research center and a coordinating agency for regional associations on Interstate Cooperation. Negotiations for drafting compacts between the states are initiated with these groups. All this cooperation works toward better relations and closer harmony between the States and keeps them up-to-date in regard to current problems and what is being done about them. The impact of the Council on the states has been tremendous and it has worked tirelessly for improved government in the states. Its publications are invaluable to scholars in political science as well as laymen and state officials. It publishes BOOK OF THE STATES, STATE GOVERNMENT, WASHINGTON LEGISLATIVE BULLETIN. The Council is the secretariat for the Governor's Conference, the American Legislators' Association and the American Association of Attorney-General, secretaries of state and others.

counselor: An attorney who gives legal advice in the preparation of cases at law. Also, a foreign service officer, second in authority to the head of an embassy or legation.

counterpart funds: One of the chief benefits of the Marshall Plan was to meet the great need of European countries to buy American goods after the destruction they had suffered during World War II, but who were limited in making such purchases in many cases by a lack of American dollars. By means of these special funds those desiring to make purchases for European recovery would find equal or duplicate funds in American dollars made available if the farmer or business man involved had deposited with his own government money in his own currency which would then be matched by such counterpart funds. Ultimately through intergovernmental bookkeeping and loans this indebtedness was balanced, but in the meantime recovery was advanced. *See* MARSHALL PLAN.

counter-revolutionary: An expression used to designate those who act against the revolutionary trend of the times, especially the nobles, friends of the King and supporters of the Catholic Church at the time of the French Revolution (1789).

County: A local administrative unit in all states except Louisiana which uses the term parish. The range is from that of New York County (Manhattan Island) of 22 square miles to that of San Bernardino with 22,000 square miles; from Armstrong, S. D. with a population of 42 and Cook County (Illinois) with 4 million persons. The governing body is usually a County Board, elected and with a membership varying from one to 84, with 70% of them having from three to five. The Board has usually administrative powers covering matters of finance, highways, charities and a large assortment of miscellaneous items. The County officials and their duties are much as follows: Sheriff to preserve the peace, carry out court orders and issue writs. Prosecuting attorney to make arrests and commence criminal actions. Coroner to investigate circumstances under which any person has died in violent or suspicious circumstances. A Clerk and a Court to keep the records.

court-house gang: Those members of small political machines in town or county who look for political rewards through appointive office, or through contracts for fuel, food, construction or printing; such as aspiring young lawyers or county seat editors, who benefit directly or indirectly from the existing regime regardless of party affiliation and fight the application of the merit system.

court-martial: A tribunal consisting of military and naval officers and men from the ranks who try a person for violating military or naval law.

Court of Claims: A federal court created in 1855 before which suits against the United States could be tried. There are still some limitations on what cases may be brought before it but any contractual claim is valid.

court packing proposals: An attempt was initiated by President Roosevelt in 1937 to "reform" the Supreme Court which it was felt at the time was blocking New Deal legislation because so many measures like, Agricultural Allotments Act (q.v.) and the National Recovery Act, were being found unconstitutional. An additional judge was to be appointed for each member, who though eligible for retirement had not done so, until a panel of fifteen judges was reached. Though there had been much popular discontentment over the "nine old men" the measure was defeated. *See* SUPREME COURT.

covenant: An agreement entered into by two or more persons, or a solemn pledge. Also used to designate the "constitution" of the League of Nations as part of the Treaty of Versailles.

craft union (trade union): A cooperative group of workers concerned with all matters having to do with the improvement of their working conditions, and all engaged in a similar type of process or trade. The craft union is considered to be organized on the horizontal basis across industrial lines in contrast to the newer industrial union (q.v.). From the "locals" within one community there rises a hierarchy, of state, national and international grouping. One sample of this is the International Brotherhood of Bookbinders, or the United Association of Plumbers and Steamfitters of the United States and Canada.

Crime commissions: Private citizens' organizations which observe local crime conditions, cooperate with civic, educational and law enforcement agencies to curtail or prevent crime and report to the public any evidence of laxity or corruption in the carrying out of this program.

Crime prevention programs: Those activities of the police and welfare organizations designed to reduce the opportunities for criminal behaviors. Athletic programs such as those conducted by the Police Athletic Leagues, Boys Club activities, Neighborhoodhouses, Scouting and related programs such as Teen Age Centers (q.v.) all assist in this work.

criminal case: A court proceeding which involves the commission or omission of an act which is an offense against the state. The state is the accuser, prosecutor and plaintiff.

Critical Period: The period from the end of the American Revolution to the ratification of the United States Constitution (1783-1789) has been designated by this term because there was considerable question whether the new nation just created would actually survive. There were many weaknesses in the Articles of Confederation (q.v.) under which the country was governed at that time, which contributed to the "criticalness" of this period, but fortunately they proved valuable in the long run for remedies were provided in the new constitution.

cross-filing: The election laws of several states allow a candidate to file in the primary elections of both major parties. This is possible in the "open primary" where there are no restrictions requiring the voters to have registered for a particular party in the preceding elections. The program is resented by those believing strongly in party "purity."

"Cross of Gold Speech": A famous speech delivered many times by William Jennings Bryan in 1896 in advocating "Free Silver" (q.v.). It contained a plea for "cheap money" (q.v.) in which he advocated that the government allow the free and unlimited coinage of silver at the ratio of sixteen to one, and attacked the big money interests who he claimed were crucifying the farmers by their control of the wealth of the country, their high interest rates or their high freight rates or their influence upon Congress. Despite the vigor of his campaign and great oratorical ability the "sound" money advocates of McKinley won.

"cross the aisle": When a member of a legislature votes with the opposition party he may be accused of having "crossed the aisle" because in many law-making bodies the different parties are literally separated by a center aisle in the seating arrangements.

"cruel and unusual punishments" prohibited: Inhumane punishment or torture is condemned by the Constitution of the United States in the Eighth Amendment. The Supreme Court has held hard and painful labor in chains for falsification of public records an action within the application of this prohibition.

Cumberland Road: A national highway authorized by the Federal government in 1806 and extending from Maryland across Ohio and Indiana. It symbolizes the idea of internal improvements at federal expense rather than at state expense and became one of the "Sectional" issues at a later period. *See* INTERNAL IMPROVEMENTS.

cumulative voting: This method of voting is being tried out as a method for giving the individual greater weight in the choice of officials. Under it the voter has more than one vote. He may give two or more votes to the same nominee or distribute them. Minority groups may stand a better chance under this system by concentrating their additional votes on a particular candidate they favor.

currency, varieties used in the United States: The commonest type of paper money in circulation in this country today is the Federal Reserve Note. Silver certificates are plentiful and United States Notes issued by the Treasury common. National Bank Notes, and Federal Reserve Bank Notes are being called in and are very scarce. Gold certificates have practically disappeared since the nationalization of gold (q.v.) in 1933.

custody: Imprisonment of a person convicted of a crime, or (q.v.) the safekeeping of one arrested and accused of a crime.

custom and usage as means of effecting Constitutional expansion: The whole system of party development is not mentioned in the Constitution, nor is there a specific basis for the cabinet, nor for the departments which they administer. The really revolutionary change in our government of turning the presidential electors into figure heads has been effected by custom. Also, since the number of Presidential appointments is now so large, recommendation by a Senator or Representative is often the most effective way of gaining office. All the indirect means employed by "pressure groups" to introduce bills are generally outside of the legally provided structure of our government.

Customs Court: One of three federal courts created by Congress not originally provided for in the Constitution, but implied through the power to collect custom duties. Its only jurisdiction is in regard to classification of merchandise and the determination of dutiable valuation of imported goods. The Court is located in New York City.

Customs Service: Next to the Bureau of Internal Revenue the Custom Service collects the largest amount of revenue received by the United States. There are collectors at all the major ports and at some of the interior points for goods may be shipped under bond and duties paid at any destination.

D

Danbury Hatter's Case (1908): A famous Supreme Court decision which held the Brotherhood of United Hatters of America responsible for "restraint of trade" when they boycotted a hat firm in Danbury, Connecticut; thus making them subject to action under the Sherman Antitrust Law. A judgment of $240,000 was rendered against the union. This immediately started labor organizations on a crusade to remedy the situation which they at last accomplished in 1914 with the passage of the Clayton Antitrust Law, which specifically excluded unions from the possibility of being held in restraint of trade, and was looked upon as the Magna Carta of the labor movement.

"dark continent" of American politics: The county government is often referred to in this fashion because of the confusion and corruption resulting from the use of the long ballot (q.v.) and because there is so often duplication of the work of the county officials by their city, town or state counterparts.

dark horse: A candidate nominated after a deadlock of the better known candidates. One who has had little publicity or consideration before the convention. Polk was the first dark horse candidate on a national scale in 1844.

Dawes Plan: A committee headed by Charles G. Dawes who proposed in 1924 that Germany's annual reparation payments be scaled down and an effort be made to balance her budget. This effort lasted as long as American loans in gold poured into Germany who used the gold to pay her reparation obligations to Great Britain and France, who in turn paid off their war debts to the United States in the gold thus obtained. The collapse of the Plan came with the end of American loans to Germany, and was followed in 1929 by the proposal of a similar plan called the Young Plan (q.v.).

daylight saving time: A practice presumably advanced for the benefit of city dwellers by which one turns the clock ahead an hour sometime at the start of the summer in order to provide more sunlight for the office workers after business hours. There is noticeable criticism from the farm population, already early risers, who are disturbed by the necessity of fitting "nature" into varied railway schedules and upsetting the barnyard routine.

death sentence clause: A provision of the Public Utility Holding Company Law of 1935 which caused all but certain types of holding companies to be held illegal.

Debt Default Act of 1934: The Johnson Act prohibited loans to any nation in default of its payment of obligations to the United States in connection with World War I and automatically ended the possibility of loans to most European Nations. It was repealed after 1941 to permit loans to nations after World War II.

debt, imprisonment for: New York State was the first state in 1831 to outlaw imprisonment for debt, and all others have since followed suit. Now debtors are free if they have violated no part of the penal code.

debt limit: The maximum amount beyond which a government agency may not borrow. Congress may vote such a limit, or a state may do so for a municipality.

debt, national: The national debt of the United States in 1950 was just under $280 billion on which the interest alone is over $5 billion. About one-quarter of this debt is in the form of redeemable bonds held by individuals. Another portion is held by federal agencies and trust accounts. The rest, or 55% is in marketable issues held by Federal Reserve Banks, commercial banks, loan and insurance companies.

decentralization: Division or scattering of power among several authorities. Removal of industrial enterprises and residential sections from key centers to avoid danger of complete collapse of industrial activity in case of atomic or any other type of bombing has been suggested.

declaration of intention: The so-called first papers of an alien starting the process of naturalization. A declarent alien is one who has taken out his first papers.

declaratory judgments: Because of the over-crowded character of many court dockets there are those who would have a declaratory judgment rendered to clarify the law and permit cases to be settled outside of court. Much as this might speed up the settlement of some types of cases there is some opposition to this cutting of red tape on the ground that a court is not able to pass on a point of law as a matter of principle since in the absence of an actual case it is difficult to perceive all the implications. Short-sighted lawyers may display slight enthusiasm for issuing these time-saving awards.

deed: A document which shows the transfer of ownership in land and houses from one person to another.

de facto government: A government which is actually governing a country even though it may have no legal authority except that acquired by the actual uprising and have had no recognition by other countries. If full legal recognition is obtained then the government is known as a "de jure" government.

defamation: The offense of injuring a person's character or reputation by false statements.

defendant: A person against whom a legal action is brought in court. The plaintiff is the person who brings the suit in a civil case, or the government in a criminal case.

Defense, Department of: As the result of a program of unification effected in 1949 a National Military Establishment was created known as the Department of Defense and including in it the Department of the Army, the Department of the Navy, the Department of the Air Force and certain other agencies. In addition to the obvious military duties of the preceding there are nonmilitary functions carried out as follows: the army engineers undertake extensive construction jobs, such as the building of the Panama Canal, the Navy has supervision of civil governments in islands such as, Guam and American Samoa, assembles hydrographic and navigational information for the maps and charts it issues, and broadcasts signals every hour from the Naval Observatory.

deficiency bills: Measures introduced to make up for an inadequate appropriation as originally passed. On a national scale all such money bills originate in the House of Representatives.

deficit bonds: Bonds may be issued in certain states to meet a situation where administrative agencies have had expenditures in excess of appropriations on such items as, the poor fund, court expense fund, rebuilding bridges destroyed by fire or flood.

deflation: A period when there is an increase in the purchasing power of money, and when the volume of money in circulation has contracted in relation to the amounts of goods available. *See opposite* INFLATION.

delegated powers: *See* enumerated powers.

delegation of power: The transfer of authority from one branch of government to another as in a case where Congress may create a specific agency and outline the limit of its authority. The National Recovery Act was found unconstitutional because Congress had given a blanket authority to all the various industrial boards involved to make codes of fair competition and enforce them. The Supreme Court decided this was an unfair "delegation of authority."

delinquent taxes: Taxes not paid when due. Fines are prescribed for short term delays, but in regard to property whose taxes have been long unpaid, the appropriate governmental authorities may order the property sold passing on to the individual involved any balance owed to him.

demagogue: A politician who attempts to win popular support by extravagant statements, by emotional appeals to prejudice or passions of the mob, by unscrupulous claims, and by a willingness to be on both sides of an issue, or to win over opposing groups by reversing his position as needed.

democracy: Rule by the people. It may take the direct form as the New England Town Meeting (q.v.) with all eligible members able to actually attend the law making sessions, or be an indirect form in which the individual elects a representative to act for him as in a municipal assembly, state legislature, or Congress.

Democratic Party: Originating as the Democratic-Republicans (q.v.) in support of Jefferson the party used the single word Democrat from the presidency of Andrew Jackson on, when the rule of the "common man" was particularly stressed. Under Cleveland, Woodrow Wilson, and Franklin D. Roosevelt further "democratic" principles were evolved especially in the attempts to curb monopoly practices and limit the power of "Big Business." Reduction in the tariff was frequently proposed and a check upon the banking interests instituted through the passage of the Federal Reserve Act. With the New Deal came a greater degree of government in business as in the creation of the Tennessee Valley Authority, the many public works projects, and the increased aid to the handicapped. The Fair Deal of President Truman brought an intensification of all these items plus additional aid abroad to fight Communism.

The Democratic Party has been practically the only Party in the South (q.v. Solid South) as the result of the Reconstruction program carried out by the Republican Party after the Civil War. The first noticeable gains for the Republicans were in the 1928 election. However the Democrats have had to face a split in their own ranks in the 1948 election over the Civil Rights issue when the Dixiecrats bolted (q.v.).

In its century and a half of existence the Democrats have made what amounts to a reversal of their position on the issue of States Rights (q.v.). Originally Jefferson was a firm advocate of strict interpretation which would limit the power of the federal government and protect the rights of the individual states. Under the New Deal the Democrats have become the advocates of a program greatly extending the power of the federal government, with the Republicans proposing the return of many controls to the states.

Democratic-Republicans (also called Republicans and Jeffersonian Democrats): Followers of Jefferson and opponents of the Federalists (q.v.) they were active from the start of our government. They were particularly for States' Rights, for the protection of the common man, and for the agrarian interests in distinction to the commercial interests of those who favored Hamilton's financial program.

democratic socialism: A term used to refer to a type of socialism under which there is partial government ownership of private enterprise in regard to certain key industries, such as banking, munitions making, utilities and transportation, established by means of the vote of the law-making body as in modern Britain and France particularly.

demonetization: The removal of certain coins from the officially designated list of legal coins. This was done in regard to the silver dollar by what was known as the "Crime of '73" because silver was more valuable as a commodity than as money, so that many people were melting down the silver dollar and therefore the government stopped trying to keep it in circulation since it would suffer a financial loss to do so. Later when a great new supply of silver was discovered the value of silver dropped greatly and the miners brought pressure upon the government to purchase the surplus silver and coin silver dollars again.

denaturalization: When the certificate of naturalization of a citizen has been revoked, the citizen has been denaturalized. Conviction of crime other than treason does not abrogate citizenship but results in merely loss of civil and political privileges. However, cancellation of citizenship does follow if it was obtained by fraudulent means, or since 1950, if the person becomes affiliated with a Communist-front organization within five years of his naturalization.

deponent: One who testifies to the truth of certain facts.

deportation: The right to send aliens regarded as dangerous to the public welfare out of the state.

deposition: Testimony taken from a witness in writing to be later used as evidence in court procedure, and subject to cross examination.

depression: A period of the business cycle following the crash or panic stage characterized by full scale unemployment, slight business activity and limited extension of credit. A situation well described by Franklin Roosevelt in 1933 when he said that the nation had nothing so much to fear as fear itself. This psychological lift plus the "pump priming of the 'New Deal'" (q.v.) did serve to break the worst of that depression.

despotism: Absolute power-autocracy. This term usually refers to a period of tyrannical rule under a monarch, as that of Louis XIV of France, or of Peter the Great of Russia, in the Seventeenth Century. It may, however be used to refer to a condition in modern politics, as in the case of a so-called dictatorial Speaker of the House (Uncle Joe Cannon) or in regard to a committee which flouts democratic practice.

destroyer-base deal: An executive agreement made by F. D. Roosevelt on September 2, 1940 with Great Britain to exchange 50 overage destroyers for bases ranging from Newfoundland to the Caribbean of which two were offered for 99 years leases. They included Antigua, St. Lucia, Trinidad, Jamaica and Bermuda among others.

detention, house of: A building operated by local authorities in which to keep juvenile delinquents, wayward girls or others being held as material witnesses in future court trials.

devaluation of money: A reduction in the gold or silver content of the standard monetary unit, and the accompanying loss of value in paper money backed by gold or silver. In 1934 the .2322 grains of gold nine-tenths fine that backed a dollar was reduced to 15.24 grains. This was equal to a devaluation of about 59%. The British and many European countries devalued their currency in 1950 in a similar fashion.

devolution: To pass the power of a central government on to local authorities as a means of decentralizing authority.

dialectical materialism: A view expressed by Karl Marx based on an aspect of Hegelian philosophy, that the production activities of man determined the social, political, and intellectual processes of life. From this Marx predicted will come an inevitable class struggle, out of which the workers will emerge as the most numerous and the most powerful group and will then finally overthrow the dominance of the capitalists and make a Communist society.

Dies Committee: *See* UNAMERICAN ACTIVITIES COMMITTEE.

dilatory motion: A delaying action in a legislature for the purpose of holding up progress in the expectation of winning concessions to get the delay stopped.

diplomatic corps: All the persons concerned with the foreign service and residing at the capital of a nation.

diplomatic immunity: Special privileges are extended to diplomats under which they enjoy freedom from civil and criminal jurisdiction. However, United States Department of State officials may turn over minor officials wanted by local authorities,

DIRECT ACTION 76

and all who serve in the diplomatic service are carefully warned to do nothing to violate local regulations.

"direct action": A policy of some radical organizations, especially the syndicalists aiming at the seizure of the economic order by "direct action," that is by resorting to intimidation or violence to gain their political objectives. *See* SYNDICALISM.

direct burden tests: A state may not discriminate in regard to interstate commerce in favor of intrastate commerce. A tax levied by a state which could in turn be levied by succeeding states would be a direct burden as would be an unreasonable charge for the use of the highways. A gross receipts tax by a state is thus held invalid.

direct election of Senators: Senators have been elected by popular vote since the ratification of the Seventeenth Amendment in 1913. Special elections are provided for filling unexpected vacancies, though governors may be authorized to fill the vacancies by appointment and have even been known to appoint themselves to the position.

direct legislation: This term refers to means by which the voter may have an opportunity for more direct participation in the running of the state governments besides voting for candidates. *See* INITIATIVE, REFERENDUM and RECALL.

direct primary: A means of nominating for office holding. Ballots and polling places are often the same as in the final election, except that all is under the direction of a major party. Opportunity to vote in a primary usually depends upon enrollment in the party in the previous registration period. Such a condition is known as a closed primary. An open primary allows any one to vote regardless of party affiliation. *See* CROSS-FILING.

disability insurance: New York State by means of a payroll deduction for each worker plus a certain amount made up by the employer accumulates a fund to be paid workers who become sick or disabled in a fashion not covered by workmen's compensation. Payments start after seven days and may be paid for thirteen weeks in any year. This Miller-Condon Law is matched by similar measures in California, New Jersey and Rhode Island.

disarmament: Reduction or limitation in the production of weapons for war. Very little has ever been accomplished in this respect except for the Five-Power Treaty signed at the Washington Conference in 1921 when the nations agreed to limitation on the construction of capital ships but allowed this program to lapse at the 1930 London Conference.

disaster unit: A group functioning under the Red Cross, or Civil Defense auspices which can be speedily alerted for assistance in case of an emergency under either peace or wartime conditions, such as flood, widespread fire, heavy explosion, or air raid attack. It may be made up of a team of doctors, nurses and technicians from one hospital unit trained especially to act together as a unit.

disbarment: Proceedings to cause a lawyer to be barred from the practice of his profession.

discharge rule in the House of Representatives: To keep a bill from being "killed" in committee, that is never being sent back to the house for a vote, the bill may be forced out of committee ("discharged") upon the request of a majority of the House, through obtaining 218 signatures. This does not happen very often.

discipline in the House of Representatives: Control of members may be attempted by a vote of censure for unbecoming conduct, but such acts of censure may be ignored if the candidate wins reelection and is seated without question in the next House. An extreme case of discipline is applied in the case of the expulsion of a member but this requires a two-thirds vote. It is possible also for the House to refuse to seat a member about whom there has been much controversy, one side claiming that this action flouts the will of the voters and the others claiming that the House according to the Constitution of the United States has the sole right to make rules for its own conduct.

discipline in the Senate: The question of disciplinary action against a Senator arouses even more discussion than the problem in the House (*see* above), for in the latter case it is felt to be just an issue over an individual, but for a Senator the plaint is that the State itself is being repudiated if the Senator should be rejected by exclusion or expulsion. In either case the action is looked upon as an extremely dangerous prerogative, because it could be abused for partisan reasons and there is no right of appeal.

disfranchisement: The removing from a person of the right to vote. Felons, idiots and the insane are uniformly denied the ballot. Paupers, vagrants, and those under guardianship are excluded in some states.

Displaced Persons Act (1948): A measure providing for the admission to the United States of the homeless refugees of Europe under carefully supervised racial, religious and occupational limits. There were 205,000 to be admitted, but so rigorous were the regulations that only about 100,000 qualified for admission the first year. This law was liberalized in 1950 and the number to be admitted was doubled.

dissenting opinion: The legal opinion of a judge who has disagreed with the other judges in the view expressed as to the decision in the case. The minority view of the court may become the majority position in some future cases. The views expressed are often as carefully studied, if not more so, than the concurring opinions (q.v.).

district attorney: A locally elected state official, also called prosecuting attorney, who represents the State in bringing indictments and prosecuting criminals, but must also be really aggressive in seeking information in the underworld and avoid playing into the hands of bosses or racketeers.

district court: The lowest court of the federal judicial system. There are over ninety of these courts distributed throughout the United States. They have only original jurisdiction (q.v.).

diversification of industry: A practice developed as a phase of the ultimate results of the Industrial Revolution, by which it was found advantageous for communities to encourage varied production activities by the factory owners for fear that workers might become too dependent upon one type of enterprise. In case of a strike all would be out of work at once, or if any cutbacks in that one type of industry occurred, wholesale unemployment would be disastrous. The textile workers centered in New England were facing that dilemma particularly in the 1950's in the face of great competition from new and more efficient mills in the South. The "new South" on the other hand was benefiting from the advantages of having begun diversification in turning from exclusive cotton production to peanut, soy bean production to dairying, and other varied activities.

divest: To dispossess, as of rights, applied to corporations ordered by the court to reduce the number of their subsidiaries.

division of labor: In its simplest form division of labor relies upon distinctions in occupation developing in the earliest stage of mankind, as for example between one who hunts and one who prepares the food. More commonly the expression applies to the reduction of a complex industrial process to a series of minute and simple operations each carried out by a separate individual who therefore needs no special skill in learning the job. The opportunity of full scale use of division of labor is looked upon as one of the important factors in setting up our modern large scale production in which skillful management requires a continuous flow of raw material into the plant and requires equally essentially a market for a mass produced product, but has been criticized for leading to monotony for the worker and standardization of production.

Dixiecrat: This term was created in the 1948 election to describe bolters from the Democratic Party in the "Dixie" States, who ran their own candidates for president and vice president on a "States' Rights" ticket. They resented particularly the stand Mr. Truman had taken on the civil rights issue. *See* STATES' RIGHTS DEMOCRATS.

docket: List of cases to be tried by a court, or a list of items of business intended for a conference or committee.

dollar-a-year man: A person in a government position who accepts only the minimum portion of the income which he might command.

"Dollar Diplomacy": *See* YANKEE IMPERIALISM.

domicile: An individual's permanent and legal abode, from which he exercises his political rights.

donkey: Symbol of the Democratic Party originated by the clever political cartoonist Thomas Nast who helped expose the Tweed Ring in New York City shortly after the Civil War. He also created the elephant as the symbol of the Republican Party.

double jeopardy: A person is held to be "in jeopardy" after indictment, and as soon as the trial jury has been sworn in, unless the jury disagrees or was not legally constituted. The person may not be put in jeopardy a second time for the same offense according to the Fifth Amendment. However if his crime included breaking both a state and a federal statute he may be tried for each offense since that does not constitute double jeopardy. Even if the offense involved two federal statutes he may be tried for each separately since he is not being tried twice for the same offense. *See* FIFTH AMENDMENT.

"doughface": Originally a political term for those "northern men with southern principles" who in the period after the Jackson Era, though holding no brief for slavery, thought that they saw as bad conditions for the factory worker in the industrial evils of the north as for the slave in the South and therefore condoned the latter situation. The term is now used to describe the progressive who has vivid dreams of needed reforms, but will assume no discipline or responsibility for carrying them out. He may condemn the Mexican War, but will have no answer as to whether the areas acquired then should have been returned then or now. He will support the Spanish Republicans blindly without seeing any Communist influence. Finally, according to Arthur Schlesinger Jr., he is a fellow-traveller of a fellow-traveller and a grave danger.

drafted: Politically the term refers to the fact that a person has been nominated due to pressure of the party and not as the result of his own desire to seek office.

Drago Doctrine: A doctrine originally stated by Senor Calvo of Argentina and adopted by Luis Drago, Argentinian minister for foreign affairs, who, however, limited the application to a protest against any foreign intervention for the collection of debts. He complained specifically in a note in December 1902 against the coercive blockade of Venezuela initiated by Germany with the backing of Italy and Great Britain. Though not all the Latin-American countries accepted the interpretation, the United States found it consistent with the Monroe Doctrine to volunteer its services in "protecting them from danger" in case such circumstances arose. The Drago Doctrine has since been absorbed in the agreements accepted by the International Conferences of American States (q.v.).

dry: A political term for those favoring prohibition. The widespread use of the term came to an end with the repeal of the Volstead Act providing for the end of national controls on the sale of intoxicating liquor. The term may have limited application to the still remaining "dry" areas in the individual states. *See* TWENTY-FIRST AMENDMENT, LOCAL OPTION.

due process clause: A safeguard of individual rights implementing the "Bill of Rights" (q.v.) by providing specifically in the Fourteenth Amendment that "no state shall deprive any person of life, liberty or property without due process of law."

due process of law, procedural: This type of due process derives its meaning from custom, tradition, legislative enactments and judicial precedents but it basically hinges around the following broad principles: a fair trial must be given, the agency handling the case must be fully authorized by law for the purpose, the defendant's side must be heard, legal assistance must be provided, such as the right to subpoena witnesses, and advice of counsel be provided for under a program covering sufficient time and effort.

due process of law, substantive: This type of protection is concerned with the actual wording of the statutes under which a person is tried. They must be exact, must provide equal protection and must contain an ascertainable standard of conduct.

Dumbarton Oaks Conference: A meeting held in Washington, D. C., in October 1944 at which a preliminary draft was drawn up to establish an international organization to replace the League of Nations. This draft with additions and alterations produced at the San Francisco Conference the following year became the United Nations Charter (q.v.).

dumping: A practice of selling a commodity in a foreign country below the price for which it sells either at home or abroad with the intention of eliminating competition by means of a temporary loss, or of unloading a surplus holding down the price at home. The first protective tariff in the United States was passed in 1816 to prevent this practice on the part of the more highly industrialized British firms intent on overwhelming our infant industries.

duress: Illegal compulsion. A contract signed under such terms is not binding.

dust bowl: An area in the Middle West which in the middle 1930's had its top soil lifted away by wind erosion with disastrous effect upon the already suffering farm population. This was felt to be due to the great overproduction of the World War I years, when an exceedingly high price for wheat encouraged marginal producers to enter the market, who, when faced with foreclosure when the normal competition of the restored European markets depressed the price of wheat, left their lands without any cover crop of grasses such as had originally protected it, and their good top soil literally blew away.

dyed-in-the-wool: A phrase used to indicate steadfastness in party loyalty.

E

easement: A liberty, right to use, or privilege of access to land, which one person may acquire in relation to the land of another.

Economic and Social Council: Article sixty-one of the Charter of the United Nations created this Council of eighteen members elected by the General Assembly for three-year terms, one-third to be chosen every year. It may initiate studies and reports on cultural, educational, health, and related matters for the purpose of promoting respect for and observance of human rights and fundamental freedoms for all, by promoting higher standards of living, full employment and economic progress and universal respect for human rights, regardless of race, sex, language or religion.

It has a Coordination Committee to render mutual assistance for all the specialized agencies which are related to it, in order to best advance their work and to avoid duplication. Some of these agencies are the World Health Organization, International Labor Office, or the International Trade Organization (qq.v.).

economic nationalism: A policy by which a nation is concerned only with its own attempts to attain economic prosperity and favors a program of non-cooperation with other countries. This was especially true of the activities of the United States about 1933 when we would not conclude any currency agreements with European countries which would interfere with our efforts to raise domestic prices, and particularly when we would not make any reductions in our high tariff duties. The policy was just as visible in narrow nationalistic actions on the part of many European countries. Such slogans as "Buy British" and "Buy French" were popularized in their individual countries until the havoc such "uneconomic" views produced were apparent to all in the collapse of foreign trade and all its related enterprises.

Another stage of economic nationalsim was ushered in by the restrictive measures of the fascist or corporate states where an artificial self-sufficiency was encouraged as in Italy and Germany. As a result of World War II we have a period almost exactly the reverse in the economic internationalism developed thru the various economic agencies created by the United Nations.

economic planning: This program is usually assumed to be one in which the government or some designated agent of it, directs the interrelation of labor, capital, and natural resources rather than allow the decisions to be exclusively made on the basis of the profit motive as would be undertaken in a completely free capitalistic society. Criticism of this type of economic planning ranges from conservatives who resent the least degree of government regulation to those who call it "fascist" because, as they claim, it leads to totalitarian regulation, to those who call it "socialistic" arguing that the next step after excessive regulation is government ownership. The term also leads to political distinctions with the Republicans tending to repudiate the "New Deal" and "Fair Deal" programs as samples of such economic planning; while the Democrats defend their position as all premised on the "general welfare" provision of the Constitution. See STATEISM.

economic royalist: A term used by Franklin D. Roosevelt in his 1936 acceptance speech in a disparaging sense about those men of wealth, or of special business interests who were opposing his "New Deal" program for benefiting the "common man."

economic stages of mankind: The development of man from his first appearance on earth has been assumed to have followed certain stages, which, however, have overlapped on one another considerably historically. They are usually given as: hunting and fishing stage, pastoral or nomadic, agricultural or handicraft, factory or industrial.

economy of abundance: This situation represents a condition where there is full production, where prices are such as can be met by the purchasing power, and there are no restrictions on quantity or on currency valuation, with all economic activity advancing at full capacity. Historically it is an ideal state to which those resentful of the "tampering" with the economic "laws" dream of if they can stop government "interference," and others hope for if nature, man, war and "social security" will only permit.

economy of scarcity: In contrast to the ideal state of the economy of abundance is the condition that exists when by unnatural means such as by a depression or by deliberate creation of shortages the quantity of goods available has been reduced in an effort to force prices up. This was undertaken in our first Agricultural Allotment Act (q.v.) in regard to wheat and pork, and to a great many "subsidized" items in later years. It is also a factor in the program of a "corporate state" like that established by Mussolini with many artificial restraints in production.

Eighteenth Amendment: An amendment to the Constitution of the United States ratified in January 1919 to go into effect the following year. It prohibited the manufacture, transportation and sale of intoxicating liquor or the importation or exportation thereof from the United States or its territories for beverage purpose. Congress and the State legislatures have concurrent power (q.v.) in this respect. Repeal was provided for in the Twenty-first Amendment (q.v.).

Eighth Amendment: An amendment to the Constitution of the United States which provided that excessive bail shall not be required, nor excessive fines imposed, nor cruel and unusual punishments inflicted. *See* BILL OF RIGHTS.

elastic clause: The 18th clause of Article I Section 8 of the Constitution is known as the "necessary and proper" clause because it grants Congress the power to carry out the preceding eighteen powers by all means necessary and proper. "Stretching" this power enabled the Federalist Party through "loose interpretation" to enlarge considerably on what they deemed appropriate for the federal government to have control. This clause has also made it possible for the Constitution to be a "living" document. For example, control of commerce has been extended to give control over aviation and atomic energy.

elastic currency: This is currency which will expand and contract to meet the needs of business. This elasticity is obtained in the United States by the issuance of Federal Reserve Notes which are partly secured by "commercial paper," promissory notes recognizing a bank's acceptance of an enterprise's desire to increase its productivity through the introduction of more capital. In a period where contraction is necessary the bank refuses loans and retires the Federal Reserve Notes when the previously mentioned "commercial paper" is redeemed, thus reducing the amount of currency in circulation from two directions.

elastic demand: The practice of purchasers increasing or decreasing their determination to buy (demand) goods considerably depending on the price change. Demand for luxuries is elastic because buyers will buy more at low prices and drop out of the market when prices go too high. On the other hand inelastic demand is that which will not change much despite price changes. For salt and coffins there might be an inelastic demand because they must be obtained regardless of price.

electioneering. Working on behalf of a candidate in canvassing for votes, or efforts to win support for the party in a coming election.

electoral college: The "electors" of each state form the electoral college whose purpose is to elect a president and vice president of the United States. They are determined by the state legislature and equal in number for each state the number of representatives and senators that state has in Congress. The political party that gains one over half the popular vote cast in the November elections gives the entire electoral vote of that state to that party. Since 1887 by the Electoral Count Act the governor of each state sends to Congress the official certificate of election. On the sixth of January the members of the two houses of Congress meet and count the votes. The candidate with the greatest number of votes is declared elected if it is at least one over half the entire electoral vote (266).

Electoral Commission: A supposedly impartial board set up in 1877 to judge the disputed election returns in the contest between Hayes and Tilden. Of the five Representatives, five Senators and five members of the Supreme Court making up the Commission seven were to be Republicans and seven Democrats with one independent; however at the last moment a replacement for an independent member resulted in a membership of eight Republicans and seven Democrats. Every one of the disputed returns was decided in the Republicans' favor and by one extra vote in the Electoral College. Hayes, the Republican, became President two days before he was to be inaugurated.

Electoral Count Act: This measure was passed by Congress in 1887 because of circumstances that had arisen over the election of 1876 when Hayes won by gaining all the disputed electoral returns in states where two sets of different results had been reported. To obviate such a repetition it was finally provided that Congress voting as two separate houses would decide which returns to accept, but if they disagreed the returns certified by the governor under the seal of the State were to be accepted. If this arrangement still failed to resolve the dispute, then the state would lose its vote.

electorate: The collective body of legally qualified votes.

Eleventh Amendment: The Eleventh Amendment to the Constitution of the United States was added in 1798 and stated that "the judicial power of the United States shall not be construed to extend to any suit in law or equity, commenced or prosecuted against one of the United States, by citizens of another State, or by citizens or subjects of any foreign state." This addition was made necessary because of a law suit initiated in 1793 by Chisholm of South Carolina against the state of Georgia. To the States' Rights supporters of that day this was a shocking procedure and under their influence this power of a citizen of one state to sue another state was removed by the ratification of the Eleventh Amendment.

emancipation: To set free, as of a slave by the Thirteenth Amendment (q.v.) or as of the enfranchisement of women in the Nineteenth Amendment (q.v.).

embargo: The prohibition of a government against the leaving of a ship for another port, or of the shipment of certain goods.

embassy: The office of an ambassador often including his residence.

embezzlement: The misappropriation of funds entrusted to one's care. Since these funds are legally in the person's possession it differs from theft where the money is acquired illegally.

Emergency Fund of the State Department: Out of this Fund the President and the Secretary of State may make expenditures in

EMINENT DOMAIN

regard to unforeseen circumstances without presenting an original account or voucher to the Treasury Department. It may be used for entertaining distinguished guests or tracking suspicious aliens or to watch secret agents.

eminent domain: The right of a government, either city, state or nation, to take private property for public use, by due process of law. Just compensation must be provided and the property must be "affected with a public interest."

emoluments: Salary and other profits of a public office.

Employment Act (1946): In facing the problems of the post World War II years Congress was concerned about a possible slow return to full peace time production which might lead to a mild depression. Some members were also worrying about a possible trend toward inflation. To compromise these two viewpoints an Employment Act was passed which disappointed those wanting a "full employment bill" with strong guarantees of government spending, but did provide for federal responsibility for a broad program under which there would be useful employment opportunities. The Council of Economic Advisors was established as an economic general staff to make appropriate policy recommendations to the president; and an annual economic report was to be required of the president. Thus was put into operation one of a dozen schemes of the government to provide for a stable economy.

employment tax (Social Security Act): Since the passage of the Social Security Act increasingly large amounts of money have been flowing into the Treasury from the one percent, now 1½%, tax collected from both employer and employee based on the amount of the employee's earnings under $3,000 (now under $3,600). It is estimated that by 1952 the total of all these collections will exceed three billion dollars. Critics of the Treasury Department regret that these funds are being used to meet current deficits. They believe that these funds should be kept available for the time when the full burden of the Social Security payments to those over sixty-five will reach its peak in the 1970's. On the other hand there are those who would question the withdrawal of such large sums of money from circulation.

enfranchise: To admit to citizenship, also to free from slavery.

A franchise is a constitutional right which a government may extend—or take away. *See DISFRANCHISEMENT.*

Engel's Law: As the result of investigations reported by Dr. Ernest Engel about 1850 a widely accepted series of conclusions resulted. The proportions of a person's income spent for food increases as the income becomes less. The operation of this "law" is an important consideration in determining the point of exemption in a tax levy, and need for relief allowances in certain cases.

Enoch Arden Law: A law providing that after five years a widow may remarry legally if her spouse has not been heard of and is presumed dead.

entail: A means of restricting the bequeathing of land so that a previously established requirement must be followed. Illegal in the United States.

entente: An agreement or understanding usually referring to relations between nations. For example Great Britain and France signed the ENTENTE CORDIALE in 1907.

enumerated powers: The listing of the eighteen powers specifically delegated to Congress in Article I Section 8 of the Constitution. Except for these powers all other authority rests with the states as residual powers (q.v.). However, through the "loose interpretation" of the Constitution from these basic powers the greatly extended power of the federal government today stems.

environmental sanitation: The overall health picture of communities today is dependent on more than merely local control. The health condition of rural areas has become of considerable significance in such matters as drainage, mosquito abatement, sewage disposal and water supply where individual action would be entirely inadequate, now with so many overlapping problems we have a problem of the integrated whole—environmental sanitation—or the encircling neighborhood health problem.

envoy: A diplomatic representative of any rank. If assigned full authority under certain circumstances he is called envoy plenipotentiary.

E Pluribus Unum: One from out of many. The motto of the United States.

"equal protection of the law": This guarantee is not explained exactly in the Fourteenth Amendment (q.v.) with the conse-

EQUAL RIGHTS AMENDMENT 90

quence that it has been up to the courts to undertake an interpretation. Since this is only possible when a specific case reaches the Supreme Court the process is a long one not yet completed in all respects. So far arbitrary, distinctly unfair and entirely unwarranted applications of inequality under the law have been prevented. Certain forms of discrimination have been tolerated. The rich pay a higher rate of income tax. Chain stores pay higher taxes in some states than single units within the state. Japanese nationals could not acquire land in California, and Communist front organizations must register with the government. However, much progress in the protection of individual rights has been made, especially noteworthy has been the obtaining of equal educational opportunities for Negroes.

"equal rights amendment": A proposed amendment to the Constitution of the United States unfailingly introduced for several decades by the National Women's Party, stating that "equality of rights under the law shall not be denied or abridged by the United States or any State on account of sex." Defeat has not weakened the hope of this group to gain their objective in time. In the field of anti-discrimination measures practically equivalent have been won for women in New York State by the Ives-Quinn Law (q.v.).

equity: Law suits may be tried under common law or equity. Equity, a branch of remedial justice, covers cases common law would not solve. Its aim is preventive not punitive. It is more drastic and more expeditious, less tolerant of delaying tactics. The courts proceed by issuing writs and with little use of juries, and depend more on written arguments.

Erie Barge Canal: The old Erie Canal completed in 1825 has been rebuilt and renamed. This waterway extends across the state from Troy to Buffalo and has been valuable in promoting the prosperity of the central part of the state; particularly because of the saving of millions of dollars of freight charges as it costs less to send goods by water than by rail.

escalator clause: A provision in the London Naval Treaty (q.v). which permitted the three signatories to increase their naval tonnage if other nations menaced their security. It opened the period of increased military and naval preparation leading to World War II.

escheat: A condition under which land reverts to the state if no heir is found available.

escrow: Money, property, or a document held by a third person for delivery to the grantee upon occurrence or performance of certain conditions; title does not pass until the conditions are fulfilled but the grantor controls the escrow.

European Recovery Program: *See* MARSHALL PLAN.

ever-normal granary: A scheme provided for under the A.A.A. of 1938 by which national acreage allotments are established. Farmers who cooperate are eligible to receive benefits in proportion to the amount of surplus crops they do not produce and to the extent of their soil conservation program. Controls are voluntary. Benefits are also based on a parity formula; that is, by mortgaging a crop to the Commodity Credit Corporation they can get a check up to ninety percent of the parity value of their crop and calculated in dollars that will have an equal purchasing value for the value of his crop in the 1909-1914 period. The basic commodities included were cotton, wheat, corn, tobacco, rice and peanuts, and later additions include hogs, eggs, chickens and potatoes.

evidence: Materials, reports, or oral accounts admissible in a court trial by means of which an effort to arrive at the truth is made.

excess profits tax: A graduated tax on profits over a certain amount intended to drain off the profits made due to a period of abnormal consumer demands and during a period of artificial shortages. Each time that Congress has imposed this kind of a tax a time of oncoming war, or recovery from war was involved— 1917, 1941 and 1944. The principle of equality of sacrifice was supposed to operate so that the business man might approximate the suffering of those in the services.

excise: An internal revenue tax levied on goods produced or manufactured within the country. The most common are those on gasoline, cigarettes and liquor, but included since 1940 are such luxury items as furs, jewelry, cosmetics and luggage.

executive agreements: Agreements the equivalent of treaties which may be executed between heads of states and the President of the United States without senatorial approval through his authority as commander-in-chief, or through some other statutory provision. The Destroyer-Base Agreement made with Great Britain in 1941 was an executive agreement which if subjected to lengthy discussion in the Senate and to the need for a two-third approval might well have resulted in having the fifty destroyers arrive too late in that critical interval.

Executive Office of the President: A regrouping of agencies by the Congressional Reorganization Act of 1939; assembled under this one designation all those bureaus necessary to carry out the executive duties of the President. More have been added and some of the war time agencies have been dropped. As of 1952 the following five remain active: White House Office (q.v.), Liaison Office for Personnel Management, Council of Economic Advisers (q.v.), National Security Board (q.v.), and the National Securities Resources Board.

executive orders: Such orders may be issued by the President in order to carry out some law or treaty or provision of the Constitution. They involve a delegation of power to an administrative agency, and as more and more departments develop to meet the increasing complications of government, they would almost seem to form a fourth branch of our government, that is in addition to the executive, legislative and judicial.

executive session: A session of Congress during which administrative business is carried out in secret.

exemption: Immunity from certain legal obligations, such as freedom from taxation of certain charitable organizations.

ex officio: To be a member of an organization or to have certain privileges "due to the nature of the position." The Secretary of the Treasury was once an ex officio member of the Federal Reserve Board by the nature of his position. Now that is specifically forbidden because it was not considered wise to have a political appointee in a position of such critical financial importance.

expediency: The following of a policy for immediate gains despite the bad effect it may have as a long term program.

export tax: A duty imposed upon goods leaving a country. This is forbidden in the Constitution of the United States though export controls may be instituted by Congress. In April 1949 controls on several hundred items then in plentiful supply were abolished thus permitting their shipment to any part of the world. In November more stringent controls were imposed on the export of highly strategic material, potentially valuable in case of war and with the intention of forestalling shipments to countries behind the Iron Curtain. Direct shipments to the Soviet Union had already been stopped in 1948.

ex-post-facto-law: A law making an action a crime which was not a crime when it was first committed. The Constitution forbids such laws. Penalties also may not be changed after the passage of the original sums so as to be ex post facto in effect.

expressed powers: *See* ENUMERATED POWERS IN THE CONSTITUTION.

expulsion of members: Congress has full authority to punish its members and with the concurrence of two-thirds of the members may expel a member as an extreme disciplinary measure, usually on the grounds of notorious disloyalty or moral turpitude. *See* DISCIPLINE IN THE HOUSE, DISCIPLINE IN THE SENATE.

expunge: To strike out or remove from the record, as part of a political debate, or in regard to the removal from the Congressional Record of some statement of personal offense retracted by the original speaker after better judgment.

extortion: The attempt to obtain something through the threat of force, illegally.

extra-constitutional: A power derived from the Constitution may be implied through interpretation but an extra-constitutional power may be one which is not explicitly denied nor expressly stated even indirectly. Jefferson doubted the right of the federal government to buy territory, but the opportunity to make the Louisiana Purchase was too good a one to miss, an amendment would take too long, so he went ahead anyway in what was really an extra-constitutional action.

extradition: The surrender of a fugitive from justice to the appropriate authorities either state or federal.

extra session: A special session called by a governor or the president at a different time and in addition to the regular session of the law-making body. The adjournment rests upon the body itself.

extraterritoriality: The right of a nation to carry out authoritative actions within another country. For example, in Turkey or China the British could try all British offenders in British courts. Most of these special privileges have lapsed since the end of World War II.

F

faction: A group within a state, either a personal clique, or a portion of a political party.

factory laws: A general designation applied to laws passed by the individual states under their residual power to regulate intrastate labor which provide for a variety of matters such as safety devices in connection with dangerous machinery, provisions for fire protection, keeping clear of staircases, regulations about ventilation or controls on the use of harmful materials.

Fair Deal: The liberal program of Mr. Truman stressing particularly the protection of civil rights, extension of social security, government aid to housing construction, and flood control, representing the post war version of F. D. Roosevelt's so-called New Deal (q.v.).

Fair Labor Standards Act: This measure, popularly known as the "Wage and Hour Law," was originally passed in 1938 and has been revised in 1949. It applies to workers in mining, transportation, and other aspects of interstate commerce. The present minimum is at the rate of seventy-five cents an hour for a forty-hour week but the coverage is rather more precisely defined than originally as "closely related process or occupation directly essential to interstate commerce."

farm bloc: After the Non-Partisan League (q.v.) declined in influence continued unrest among the farmers in the West led to the creation of a farm bloc consisting of Senators and Representatives of both Republican and Democratic parties who forgot party differences to promote laws of benefit to the farmers. Some of these laws of the 1920's were to place limitations on speculation in grains, or to prohibit unfair practices in the stock yards, or to exempt cooperatives from the operation of the antitrust laws.

Farmer Labor Party: The attempt to organize a party of farmers and industrial workers in 1920 was felt by many to be foredoomed because of the opposing interests of the two groups. The one-quarter million votes out of twenty-six million won by their presidential candidate, Arthur Christiansen, seemed to prove the point, though the party's influence in Wisconsin was considerable.

fascism: A system of government in which industry, law and all phases of society are under a dictator and his party. The idea originated under Mussolini in 1922 and was copied by Hitler in the 1930's with some remnants of its program remaining to the present.

"Father of the House": After the November elections a new Congress must be convened in January, part of the necessary procedure is the swearing in of members-elect. To accomplish this after the new Speaker of the House has been elected he takes the oath of office from the member-elect who is oldest in point of service in the House, who is called the "Father of the House." The Speaker then proceeds to swear in all the other members of the House.

favorite son: A candidate for nomination or election whose only support may be that of his own local representatives.

featherbedding: A practice imputed to union workers of make-work, or stand-by arrangements by which an employer pays for services not performed. A real musician must be hired if recordings of an orchestra are used on the air. Fear that technological improvements might throw men out of work if they were not counterbalanced by such restrictions has been offered as justification for these practices.

Federal Bureau of Investigation: This agency is a subdivision of the Department of Justice. Its job is to track down "public enemies" and ferret out spies. It investigates only. The G-men are called in only when the local authorities request it or are incapable. The Bureau does not prosecute or punish. It has field divisions all over the United States.

Federal Communications Commission: In 1934 the control of telephone, telegraph and cable companies was taken from the Interstate Commerce Commission and merged with the Federal Radio Commission to form the Federal Communications Commission, which was given additional control of foreign communications also. The commission consists of seven members appointed for seven years by the President with the approval of the Senate. Licenses subject to periodical renewal are required for broadcasting and television stations, including wave length assignments, hours for use and strength of equipment, limitations on time given for advertising, and for public service programs.

Federal Crop Insurance Corporation: An agency within the Department of Agriculture which insures growers of wheat, cotton, flax, corn and tobacco against losses from unavoidable damage caused by insects, plant disease, bad weather or accidents. Its program supplements a phase of the Agricultural Adjustment Act in attempting to keep the farmers' income stable.

Federal Deposit Insurance Corporation: This agency of the government was created to pay off the depositors of an insured bank member which went bankrupt. The Banking Law of 1933 established the organization which collects from all its members a premium of one-twelfth of one percent of its deposits which is set aside in a fund out of which the insured depositors may be certain of obtaining their own funds, formerly insured up to $5,000, now up to $10,000.

federal-local cooperation in law enforcement: Marked improvement has developed in the twentieth century in better relation between the federal and the local officials in many fields of cooperation. This has been particularly noticeable in the following examples: National Kidnapping Act 1938, the National Motor Vehicle Theft Act of 1919, the Fugitive Felon Act of 1934, the Defense Highway Act of 1941, the Hill-Burton Hospital Act of 1946. Agencies of the federal government have cooperated closely, such as the Federal Bureau of Investigation, which has helped as a clearing house of information and identification; others such as the Bureau of Standards, or the Bureau of Chemistry and Soils of the Department of Agriculture, cooperate with the appropriate local agencies. The Civil Service Commission may actually conduct examinations for municipal authorities, or make its own civil service lists available for placement purposes to city or state agencies.

Federal Power Commission: An independent organization created in 1920 and reorganized in 1930, it regulates wholesale rates of electric power transmitted across state lines. Through joint boards and voluntary agreements it has taken the initiative in determining valuation of property and calculating a fair return on the investment, and encouraged better accounting methods to help stabilize the entire industry. It also conducts surveys as to the water resources of the country, and most recently has assumed the duty of the regulation of the transportation of natural gas in interstate commerce.

Federal Register: Established in 1936, this publication is a daily compilation of presidential proclamations, executive orders, administrative departments' rules, and decisions of quasi-judicial agencies. All these items become a permanent record of executive activity paralleling the purpose of the "Congressional Record" for the legislative agencies of our government, and the "United States Reports" for the judicial activities.

Federal Reserve Notes: These are the most numerous of the bank notes in circulation. They were formerly secured by a 40% backing of gold, the gold already held by the government through its policy of nationalization but for which "gold certificates" were issued to the appropriate Reserve Bank. The percentage of gold backing them has now been reduced to 25% (1945). The balance of the backing is made up of "commercial paper," that is, bills of exchange, promissory notes or similar credit instruments "as good as gold."

Federal Reserve System: This system includes the Board of Governors, the Federal Open Market Committee, the Federal Reserve Banks, and their twenty-four branches, and the Federal Advisory Council and all the member banks of the United States. It regulates banking practices in the United States so that sound conditions will exist, sees to it that the depositor and the public's interests are equally well protected and controls the general credit situation.

Federal Security Agency: An independent agency created in 1939 to supervise the work of the Public Health Service (q.v.), the Social Security Administration (q.v.), the Food and Drugs administration (q.v.), the United States Employment Service (q.v.) and the United States Office of Education—*see* OFFICE OF EDUCATION. In the plans for reorganization of many government departments in the 1950's it was under consideration that a new department be created, that of Public Welfare or perhaps Social Service and Education, and that most of the units in the Federal Security Agency be moved to it and that its head thus attain cabinet rank.

Federal Trade Commission: A Commission established in 1914 to supplement the work of the Clayton Antitrust Law which listed the unfair business practices which might lead to combinations being found in restraint of interstate commerce. It may prevent price discrimination, or fraudulent advertising by first using "cease and desist" orders, and then by having recourse to law suits when firms do not obey. With larger appropriations and better selected personnel, it is felt that the Commission has an opportunity of a much larger field of activity before it.

federal union: A federal government in which several states unite under a common sovereignty and establish a central government to administer certain specific functions, but with the subdivisions, state, province, or canton, retaining some degree of power. Examples include United States of America, Dominion of Canada, and modern Switzerland.

Federalist Party: The first political party to assume power in the United States. Under Alexander Hamilton's leadership a strong financial program was undertaken which depended on the loose interpretation of the power of Congress (*see* "ELASTIC CLAUSE"). The establishment of a National Bank, the collection of a Tariff and of an Excise Tax, and the Assumption of the States' debts, all helped to strengthen the federal government and the Federalist Party, winning the support of the commercial interests and of "the rich, well born and the able." Federalist prestige declined with the election of Jefferson in 1800, and the party disappeared completely after the calling of the Hartford Convention (q.v.) and the opposition to the War of 1812. A new party organized about 1828 was in a sense a successor to the Federalists, the Whig Party (q.v.).

fee: A charge made by the government because it has rendered some specific service to the payer. The service is usually one for protective or regulatory purposes not intended as a source of revenue or for merely commercial reasons. Examples would include the fees charged for recording a deed or mortgage, issuing a marriage license or a permit to operate a certain type of business.

fellow-servant rule: In the period before workmen's compensation laws were in effect, if a man were hurt on the job due to the carelessness or negligence of a fellow employee, he had no redress against the employer. This was referred to as the "fellow servant rule" but has since been discarded by provision for payments regardless of the contributory negligence of anyone.

fellow traveler: One who is suspected of sympathizing with the aims of the Communist Party though not an official member, but one who may act through any of the various Communist Fronts.

felony: Any of various crimes serious in nature and involving more severe penalties than misdemeanors.

fence, to be on: A candidate will be considered to be on the fence when he does not take a definite stand on a particular issue. An individual may be on the fence when he has not yet determined his party affiliation or his choice of candidate.

F.E.P.C.: *See* COMMITTEE ON FAIR EMPLOYMENT PRACTICES.

fiat money: This type of money represents inconvertible notes issued by a government. They may serve as a satisfactory medium of exchange as long as they are acccpted at full face value by the public, but once distrust arises the value falls rapidly as is witnessed in the Civil War period when the Greenbacks commanded only a fraction of their original value.

fiduciary: A person or organization in a position of trust or confidence who manages financial transactions or property for others.

fiduciary money: Money not fully backed up by gold or silver. In this sense of the meaning, a Federal Reserve Note which is backed only by a certain percentage of gold (held in reserve) and the remaining percent by "commercial paper" is a sample of fiduciary money in the United States.

field services: When a central bureau has agents who carry out its program directly to the people a field service is usually in operation. The Federal government has many such activities throughout the United States under the supervision of the Geological Survey, the Social Security Administration (q.v.), the Department of Agriculture and many other bureaus.

Fifteenth Amendment: The third of the amendments to the Constitution of the United States introduced as a result of the Civil War and ratified in 1870. It states that the rights of citizens of the United States to vote shall not be denied or abridged by the United States or any State on account of race, color, or previous condition of servitude.

Fifth Amendment: One of the first ten amendments to the Constitution of the United States added in 1791 as part of the Bill of Rights. "No person shall be held to answer for a capital or otherwise infamous crime, unless on a presentment or indictment of a grand jury, except in cases arising in the land or naval forces, or in the militia, when in actual service in time of war or public danger; nor shall any person be subject for the same offense to be twice put in jeopardy of life or limb; nor shall be compelled in any criminal case to be a witness against himself, nor be deprived of life, liberty, or property, without due process of law; nor shall private property be taken for public use without just compensation." *See* DUE PROCESS OF LAW, EMINENT DOMAIN.

fifty-four forty or fight: A slogan used in the 1844 elections based on the claim of the United States to the whole of the Oregon Territory whose northern boundary coincided with the southern boundary of Alaska, that is, the 54°40′ parallel. The United States and Great Britain had occupied the area jointly since 1818. Since about this time the trouble with Texas had resulted in one war, the dispute over Oregon was easily compromised and the 49° parallel was extended to the Pacific dividing the territory in half in 1846.

filibuster: An oratorical obstruction by which a speaker holding the floor could delay or prevent the passage of a measure to which he was opposed. A small group of senators could work together delivering relays of speeches thus holding the fort indefinitely. La Follette once held the floor for eighteen hours. Because of many similar occasions in 1917 the "Cloture Rule" (q.v.) was passed in the hope of limiting debate, but as it requires a two-third vote and two days to put into effect it has not curbed the practice completely.

filing for office: Candidates for office must in all but a few towns and small school districts personally declare themselves candidates for office and file with the appropriate official, the secretary of state, county or city clerk, their intentions to run for office. If too large a number of candidates file for office usually a run-off primary is provided for. One way to try to limit the number of applicants is to provide as they do in England that the candidate post a fee which he will lose if he does not obtain a minimum number of votes, or there may be a requirement that he obtain a certain number of signatures on a petition before filing is possible.

filtration: A municipal device for water purification usually using some type of slow sand filter which permits the water to seep through several layers of sand, gravel and broken stone. Beds must be cleaned regularly of the material that has been screened from the water.

fineness of coins: The proportion of pure metal to the alloys contained in coins. When gold coins were allowed to circulate in the United States before 1933 they were "nine-tenths" fine, that is 90% pure gold and the rest an alloy to make the metal harder. The British sovereign when it too was in circulation was eleven-twelfths fine.

fireside chat: A description used to designate the more informal type of radio speeches of Franklin D. Roosevelt in the early years of his term in office when he was attempting to overcome the spreading evils of the depression period by making the public appreciate that the only thing they had to fear was fear itself.

First Amendment: The first addition added to the Constitution of the United States in 1791 forming part of the Bill of Rights (q.v.). "Congress shall make no law respecting an establishment of religion, or prohibiting the free exercise thereof; or abridging the freedom of speech, or of the press; or the right of the people peacably to assemble, and to petition the government for a redress of grievances."

fiscal year: Any period of twelve months considered as a year for financial operations, and budget and accounting purposes. In federal finances the year runs from July first through June thirtieth. Great Britain starts her financial year April first.

five-minute rule: A rule of the House of Representatives to limit debate under certain circumstances, in the committee of the whole, when an amendment has been proposed, "the member who shall first obtain the floor shall be allowed to speak for five minutes."

flexible tariff: A tariff system which provides that a tariff duty may be raised or lowered for the purpose of expanding American export trade or of alleviating current abnormal conditions. The 1930 Tariff Law is still the basic law of the United States, but the President may raise or lower duties 50% because of the "flexible" provision.

floating: A term used in financial circles to indicate the public marketing of securities, or more technically in referring to a debt which has not been secured by bonds, but which is to be repaid in a short period of time.

floating debt: The debts of a nation which are unpaid and for which no definite arrangements have yet been made. The debt becomes a funded debt when funds are borrowed or provisions are authorized for ultimate payment.

flood control: Activities aimed at the regulation of the excessive flow of water in shallow river valleys or other regions where an overflow is likely. Over a thousand miles of dikes and levees line the Mississippi's banks for this purpose. The Tennessee Valley Authority (q.v.) has, with its great building program of dams and lakes, provided control of incalculable value for the once uncontrollable Tennessee River. Army Engineers fight this danger constantly all over the United States. The Soil Conservation and Domestic Allotment Act has furnished the farmers with many incentives to plant crops that will hold back the waters that would otherwise find their way into stream or rivulet to become potential flood threats. Recent disasters have pointed up the need for federal action in regard to the proposed Columbia

Valley and Missouri Valley Authorities. The Flood Control Act of 1944 has authorized the Department of the Interior to select the best agency for this job.

Food and Agricultural Organization: An agency authorized by the General Assembly of the United Nations to collect and distribute information and make recommendations in regard to conservation, processing and marketing of products, improvement of forests and fisheries in order to wipe out starvation and to improve nutrition throughout the world. The individual nations must each have the proposed legislation ratified by their own legislatures, but valuable suggestions may be offered by means of experience described to and disseminated by the FAO.

Food and Drug Administration: A division of the Federal Security Agency created in June 1940 to enforce the Food, Drug and Cosmetic Act. It is responsible for the inspection of factories producing such items in order to check adulteration or misbranding. The prevention of false advertising in connection with these items comes under the supervision of the Federal Trade Commission. Occasionally the two agencies exercised concurrent jurisdiction in these overlapping fields, but since 1946 the Food and Drugs Administration has been given full authority in its field to avoid duplication of efforts in protecting the consumer.

food stamp plan: A plan in operation during the middle thirties, it was intended primarily to benefit the person on so-called home relief providing that when he received his regular allowances for food purchases he would be given stamps with which he could obtain another 50% of food which had been designated surplus by the Department of Agriculture. During the temporary period of its use the food stamps did bring additional nutritional benefits to a group who might otherwise have been forced to go without, and by withdrawing certain food stuffs from the market did assist the farmer to obtain a better price for the remainder of his crop. The stores receiving the stamps could later redeem them through a clearing house maintained by the Federal Reserve System.

forced labor: Labor of an individual compelled to work against his will. Slave labor. The National Labor Relations Act specifically states that no one may require an individual to work against his will. Persons may stop work where conditions are abnormally dangerous without such action being deemed a strike.

foreclosure: A judicial proceeding by which a debtor (mortgagor) is compelled to pay the required installment or debt, or forfeit the mortgaged property. The judgment issued against the debtor may under some circumstances provide that the property may be redeemed under proper notice of intention, or may result in the sale of the property and the satisfaction of the debt to the extent possible.

foreign exchange: The process of changing the money of one country into the money of another in making settlements in international trade. This may be accomplished through instruments known as bills of exchange which are claims for payment in foreign currency. If a person of one country buys such a bill and a person of another country owes a similar amount abroad a bookkeeping arrangement clears the transaction. This may be carried out on a large scale between many countries with the final balances being cleared by the shipment of gold.

Forest Service: The National Forests, of which there are over 150, exceed in extent over 180 million acres and are supervised by the Forest Service. Mature timber may be cut, thinning operations undertaken, and reforestation advanced. Recently 145 million trees were planted in one year. The planting of a belt of trees has been undertaken to be 100 miles wide from North Dakota to Texas where drought resistant trees will provide a valuable conservation device under Forestry Service supervision.

forfeiture: That which is lost or alienated as in the case of civil rights under circumstances provided for by law.

"Founding Fathers": Those statesmen who supported the American Revolution, and more particularly those who participated in the work of the Constitutional Convention in 1789. The attempt to guess or figure out what they may really have intended to have been the meaning of controversial sections of the Constitution has been the subject matter of countless debates and many volumes of constitutional interpretation.

Four Freedoms: A program advocated by President Roosevelt in an address to Congress on January 6, 1941, in which he stressed the need for freedom of speech and expression everywhere in the world, and for freedom of every person to worship God in his own way, and freedom from want, or better economic understanding between the nations of the world, and freedom from fear, meaning a world-wide reduction of armaments to such a point that no nation will be in a position to commit an act of aggression against any neighbor anywhere in the world.

4-H Clubs: Educational clubs of young farmers sponsored by the Department of Agriculture and the county agents to encourage good citizenship and an appreciation of improved methods of crop production and animal husbandry. The symbol of the program is a four leaf clover on each leaf of which is an H which indicates the goal of betterment in health, head, hand, and heart.

Fourteenth Amendment: The second of the three amendments added to the Constitution of the United States as a result of the Civil War, ratified in 1868. Section 1) Defines citizenship (q.v.) and places restrictions on the States in regard to the civil rights of citizens providing that no person shall be deprived of his life, liberty or property without due process of law (q.v.). Section 2) Provides for penalties to be applied in the reduction of the number of Representatives a state may have if the right to vote in any election for the choice of electors for President of the United States is denied to any male inhabitant of such state, being twenty-one years of age and a citizen of the United States and had not been in rebellion against the United States.

Section 3) This section disfranchised those who had fought with the Confederacy, but did provide that Congress could remove such a disability. Section 4) Repudiated the debts of the Confederacy and held all their obligations null and void.

Fourth Amendment: One of the first ten amendments added to the Constitution of the United States in 1791 as part of the Bill of Rights: "The right of the people to be secure in their persons, houses, papers, and effects, against unreasonable searches and seizures, shall not be violated, and no warrants shall issue, but upon probable cause, supported by oath or affirmation, and particularly describing the place to be searched, and the person or things to be seized."

fourth estate: The press has claimed this designation for almost a century as an indication of its unique position for in medieval times in France the country was represented by three Estates, Nobles, Clergy and the Common Man.

franchise: A special privilege granted by a local government to an individual or corporation which extends to them the right to use some public property. These privileges may include the right to operate a bus line over a specified route, a railroad right of way, the construction of a gas works or of a pipe line or the laying of gas mains or of electrical wiring. Often the fees paid for these franchises are a valuable source of municipal funds.

Franchise also refers to the right to vote.

franking privilege: The right enjoyed by members of Congress and officers and agencies of the federal government to send material through the mail free by substituting a frank or mark in place of postage.

fraud orders: The Postmaster General may issue orders forbidding the acceptance of mail from, or the delivery of mail to a corporation he has evidence against for some action contrary to the public's interest.

Frazier-Lemke Act of 1935: In an effort to combat some of the evils resulting from the Crash of 1929 a measure had been passed suspending foreclosure of mortgaged farm properties, but this law had been found unconstitutional as taking property unfairly. A new law bearing the same name was passed later which only delayed the foreclosure for three years and provided that the owner pay a reasonable rent to the mortgagor during that interval. After the three years the creditor could demand the sale of the property at auction after reappraisal, but for ninety days thereafter the farmer could recover full title by paying the sale price plus interest.

free coinage: The right to take unlimited amounts of a metal to the government for coinage into coins. The privilege as applied to gold has always been accepted in the United States, and was urged for silver in the Populists' demands (q.v.) especially in the 1896 campaign. *See* FREE SILVER.

freedom from arrest: Congressmen while attending a session of Congress or on their way to do so are not subject to arrest for minor offenses and may not be forced to answer court writs in civil cases. In any indictable crime they are at all times subject to arrest.

freedom from double jeopardy: An accused person may not be tried twice for the same offense, but in connection with the same circumstances may have committed two crimes and therefore be subject to a second trial but for another crime. *See* FIFTH AMENDMENT.

freedom from self-incrimination: To protect the accused person the Fifth Amendment provides: "no person shall be compelled in any criminal case to be a witness against himself." This applies to any sort of proceedings which might later be used in a criminal prosecution. Involuntary confessions are not acceptable as evidence since they have been found equivalent to forcing a defendant to testify against himself. A voluntary confession is acceptable.

freedom of debate: The right belonging to a legislative body in a representative government to discuss, deliberate and act under rules of its own making and not curbed by any other government agency. Individual members cannot be called to account for what they say by any other authority than that of which they are a part.

"freedom of entry": This expression has been created to indicate with what ease a new enterprise may enter the competitive field. Theoretically in the American free enterprise system there are no limits beyond the legal requirements of incorporating, having access to the needed raw materials and satisfying the local building and labor requirements. On the other hand those on the outlook for monopolistic practices find there are some lines of enterprise where it certainly is not easy to attempt to start a new business in competition with a well established business. The successful accomplishment of this difficult task was recently shown when an enterprising electric light bulb producer broke into a very tightly controlled field. This action appeals to those who feel that "potential" competition is an important bulwark of American capitalistic society.

freedom of the press and of speech: The right to publish any newspaper, magazine, book or pamphlet without censorship or registration, or to say anything one wishes, except what might be subject to suits for libel. The possible restraints that may be placed upon this freedom have caused much discussion since the point at which freedom ends and license begins is not easily determined. However, by interpretation the following limitations have been generally accepted: not to utter indecencies, incite to insurrection, encourage disobedience of the law, or defame the government, or aid and abet the enemy.

freedom of religion: This represents a goal that has been the aim of Americans since the start of our government and was specifically guaranteed in the First Amendment to the federal constitution, and has many safeguards provided for by state laws. It provides for the right to worship freely according to the dictates of one's own conscience, and implies the separation of state and church (q.v.). People of every or no religion have equal standing in the eyes of the law. While assuring religious freedom some circumstances have arisen where conflict with the law has occurred. For example polygamy, tolerated by the Mormon religion, was forbidden by federal law. Several conflicts have reached the Supreme Court over the beliefs of the Jehovah's Witnesses, but the Court has ruled for complete freedom of religion where no violation of law, no breach of the peace, or no offense to public morals has occurred.

"Freedom Train": In 1947 a Diesel locomotive and seven railroad coaches left Washington, D. C., for an extended tour of the United States, containing a wonderful collection of documents that gave evidence of the means by which our most precious rights and privileges of freedom were protected. In well safeguarded display cases were shown the Declaration of Independence, the Constitution of the United States and the Bill of Rights. Enthusiastic crowds poured through the train all over the United States.

free enterprise: *See* FREEDOM OF ENTRY.

freehold: A property qualification for voting during colonial times and continuing in many states up to the 1850's.

free list (free goods): Those items that are admitted as imports to a country without the necessity of paying customs duties.

free port: A portion of a harbor designated for goods to be reexported and therefore admitted temporarily duty free. The goods may be unloaded, stored, reshipped, but the "original package" is held to be unbroken.

free silver: A term referring to the desire for unlimited coinage of silver dollars, a policy favored by the farmer and the debtor classes in the last quarter of the nineteenth century, and partially attained by various silver purchase acts (1878, 1890 and 1934) when the government agreed to buy limited amounts of silver for coinage into dollars or to be used as backing of silver certificates. The greatest peak of the demand for free silver was in the campaign of 1896 when the defeat of William Jennings Bryan practically ended the issue. *See* FREE COINAGE.

Free-Soil Party: A minor political party opposed to the extension of slavery in the newly created territories being carved out of the Louisiana Purchase or the Mexican Cession. They represented a compromise between the absolute position of the abolitionists [politically known as the Liberty Party (q.v.)] and the southern position of allowing slavery to exist anywhere. The Free-Soilers nominated Van Buren in 1848 who drew votes from the Democratic candidate Lewis Cass in New York and thus threw the election to the Whig candidate Zachary Taylor.

free trade: A situation where a country does not impose duties on the importation of goods from foreign countries, or else collects such a low tariff that there is no effect of reducing the potential competition of such goods in her domestic economy.

fry the fat: An American slang expression meaning to secure political contributions from wealthy individuals, or from corporations in return for favors advantageous to the contributors. *See* CORRUPT PRACTICES ACT, which stop much of this.

fugitive from justice: One who has fled from the state in which he is accused of having committed a crime in order to avoid arrest, or to avoid giving testimony. The consent of the governor of the state to which he has fled is required to force extradition or return of such a fugitive.

Fulbright Act: This measure makes it possible to send several hundred student research workers to countries which purchased American war surpluses such as Great Britain, France, Norway, Italy and Greece. This financing was provided because of the need for broader international understanding, and because of the increased shortage of dollars. The Europeans get much needed dollars and the Americans have a chance to study abroad. Some Europeans may come here too. The grants are only for graduate study in connection with some recognized institution.

"full dinner pail": This slogan was one of the major planks of the Republican Party platform at the start of the Twentieth Century in its effort to win working class support by implying Republican responsibility for full employment through favoring private enterprise and the growth of business and thus making possible high wages. Its variations have appeared as "a chicken in every pot," or "a car in every garage."

full faith and credit clause: This clause from the Federal Constitution requires that each state recognize the legal papers, wills, charters of every other state when they are duly authenticated. Some exceptions have arisen as to divorce when one state does not accept the residence requirement as fully met.

functional representation: An idea not taken very seriously in the United States would provide that the legislative bodies be chosen on the basis of representation by groups of workers, such as textile workers, farmers, transportation workers, or professional groups rather than on a geographical basis. One of the commonest objections to proportional representation was that it might tend to develop just some such type of functional divisions, and by giving direct representation to special economic groups create "splinter" parties unable to work together.

funding a debt: A financial arrangement entered into to save a government, or a corporation expenses by the reissuing of bonds at a lower interest rate, or the conversion of a floating debt, one not secured by bonds, into a permanent one.

Fusion: It may become politically expedient for a group of minority interests to band together during a period of widespread corruption and graft. This combination, or fusion may result, as in New York City, in the defeat of the entrenched party. Mayor LaGuardia won with the support of the Republicans, the American Labor Party and reform Democrats, and repeated the victory a second time.

G

game warden: A local official who sees that the laws for the protection of game and fish are carried out. He may also check up hunting and fishing licenses and see to it that the "closed season" for certain animals is observed.

garbage-disposal plants: A new device for protecting the city's health has been the construction of elaborate buildings for quick disposal of garbage. They may be the "reduction" or incinerator type. In the first the grease is extracted with solvents and is sold, the balance may be sold for fertilizer. This is an expensive and disagreeable process and many cities have dropped such a method. In the other process very high temperatures are used (1200 degrees) and the residue is more easily disposed of, though a source of income through the sale of the by-products is lost.

garnishment: The right to take a certain percentage (usually not over ten percent) of a government employee's salary because of a judgment rendered in court against that individual.

"gateway amendment": A term used for an amendment not yet introduced into Congress but which would be a proposal to expedite the adoption of further amendments to the Federal Constitution by means of requiring a simple majority approval in the two houses of Congress, rather than the present two-thirds vote, and to provide for popular ratification in place of that of the state legislatures or conventions. Proposed amendments would be started as the result of National Constitutional Conventions meeting at stated intervals.

gavel rule: Such an expression indicates that the presiding officer has assumed the power to force his decisions upon the gathering. What he says is so even though he decides contrary to rule or in violation of individual rights.

General Assembly of the United Nations: This assembly provides the most democratic element in the varied United Nations hierarchy, because on it every member is represented and has only one vote. Acting as a "Town Meeting of the World" it may discuss any problem affecting the peace of the world and send recommendations to all the UN agencies. It has other advisory duties in the appointment of the Secretary-General, admission or expulsion of new members, election of non-permanent Security Council members, and the determination of the budget. It also may create any subsidiary organization of the United Nations. There were over sixty members by 1951 with a dozen more waiting for admission during 1952 delayed because of international politics.

general court: The name given to the legislature in New Hampshire and Vermont.

general fund: The accumulation of various types of income of a city government exclusive of taxation. It may include rent from docks or for space in subway stations or fees and franchises.

general property tax: A tax on the estimated exchange value of property levied at a common rate for all property in the same taxing area, and paid by the owner of the property. It is the largest source of income for county, city and other local units, though authorized by the state government.

general strike: A strike occurring in all types of industry at once. One of the most famous was that in England in 1926 when the public rallied to the operators' assistance in providing essential services; college students running busses and similar practices. Such a strike is usually held illegal for the same reasons as those applied against a secondary boycott; that is, it means disciplinary action is being taken against a group of employers who are not directly responsible for the calling of the strike and against whom their workers have no grievance. It is a powerful weapon if used effectively and radical labor organizations advocate it though it has actually served as little more than a threat.

general welfare clause: There is a provision in the Constitution (Article I, Section 8) which gives to Congress the power to tax "to pay the debts and provide for the common defense and the general welfare of the United States." Those who interpret the clause strictly feel that taxation can only be used for specific functions granted to Congress, others, however would accept a much broader view that any kind of appropriation for the benefit of all the people would be proper and constitutional.

genocide: Mass murder of a people for reasons of race or religion. The Nazis used such methods in the extermination of the Jews in the concentration camps with such evil effect that the United Nations has since outlawed such action.

gentlemen's agreement: An understanding usually between statesmen that certain terms of foreign policy will be upheld without the need for a formal treaty. This was true of the understanding between the United States and Japan in 1907 when Japan's immigration to the United States was to be limited by Japan's own arrangements not to issue her people any passports. We broke the agreement when we established our Immigration Law of 1924 excluding all Asiatics.

geographical differential: A rate of pay, higher or lower than that commonly accepted elsewhere due to allowances for more expensive urban living or to the introduction of industrial employment as in the former agricultural areas in the South.

gerrymandering: The manipulation of election districts for unfair party advantage. It started, it is said, with Governor Gerry (Mass. 1812) who, in order to rearrange party groupings so as to defeat his opponent, outlined the boundaries of a district which an observer thought looked like a salamander, which elicited the reply, "No, not a salamander, a gerrymander." Today this same practice of creating curiously shaped districts, such as "shoestring," or saddlebag districts to best utilize party advantage still goes on whenever reapportionment of state or federal districts is necessary. Curiosities other than shape exist too. In a recent House the "misrepresentation" was such that one of the largest districts had a population more than eight times the smallest; rural areas have more weight than their numbers represent.

gift tax: A federal or state tax levied on gifts of property. These taxes were established to prevent an individual from avoiding payment of an inheritance tax.

gobbledygook: The involved and stilted verbiage of many government orders and communications. An expression created by Maury Maverick to apply to this language of the bureaucrats.

gold certificate: From 1863-1907 gold certificates were in circulation in $20 denominations. They were "receipts" for gold bullion held by the Treasury and had 100% backing. From 1907-1934 they were also issued in $10 units but after gold was nationalized they were recalled except for special use within the Federal Reserve System.

gold clause cases: After the devaluation of gold in 1933 and its nationalization by the Federal Government, the gold certificates still in circulation stated on their face that they were redeemable in gold. This was no longer possible so a suit reached the Supreme Court to settle the constitutionality of the government's action. The Court upheld the government's invalidation of its contract, the gold clause, on the grounds that the citizen bringing the suit could show no economic loss since he had available the same monetary value as before, only in gold certificates not in gold. In a similar case a holder of a bond also sued to recover gold as in the "contract" but that decision was practically the same: only where economic loss could be proven was redress by the government necessary.

gold standard: A monetary system which provides for gold as the single standard of value, and under which all legal currency may be redeemed in gold. The United States has been under a a modified gold standard since 1933. All gold has been nationalized so that our currency may not be redeemed in actual gold but in gold certificates the equivalent of gold.

"Good-Neighbor Policy": A program introduced more effectively after 1933 by the Roosevelt administration to improve our relations with Latin American countries and provide for multilateral protection rather than the "Big Brother" policy of the early 1900's, which had antagonized many of the Latin American countries, despite its avowed purpose of helping them. *See* INTER-AMERICAN COOPERATION.

good offices: This represents one of the most common methods of settling disputes either on an international or local level. A third state or neutral observer offers to act as an intermediary for transmitting proposals, or to provide for a meeting place for representatives of both sides to hold discussions.

government by injunction: A term of criticism used about the

Federal Government before the passage of the Norris-LaGuardia Act (q.v.) of 1932 because it was felt by many liberal and labor groups that it was too easy for corporations to obtain injunctions (q.v.) from federal judges to have unions stop certain actions such as agitating for strikes, and too easy to find an individual in contempt of court if they ignored the injunction since the same judge who had issued the injunction could without a trial find the person in contempt. The imprisonment of Eugene V. Debs was because of his breaking the injunction issued against him in the Pullman strike of 1894.

government-owned corporation: Rather than create a new department, or subdivision of an already existing department, the practice has developed recently of creating a government corporation. This unit has a certain degree of autonomy, and enjoys a greater degree of freedom of action, and is not subject to as much red tape as the older type of administrative agency. It is a legal entity and may sue and be sued. Its stock is owned by the United States. Usually the employees of such corporations are not under Civil Service regulations though often individual requirements are stricter than those of equivalent positions under Civil Service examinations. In 1931 there were ten such government corporations, in 1944 there were forty-four, though some have been liquidated since the war. Among the most prominent remaining are: Tennessee Valley Authority, Reconstruction Finance Corporation and the Federal Deposit Insurance Corporation.

governor: The governor, chief executive of the state, is the title used in all forty-eight states, but great variety is shown in the type of governorship provided for according to the state constitutions, with some strong with many powers assigned and more assumed, and others just "weak." Primarily a party leader, the governor in most states has found his position as an administrator becoming more and more complicated. Since the Civil War he has found himself more and more in the position of the state's business manager authorized to prepare budgets and act as supervisor of a growing number of state functions, such as highway construction, utility and insurance company regulation, health and labor department activities. Though some states are already following the trend of giving their executive large appointive powers for centralizing responsibility as in New York, New Jersey, Virginia and Tennessee, other states still have numerous elected state officials outside the governor's jurisdiction, and much systematizing will become necessary with the growing complexity of government. Most of the states have a four year term of office, though the average for actual office holding is only a little over three years. Many state constitutions prevent eligibility for reelection in succession to the first term.

graft: The acquisition of wealth or valuable privileges by dishonest or unfair means at the expense of the public on the part of officeholders, or persons who possess political influence.

Grain Futures Act of 1922: In an effort to protect farmers from unfair speculation in the crops they expect to market in the future, the Commodities Exchange Authority of the Department of Agriculture requires that all brokers dealing in grain and other commodity-futures transactions must register. This licensing and supervising prohibits corners in staples, unfair market manipulation, and the dissemination of false information.

grandfather clauses: Provisions in the constitutions of seven southern states at one time or another stated that in general persons could qualify as voters without satisfying any other requirements if their ancestors were eligible to vote before the adoption of the Fifteenth Amendment (1867). This discriminated in favor of the white voters but was not found unconstitutional until 1915.

grand jury: The duties of the grand (large) jury are derived from English common-law procedure and still serve their original purpose of safeguarding the individual's rights. No one, then or now, may be proceeded against for a "capital" crime unless on a presentment or indictment of a grand jury. The federal grand jury consists of from twelve to twenty-three persons before whom the public prosecutor or district attorney makes accusations of crimes. After discussion the jury either dismisses the case on the basis of insufficient evidence, or issues an indictment. Under some conditions the process may be slow and cumbersome, and some states have substituted the filing of an "information" or an affidavit against the person under suspicion by the county prosecutor. This simplification could not take place under federal procedure unless an amendment to the United States Constitution were obtained.

grandstanding: When a politician in making a speech plays up to some group for special approval, he is accused of grandstanding or making a bid for their particular support.

Granger laws: These laws were passed in the states of Minnesota, Iowa and Wisconsin in order to provide for the regulation of the railroads because of their unfair practices particularly toward the farmers who were dependent upon the roads for getting their goods to market at a cost that would leave them some margin of profit. At first the Supreme Court upheld the constitutionality of the state laws (Munn vs. Illinois 1876) but later reversed itself on the ground that the states could not interfere in interstate commerce. As a direct outcome of this decision Congress was urged to pass the act creating the Interstate Commerce Commission (q.v.).

Granger Movement: The National Grange of the Patrons of Husbandry was a secret fraternal order with elaborate rituals established in 1867. It had a program of economic reform that led to much pressure on Congress and the passage of legislation beneficial to the farmer, such as railroad regulation and curtailment of monopolies. The movement declined as a political force after 1875, but has retained its name in some communities as a social center.

grants-in-aid: Financial contributions by the Federal government to the states for various purposes usually conditioned by some regulatory practice. *See* SMITH-LEVER ACT.

grass roots: To appeal to the "grass roots" of the country is assumed to mean an attempt to get at the basic views of the average individual at the lowest level of the political ladder. In our early political history the expression would more likely have referred to the country districts from whence has probably come the origin of the term "grass" in the expression which today applies equally well to the city or industrial interests when a basic or fundamental opinion is sought.

grave yard committee: In most state legislatures there is a judiciary committee which is usually made up of experienced lawyers who have many serious doubts as to the legality or the correct wording of a large number of the bills assigned to their committee after their first reading in the legislature. So few measures gain their recommendation that they are popularly known as the grave yard committee because they kill so many bills. *See* "KILL IN COMMITTEE."

Greenback Party: A minor Party in the period about 1876-1884 which favored the continued issuance of fiat money (greenbacks q.v.) since they represented a debtor class who wanted inflation as a measure of relieving agricultural distress by means of raising the prices of their produce. They at times favored other reforms such as a graduated income tax and regulation of interstate commerce. After a slight lapse in activity, when the greenbacks were stabilized (*see* RESUMPTION ACT), they were absorbed into the Populists Movement (q.v.).

Greenbacks: A paper currency issued as a means of financing the Civil War. In 1879 a fund was authorized to provide $100 million in gold backing. This was resented by those elements of the population who favored cheap money (q.v.). *See also* GREENBACK PARTY.

grey market: A grey market represents the buying and selling of goods in a fashion not strictly illegal, but violating the spirit of certain restrains or rationing decrees, and obtaining exorbitant prices by unfair means.

"groomed for office": A potential candidate may be groomed for office by giving him a prominent position in the public eye, as chairman of committees or conferences or investigating groups or in any way getting his name frequently in the press or on the radio or television.

group insurance: A group working in a particular plant or institution, or in a special city department have had a form of health insurance made available to them in many communities with the municipalities helping to keep the premiums low and often providing for payroll deductions. Since this is done on a voluntary basis it has not been subjected to the attacks that a compulsory program of "socialized medicine" has had to endure. The "Blue Cross" with coverage for either hospital insurance or medical care in addition is a similar voluntary program.

"Grundy" Tariff: The Hawley-Smoot Tariff of 1930 which is still basically in effect is a high protective tariff though the President has the power to raise or lower duties under reciprocal tariff agreements (q.v.). It was named after a tariff lobbyist who admitted to getting funds for the Republicans in return for favors in tariff legislation.

Guam: This island, the largest in the Marianas, 1450 miles east of Manila, was acquired by the United States as a result of the Spanish American War in 1898. It is important for its strategic location as an American naval base, and as a potential base for naval operations. It consists of about 200 square miles of territory with a population of 59,000 (1950). It is administered by the Navy.

guaranteed annual wage: A proposal under which an employee is guaranteed a specific number of weeks' work during a year or a minimum annual wage for a specific number of weeks of work. It is favored by many who feel it is a means of job security, and could be a means of stabilizing our economy so as to eliminate the extremes of the business cycle, and encourage individual self-help by systematic saving through regular employment.

guerrilla warfare: Irregular fighting by small groups often in secret hand to hand combat, or in hit and run attacks under informal organization.

Guild Socialism: A type of socialism in which each industry would be owned and managed by all the workers in that industry, manual, clerical and supervisory, and with an emphasis on advancing creative ability. The state would act as a coordinator of all the separate guild activities and attempt to safeguard the interests of society as a whole somewhat in the fashion of the medieval craft guild. The syndicates have a resemblance to the guilds except that they lack the coordinating activities.

Guild System: A voluntary association of individuals banded together during the Middle Ages according to specific crafts. Originally for religious and welfare benefits to the members, and chartered by the royal authorities, they set up standards to insure good workmanship and to prevent monopoly. The rise from journeyman following a long period as an apprentice was climaxed by the production of a "masterpiece," indication that the candidate was really worthy of admission to the ranks of master. Though resembling the modern unions in some respects it is to be noticed that the master was his own boss and usually had his shop in his own home, where he produced only upon individual order. The Industrial Revolution bringing an end to the "Domestic System" and introducing the Factory System caused the guilds to die out.

"guilt by association": The idea that a person could be held responsible for his views if they were expressed by a group with which he was merely thought to be affiliated, probably had its origin in the practice of the Soviet Union where individuals were held accountable for the opinions and actions of relatives, or friends; children of "bourgeois" parents were disfranchised at one time, relatives of priests were kept under "observation," hostages at home were in danger of reprisals for actions of relatives abroad. In the 1950's many Americans regretted that this idea of "guilt by association" was gaining some headway in America in regard to finding Americans guilty in the same fashion if they were members of an organization placed on the "subversive" list by the Attorney-General. This would be a contradiction of the position of Justice Holmes that actions not thoughts produce traitors, but conforms to some of the more recent ideas that to look upon treason only as an "overt act" is philosophically, morally and legally inadequate in the present critical position of the world.

H

habeas corpus: A writ that guarantees that any person under arrest has the right to an immediate hearing before a court in order that it may be determined that there is sufficient cause for his continued detention. A state court will issue such an order where state law is involved, and a federal court where the national government is concerned.

Hague Conventions: Resolutions adopted by the Second Hague Conference in 1907 to regulate warfare, to protect noncombatants, and to eliminate barbarous practices, and promote the settlement of disputes by arbitration.

"Half-breeds": A group within the Republican Party who tried to challenge the supremacy of the party regulars known as "Stalwarts." They favored conciliation toward the South and civil service reform. Having supported Hayes in his position that his country came before his loyalty to his party, they looked with disfavor upon the attempt of the Stalwarts to win a third term for Grant in 1880, resenting the "deals" and corruption that had been exposed under Grant.

"hard money": Money represented by coins, especially by the silver dollar in the West. Also, money that has an adequate backing so that it has a stable value in domestic and foreign exchange. For contrast *see* CHEAP MONEY.

Hare System: *See* PROPORTIONAL REPRESENTATION.

Hartford Convention: A meeting of delegates from the New England states during the closing years of the War of 1812 to express that section's dissatisfaction with the conduct of the war and the activities of the administration. Just as they were about to consider terms of secession in "such amendments to the Constitution as may secure them equal advantages," news of the end of the war arrived (1815) and the Convention passed out of existence.

Hatch Acts: These are two measures passed by Congress in 1940 to attempt to eliminate corruption in politics by placing restrictions on the amount of money to be expended on political activities and upon the sources from which it was to be obtained. Individual contributions to a political committee are limited to $5,000 and a three million dollar limit is placed on the amount to be spent by such a national committee. These laws also attempted to prevent government workers from using political influence, and provided safeguards so that government workers could not be forced to make political contributions to retain position or advancement.

hat in the ring: A candidate by putting his hat in the ring is announcing his willingness to run for office.

Hawaii: A territory of the United States, Hawaii consists of many islands with an area of over 6,000 square miles and with a population of about half a million. It was annexed by a joint resolution (q.v.) of Congress in 1898 at the request of its own people, having been independent previously. An Organic Law of 1910 established its government as a territory with a governor appointed by the President of the United States, and a territorial delegate who sits in Congress but may not vote. The Constitution of the United States applies in full since it is an incorporated territory (q.v.). *See* HAWAIIAN STATEHOOD CONTROVERSY.

Hawaiian statehood controversy: Hawaii, acquired by the United States in 1898, is an incorporated (q.v.) territory which has been seeking statehood since 1920 in over thirty measures introduced at various intervals in Congress. Many have passed in the House but have been held up in the Senate. For the case against statehood the claims have been made that Hawaiian territory is not contiguous, that its polyglot population is unassimilable. Some express opposition for fear a conservative agricultural group may gain two senators representing the dominant sugar and plantation interests. Others fear disadvantages because as a territory, Hawaiian imports from the United States afford wholesale importers a five to fifteen percent discount that would be lost as a state. Those in favor of the admission of Hawaii as a state refer to the half million population and the more than one hundred million dollar trade in each direction, and to the great loyalty of the people during World War II.

Hawley-Smoot Tariff of 1930: The Republican Congress was called into special session 1929 to "do something" about revision of the tariff schedules. Despite vocal criticism of opposing groups such as the farmers who were by no means convinced that higher duties would help them any, and of some bankers, importers, and manufacturers who met no real foreign competition, Congress proceeded to raise the duties on farm commodities, raw materials, minerals, textiles and dyestuffs. In general this tariff raised the average level from thirty-three percent under the previous act to forty percent. The Tariff Commission (q.v.) was retained with the power to investigate production costs and to recommend the raising or lowering of rates. *See* FLEXIBLE TARIFF, RECIPROCAL TRADE AGREEMENTS.

Health Insurance Plan (National): This was a program advocated by both President Roosevelt and President Truman with considerable backing by those who felt a payroll deduction scheme contributed to by both employer and employee would finance many medical benefits not otherwise available to the individual. The Plan was to be administered by the Federal government but state collections were to be kept within the state. The opponents of the program won out partly through fear that the scheme would be compulsory and because they feared it might succumb to the difficulties of some government-run projects and be burdened with bureaucratic red tape, be costly, and be a handicap to the medical profession.

hearing: A meeting called for the purpose of obtaining information either on the part of a court or a committee of a legislature desirous of sampling the varied opinions of the public on a proposed measure.

Hemispheric Security: This is the policy that was supposed to have been initiated by Monroe by means of his famous Doctrine (1823) though John Quincy Adams originated the policy of keeping the United States free from possible European entanglements, by guaranteeing that South American countries retain their independence. Theodore Roosevelt, by means of his "Big Stick" policy, continued the same idea. Subsequent conferences for defense during and after World War II have in a sense continued the same practice but with greater emphasis on the idea of equality between the nations participating in the program. *See* INTER-AMERICANISM.

"high crimes and misdemeanors": This expression quoted from the Federal Constitution defines the condition under which any proceedings may be instituted against a federal executive or judicial official for removal from the position he holds, that is, impeachment. If indicted by the House of Representatives the Senate conducts the trial.

"higher law doctrine": William H. Seward as a firm believer in the abolition of slavery made his position clear in a speech before the Senate in 1850 when he declared that since the Constitution of the United States did not specifically outlaw slavery one was entitled to go to a "higher law," or the law of nature to justify the wrongness of slavery. His position was denounced as treasonable and was one of the reasons why the Abolitionists were looked upon as extreme radicals in that period and suffered many, even one fatal attack, for holding to such a belief.

high pressure systems: Large cities with a congested area of very high buildings require special provisions for fighting fire. New York City, and a few other cities have constructed special high-pressure systems in critical areas, which within a minute can develop water pressure up to three hundred pounds per square inch. Special mechanical devices have to be provided to direct the stream of water on the required spot. Often neighboring bodies of water are drawn upon for supplies rather than the city water supply system.

high seas: The unenclosed waters of the sea, and, by ruling of Congress, including the Great Lakes, on all of which the United States Admiralty has jurisdiction.

hoarding: The obtaining and keeping hidden of money or goods which are or are expected to be in short supply to gain advantage over those willing to abide by legal or reasonable distribution methods. Fear of such action in regard to gold after the Crash of 1929 led the Federal Government to demand that all gold coins be turned in to the banks. *See* NATIONALIZATION OF GOLD.

holding company: When trusts (q.v.) were declared illegal in 1890 an attempt was made to gain the same end, business consolidation, by creating a holding company. This is a corporation which possesses stock of other corporations, or subsidiaries from which the larger organization receives dividends, management fees, and interest payments, but which is not actually an operating company. Such companies are subject to special regulation under the Public Utility Holding Company Act of 1935, which may cause the dissolution of all but a single integrated holding company, since holding companies of a second degree are illegal under the "death sentence clause" (q.v.).

home rule: A situation by which a local administrative unit obtains the right to conduct its own government. New York City enjoys home rule by means of a charter granted by the State Legislature.

Homestead Act: An act of 1862 offering 160 acres to anyone who could pay a registration fee of ten dollars and perform a limited amount of work upon the land during a period of five years.

"honest graft": The benefits obtained by "insiders" or others by association with municipal officials who may allow valuable information to "leak" out. If a school or park or highway is about to be built upon certain property which the city has not yet purchased, "interested" persons might just happen to buy it up first and cause the price to advance considerably if "honest graft" had operated in time for them to have learned of the situation. Contracts may be awarded to the only firm which "happened" to be able to produce goods of a peculiar type which they alone produce and which by chance the city "happened" to need. All these situations produce "honest graft" in the sense that no actual laws are broken though ultimately an aroused citizenry may protest the honesty involved.

Hoover Commission: A twelve-man group of civilian experts was created by the Eightieth Congress in 1947 to thoroughly examine the operation of the executive branch of the government and make recommendations for reorganization. Each Committee report was the result of the findings of a task force of additional experts who probed deeply into, and made a detailed examination of every subdivision of our administrative agencies. By 1949 voluminous reports were being issued and books of analysis were speedily being published. Some suggested reforms were promptly carried out by Congress, but others represent long range planning and some have aroused opposition. The whole project represented a gigantic housecleaning with many favorable direct and indirect results. Especially after the start of the situation in Korea, it became essential to remedy what the Comptroller-General called "a hodgepodge and crazy quilt of duplications, overlappings, inefficiencies, and inconsistencies with their attendant extravagance."

"hopper": The large box hanging at the end of the Clerk of the House of Representative's desk into which all new bills must be first deposited until assigned to a committee for study and debate.

horizontal combination: A form of industrial organization in which businesses or factories engaged in the same activity are united under a single control. An example might be a nation-wide chain of shoe stores all branches of one concern. For contrast *see* VERTICAL INTEGRATION.

Hospital Act of 1946 (Hull-Burton Act): In line with a program of federal-local cooperation, this act was proposed to bring much needed relief in local areas by having federal funds made available by a supplementary device like the grants-in-aid already paid by the national government for agricultural and vocational education and aged and disability allowances. The local government must match the federal funds and must also obtain state approval determined on the basis of prescribed minimum standards.

"hot pursuit": A legal term under which a law enforcement officer may follow an alleged criminal across a state boundary and make an arrest, and then turn the prisoner over to the local authorities. Normally states have jurisdiction only within their own borders.

House of Representatives: The larger house of Congress has had a permanent membership of 435 since 1910, but with the ratio of population to representatives gradually rising until now it is approaching 350,000 per representative. The House has certain exclusive privileges, such as that of initiating money bills, or of the impeachment of certain federal office holders and the President of the United States, and the right to elect a President if a majority of the electoral college votes is not obtained by any candidate. In this case the delegation from each state casts one vote. The House has the full right to determine its own rules of procedure which it does every two years when the new House is organized. *See* RULES COMMITTEE.

Housing and Home Finance Agency (1947): After many difficulties with housing problems a coordination of the New Deal agencies of 1934, and the Defense Housing and the Veterans' Housing Authorities was attempted. In 1949 Congress provided that the federal government contribute $308 million annually for forty years to subsidize rents of low-income families, and to build more housing units. It also provided that slum clearance be aided by a $1½ billion grant over five years, with the federal government paying one-third of the expense and the local community making up the difference. Finally in 1950 a further grant of $300 million was made to loan colleges and universities funds to provide faculty and student housing.

Housing Expediter: According to the Housing and Rent Act of 1949 the Housing Expediter administers Federal rent legislation with five-member local boards appointed by the Expediter from names submitted by the state governors. He was to revise rent controls so that landlords would receive a "fair net operating income." Decontrol was to be arranged when a state governor advised that the legislation of his state was adequate for control or that such control was no longer necessary in that state.

humanitarian: Movements or actions having to do with the improvement of mankind by philanthropic individuals, or more recently by government administration in regard to grants for aged, blind or dependents.

hyphenated Americans: Americans of foreign birth or of foreign born parents who retain a concern for that foreign land at the expense of the United States.

I

"identical pricing": The practice of retail stores fixing prices for the same item at the same amount as in other stores selling the same article. The Federal Trade Commission (q.v.) has found "the economic effect of identical pricing achieved through the parallel action of similar sellers amounts to collusion" and it is therefore held to be a violation of the Clayton Antitrust Law and subject to prosecution. The businesses concerned attempt to defend themselves by saying that all are affected in very much the same way by all other types of expenses, and that in most cases they have individually arrived at the economically sound price at which they hope to make a reasonable profit. The issue is looked upon critically as a phase of the very important problem of how far the government may go in its efforts to curb the growing trend toward monopoly some foresee.

ideology: Doctrine or political ideas of a group or class or party.

Imhoff tanks: A chemical treatment used in reducing the organic content of the sludge resulting from the screening of sewage, in connection with the operation of sewage disposal plants by city governments.

immigration: Voluntary movement into a country of people coming as permanent settlers. The United States has introduced restricting regulations since 1922, limiting the total annual quota to 150,000, excluding those who may come in freely from any part of the western hemisphere. *See* NATIONAL ORIGINS LAW.

immunity: Exemption from the application of a rule or a jurisdiction, as Congressional immunity, or diplomatic immunity, involving freedom from arrest under certain circumstances.

immunization: Protection against disease acquired by means of the production of antibodies within the immune organism in reaction to living or dead pathogems or their poisons introduced by infection or injection. This represents a service which many of the city hospitals provide for the children of the community.

impanel: Drawing by lot the names to form the jury or panel. An individual's place on the jury may be challenged if suspected of bias, "challenge to the favor," or "challenge for cause," any other designated reason, or a limited number of arbitrary challenges may be allowed without any announced reasons.

impeachment: A formal accusation made against a civil official by the lower house of a legislature to the upper house which conducts the trial, and upon finding the individual guilty of high crime or misdemeanors (treason or bribery) may remove him from office, after which he becomes liable for criminal action. The House of Representatives impeached President Andrew Johnson and he was brought to trial by the Senate which by a very close vote acquitted him. There have been extremely few cases of impeachment in the federal government.

"implied powers clause": Congress has extended its powers greatly through the process of "loose interpretation of the Constitution" (q.v.) in regard to the eighteenth power, the "necessary and proper" clause, which makes it possible for Congress to enlarge upon its activities greatly.

impropriety: Anything that is improper or indecent. Used in politics in regard to the acceptance of "gifts" or services on the part of legislators, which may not actually constitute corruption but comes in the estimation of many very close to it.

impugn: To call in question. Frequently used in attacks upon corruption where the actions of some politicians are questioned on a level of decency and honor.

inauguration: The ceremony undertaken when a president or governor is sworn into office. In that of the President the date has been changed from March 4th to January 20th by the Twentieth Amendment.

Incentive System: A means of increasing production developed particularly by Lincoln Electric Company, who claim that they are now producing a much greater amount at a greatly reduced cost. The incentive to the worker is the promise of a big year-end bonus over and above his take-home pay. The distribution in 1946 was of over $2.8 million. Such bonus payments in that plant raised the annual average wage from $2,100 in 1919 to $5,800 forty years later with many skilled workers earning $6,000 to $7,000 a year.

incidence: The point where the actual burden of taxation falls, may be either direct, paid by the person who cannot shift the burden as in a land or poll tax, or indirect, collected at some stage of production or distribution, as a tariff, and though ultimately paid by the consumer the incidence at the time seems indirect.

incidental motion: In parliamentary procedure this is a motion which arises relative to the order or conduct of business, as for example a motion to suspend a rule, allow a paper to be read, raise a point of order or appeal a decision from the chair.

Income tax: The Sixteenth Amendment added to Federal Constitution in 1913 provides that Congress shall have the power to collect taxes on incomes from "whatever source derived." This avoided the difficulties that had existed earlier when the Supreme Court had reversed itself as to whether an income tax was a direct tax or not and whether it would need to be apportioned among the states in proportion to the population.

incorporated territory: A territory of the United States which Congress has expressly recognized as a part of the United States and to which all the provisions of the Constitution of the United States apply both fundamental and formal. Hawaii and Alaska are incorporated territories. *See* INSULAR CASES.

incorporation: The creation of a corporation, that is an artificial person, by an act of a state legislature, usually at the initiation of the three "incorporators" who must indicate the type of business to be undertaken and the capitalization of the enterprise. The federal government may also perform the act of incorporation in regard to its own administrative bodies, such as the Federal Deposit Insurance Corporation and the Reconstruction Finance Corporation.

incumbent: The holder of an office and therefore the one to be subjected to attack by the political party seeking to gain office.

indemnification: Reimbursement or payment made to an individual for some loss or damage as payment by the United States for destruction to private property during maneuvers of a regular Army outfit.

independent: A voter who is not a member of any official party, or if a member, one who still decides to vote for any candidate running regardless of party affiliation. If such an independent never joins a party he will in some states lose his right to vote in the primaries.

independent union: Most unions are affiliated with one or the other of the two great labor consolidations, the American Federation of Labor or the Congress of Industrial Organization; but a few unions due to their technical nature or their inability to decide which of the labor groups to join have remained unaffiliated or independent. Numerically the largest of these independents is the Railroad Brotherhood (q.v.), the so-called Big Four, and the largest single independent union was the National Federation of Telephone Workers. There is another group that might claim to qualify as independent unions, the company union (q.v.) which has been found legal under the Taft-Hartley Law where they were formerly held unsatisfactory as bargaining agents for workers.

indeterminate sentence: A judge in pronouncing sentence upon a prisoner may not set a fixed period of imprisonment but within certain legal limits leave the final decision to interested administrative agencies.

Indiana Ballot: A form of ballot used in a great many states which places the names of the candidates in party columns, the first of which goes to the party winning the last election. Fifteen states use the party emblem at the top.

indictment: The formal accusation by which a person is charged with having committed a specified crime. The prosecuting attorney sends the indictment to the grand jury, who, if they decide the accused must stand trial, return the indictment as a "true Bill," which charge results in the later trial of the individual when arrested.

indirect tax: A government tax upon merchandise paid by a producer but added to the price of an article so that it is ultimately paid by the consumer. Examples include cigarette and gasoline taxes. Many reformers feel that the public should be more alert to the burdensomeness of this type of tax because of its inflationary tendency and because it may hide the full weight of the tax program.

indispensable man: An expression used to indicate a government official without whom the state or country could not get along. Franklin D. Roosevelt disclaimed this label but his party encouraged the idea in the 1944 election in the midst of World War II.

industrialization of farming: Especially in the West where there is much large scale farming the modern farmer has much capital invested in his expensive machinery, he hires many farm laborers, manages complicated affairs far removed from the traditional view of one man toiling alone on his own acres. This new farmer has his account book, his payroll to make up and needs to be as good a businessman as his urban brother.

industrial union: A union formed of all the workers employed in an entire industry, skilled and unskilled, is called a vertical union in distinction to the craft union made up of workers in a similar trade or occupation and designated as horizontal union because of its national organization across the whole country. The United Mine Workers of America was one of the first industrial unions to be created, and others of this type include: United Automobile Workers, United Rubber Workers, and the Aircraft and Agricultural Implements Workers. Ten such industrial unions took the name of the Congress of Industrial Organization (q.v.) in 1938 and have been rapidly increasing their membership, reaching especially the formerly unorganized and unskilled worker.

industry-wide bargaining: A new type of collective bargaining developing in the twentieth century where the union-employer negotiations are carried on all at one time for a number of like enterprises. In some cases as in coal and men's clothing all employers are directly represented on one bargaining committee. In other instances individual companies may agree to accept the terms the largest company first agrees upon.

infant industry: A term applied to a newly established enterprise while it is attempting to increase its production and its profits. The reference is usually made to those businesses requiring "protection" from the harmful effects of competition of cheaper foreign goods. This protection is accomplished by putting duties sufficiently high on certain imported goods so that they cannot compete in the domestic market. Gradually there is growing up a body of criticism that suggests that after years of benefit the "infant" might grow up.

inflation: A situation in which there is a relatively rapid rise in prices resulting from a demand for goods in excess of their supply. Closely allied with this condition is an excess in the supply of money in proportion to the quantity of goods and services offered.

infringement: Trespassing, as upon property, or encroaching upon patents issued to another.

inherent powers: The Constitution of the United States lists the undisputed powers of Congress as the "enumerated" powers (q.v.). Custom and usage have extended their application through the "implied" powers, based on the "necessary and proper" clause (q.v.). However, since the 1930's there have been those who have tried to advance the idea that Congress has still another type of power—inherent powers, which they consider are those that fall to it through its very nature as a legislative body. Others counter this assumption by claiming such power would fall naturally into the hands of the States by means of their "residual" powers (q.v.). Following the Crash of 1929 there were those who claimed Congress had the inherent power to act where the problems proved too big for the States to handle, as in the field of agricultural assistance or that of unemployment relief. However, the Supreme Court found the Agricultural Adjustment Act of 1933 (q.v.) unconstitutional as interference in intrastate commerce, and Unemployment Insurance as provided for under the Social Security Act (q.v.) is carefully administered under States' standards which are only held to certain minimum provisions by the Federal government.

inheritance tax: A progressive tax levied upon the property which the individual heir receives from the estate of a deceased person. This is different from an estate tax which is levied upon the total value of the whole estate.

"initialed": The practice by which a treaty is signed by the negotiators to be transferred home for government approval. Ratification is the next step which in the United States is by a two-thirds vote of the Senate. Executive agreements or modi vivendi may circumvent the need for formal agreement.

initiative: The method by which the voters themselves may propose a new law by means of a petition. First used in Oregon in 1902. In the different states there are different qualifications as to how these petitions are to be prepared, the number of signatures required varying from five to ten percent of the voters in the state. The aim is to afford the electorate more direct control over legislation. No attempt has yet been made to employ such a method in regard to the federal government though progressive groups have recommended an amendment for such "direct legislation." Over half the states do use it but none has introduced it since 1918.

injunction: An order issued by a court demanding that certain activities cease under penalty of contempt of court. *See* **NORRIS-LA GUARDIA ANTI-INJUNCTION ACT.**

Inland Waterways Corporation: A government-owned corporation created by Congress in 1924. It operates a fleet of barges on the Mississippi and Warrier Rivers deriving its income from its fees.

inquest: An official inquiry into the cause of death usually held before a jury.

insolvent: The condition which exists for a business when its liabilities exceed its assets.

institutionalization: Acting by practice and custom—blind following of the traditional way of doing things, a characteristic of many political conservatives.

Insular Cases: A group of cases reaching the Supreme Court in 1901 establishing a distinction as to the rights enjoyed by individual citizens of an incorporated territory and an unincorporated territory. Among the latter which at the time included Hawaii, Philippines, and Puerto Rico, it was held that they were not "parts" of the United States and it was only to the United States proper that those sections of the United States Constitution applied which were both fundamental and formal. The unincorporated territories were to enjoy the fundamental only. Though the decisions provided no list to define this distinction it has been accepted that import duties could be imposed on goods coming from such territories, that the Constitutional requirements for trial by jury need not be carried out, and that citizenship is not automatically conferred. The Filipino was a citizen of the Philippines, not of the United States, before independence was given them. Hawaii became an incorporated territory in 1900, Alaska much later.

insurance policy: A contract between an individual and an insurance company to perform certain stipulated acts, such as provide compensation in case of losses due to fire, accident, sickness, burglary, or of damage to automobile, ship or stock of goods; or as war risk, hurricane or for employees' liability, or to provide for dependents. Besides all the private companies writing such insurance, state banks now provide a form of life insurance as does the federal government through the Veterans Administration.

insurgent: A person who may temporarily revolt from his party as did some Republicans in 1910, and in 1912 when they followed the Progressives' (q.v.) banner.

integrity: Probity or soundness. In campaign oratory a word much used to describe candidates or the program of the parties.

Inter-American Cooperation: With the lapse in our earlier policy of being a "Big Brother" to the Latin Americans (*See* PAN-AMERICANISM) we have entered upon a period of more cordial relations with our South American neighbors. Multilateral agreements proposed and agreed to equally by all the Latin American countries have lessened the resentment which at the start of the century aroused bitter reference to the "Colossus of the North" or to "Yankee Imperialism" (q.v.).

A series of Inter-American Conferences have reinforced the "Good Neighbor Policy" started in the 1930's. At Montevideo (1933) the United States declared it would not again use armed intervention, and where such need arose it would be the joint concern of the whole continent. At Lima (1938) the twenty-one republics reaffirmed their respect for international law and agreed that a threat to the peace of any nation was the concern of all. In the Act of Chapultepec (1945) the "Continentalization of the Monroe Doctrine" was complete and guarantees were established of the "inviolability of the territory, and the sovereignty, and the political independence of an American state against aggression by any American, European or other power." This policy was later accepted by a provision for "regional understandings" in the Charter of the United Nations.

Inter-American Treaty of Reciprocal Assistance: In 1948 the United States and thirteen Latin American countries ratified a Treaty which provides that an armed attack against one is against all. A vote of two-thirds of the nations participating will make a policy binding upon all except that no state is required to use armed force without its consent. United States was to be permitted to police the continent.

interdependence, economic: The reliance of one group of the community or of one country upon another in matters of specializing in skilled occupations or in the exchange of raw materials. The ideal of world government rests upon a complete development of such economic dependence with each area producing or marketing that which they are best adapted to, regardless of whether it encourages any self-sufficiency; for by these means they see the possibility of the removal of trade barriers that have been having the opposite effect of creating economic independence or nationalism with the imposition of tariffs, or quota limitation on imports.

Interior Department: The duties of this department created in 1849 have to do with matters of domestic concern that in other countries would come under the "Home Office." Public lands, Indian affairs, the Bureau of Mines, National Park Service, Fish and Wild Life Service, and the Bureau of Reclamation represent some of its varied activities.

interlocking directorates: A device once used to avoid prosecution for monopolistic practices by having some members of a particular Board of Directors also members of several other Boards. Members of still other Boards would be accorded membership in the original organization. Through this procedure a unity of policy could be worked out that might fix prices or other actions that would be monopolistic in effect. Such coordination is now held an unfair business practice under the Clayton Antitrust Law.

internal improvements: A means of benefitting the country within its own boundary by highways, canals or other ways of communication authorized at a public expense. This subject became a sectional issue (*see* SECTIONALISM) as early as the 1830's when there was much debate whether such improvements should be financed by the United States or by the individual states. The West lacking means of raising money for this purpose and in dire need of good connections with their markets in the East favored the program. (*See* CUMBERLAND ROAD.) States like New York, completing the Erie Canal at her own expense, or Pennsylvania, having financed a network of canals opposed the program foreseeing a double tax on their citizens if they were to be taxed for a federal program also. The issue was not completely dead even in the Twentieth Century for the costs of irrigation and conservation projects aroused similar support and opposition arguments.

Internal Security Act, 1950: This McCarron Act created a Subversives Control Board to decide what organizations are Communistic, or Communist fronts, and requires the registration of all such groups. It also requires internment (q.v.) of all Communists in time of emergency. The possible threat to individual civil liberty in this and the Smith Act (q.v.) has been of concern to many liberal groups.

International Bank for Reconstruction and Development (IB): A specialized agency of the United Nations active since 1945 to promote the investment of capital for productive purposes in the member countries. Loans to individual countries of many millions have been made for the modernization of industry, for the construction of hydroelectric plants and similar worth-while enterprises approved by the fact-finding officials of the IB.

International Court of Justice: This court created by the United Nations is practically a continuation of the former court established by the League of Nations, the Permanent Court of International Justice. Its judges are elected by the General Assembly and the Security Council of the United Nations and are prepared to settle international disputes facing any nation but not involving domestic affairs.

International-governmental Maritime Consultative Organization (IMCO): This is one of the newest of the specialized agencies of the United Nations established to advance ocean shipping. It hopes to make recommendations which will remove unfair, restrictive practices, and improve safety, in regard to construction and operation of ocean-going vessels.

International Labor Organization: An agency established under the League of Nations and continued under the United Nations. It aims to improve conditions of workers by research and recommendation. It holds a General Conference once a year to which each member country may send four delegates, two nominated by the government, one by labor and one by management. Its work is only advisory but may lead to the passage of beneficial laws if the delegates are able to have the results of the research and pooling of information of the Labor Organization carried out.

international law: The body of rules generally recognized as binding upon a state in relation to another might be held as a definition of international law; but this has been questioned since there is actually no international force adequate to enforce acceptance; therefore such "law" would be held to be mere morality or standard of conduct which states are willing to follow. International administrative law deals with the rules made by administrative commissions and bureaus established for the regulation of common material or intellectual interests such as Universal Postal Union, or the decisions made by the Hague Court of Arbitration, or the Permanent Court of International Justice.

International Monetary Fund: A subsidiary organization of the United Nations set up by the Monetary and Financial Conference at Bretton Woods, New Hampshire, in July 1944, which the United States joined; thus agreeing to promote currency stabilization and to make unnecessary unilateral action by a nation to depreciate its currency, or impose trade quotas or exchange controls; and further agreed to "hasten the removal of artificial barriers to international payments."

Financial experts provide advice on matters of tax reform and the need for operations in currency exchange from the huge funds it maintains for that purpose.

International Refugee Organization: The work of the United Nations Relief and Rehabilitation Administration was to have come to an end when World War II was over but unfortunately there were still thousands of refugees needing care so that IRO from 1948-1951 maintained centers for the care of displaced persons and for rendering them assistance in gaining repatriation and resettlement.

International Trade Organization: One of the specialized agencies of the United Nations whose members hope to initiate a program to lower tariffs, to remove trade obstacles and to settle trade disputes. When these agreements including items which would tend to prevent discrimination or unfair practices are ratified by the individual nations accepting them, it is hoped that the whole process will become a valuable means of expanding world trade.

internment: Detention in a camp or special area, of aliens or of persons held to be disloyal to the government.

Treatment accorded by a neutral nation to military personnel or equipment where there has been violation of neutrality.

Interstate Commerce Commission: Originally created in 1887, the Commission's power has been extended by more than six additional laws distributed over the period from 1906-1942. Its work is now largely with "common carriers," bus lines, sleeping car companies, and express companies. The eleven commissioners constitute a quasi-judicial agency, whose decisions are equal with those of a federal district court. They determine whether freight or passenger rates should be raised or lowered, reprimand lines with trains continuously late, or having unsanitary conditions in the trains, give permission to float new stock issues under certain conditions, and may allow mortgages to be assumed.

interstate compacts: Agreements among the states authorized by the Constitution with the consent of Congress, and covering a wide range of subjects such as creation of a Port of New York Authority, arrangements about water power, conservation, flood control and development of ports, parks and parkways.

intimidate: To threaten with violence or with other type of pressure equally disagreeable to the individual. The Ku Klux Klan, after the Civil War, intimidated many Negroes so that they did not dare to vote.

intrastate commerce: This is commerce carried on exclusively within the state and therefore subject to the regulations of the individual state. However, the Supreme Court has taken the position that railroad rates on lines entirely within one state may still be made to conform to the schedules established by the Interstate Commerce Commission regulation; and navigable streams whose waters at any time join those of another state are subject to federal regulations also.

inventory: An itemized list of goods on hand, and which may appear in a corporation summary of its assets. Inventory hoarding may occur where there is an expectation of a rise in prices.

investigating committees of Congress: These committees are created by resolution of Congress with their powers, duration and duties specifically defined. The right to issue subpoenas may be granted. Witnesses are forced to take an oath as to the truth of their statements. Refusal to answer questions makes one guilty of a misdemeanor.

investment bank: A "bank" or investment company subject to special regulation by the federal Investment Company Act of 1940 under which the activities of every firm trading in securities are subjected to careful scrutiny by the Securities and Exchange Commission. Each such firm must also satisfy Congressional requirements in regard to use of proxies, in regard to transactions with affiliates, and obey all measures to prevent any fraud to be exercised upon its clients. These companies do not receive deposits as ordinary banks do, but make their profits by buying securities in large quantities for resale in smaller amounts.

investment trust: A financial organization in which an individual may invest and which in turn invests its accumulated funds in a diversified group of securities of other corporations. It permits the unskilled investor to distribute his risks without the necessity of investigating in a number of different stock issues himself. The capital of such an institution is obtained from the sale of its own stock, whereas on the other hand, the investment "bank" (q.v.) sells stocks or bonds of other corporations particularly in their initial offerings.

"invisible government": Ordinarily the boss of a local political machine does not hold office as an elected official, thus all his activities are in a sense invisible, not official. He may insist on the appointment of "his" men, or force the retirement of those who do not obey the party discipline. He may award "favors" and wield considerable influence in policy making, but always behind the scenes. Elihu Root as early as 1915 used this term in describing the period when Platt and Conkling practically "ran" New York State.

"Iron Curtain": As the Soviet Union extended its influence to the satellite (q.v.) countries bordering it on the West, the same type of restrictions practiced there were gradually extended to her neighbors. Ease of entry was restricted, information was carefully controlled, as were the press and radio. Travel within the country was greatly curtailed. To symbolize this double action of cutting the world off from Communist dominated areas and of isolating the people of such areas from Western contact, the expression "Iron Curtain" was effectively created. Various devices are now operating to break through this barrier, such as the "Voice of America" broadcasts, and Radio Free Europe.

irreconcilables: Persons who refuse to make any concessions in regard to a special issue. The term was used particularly about a famous group of senators who would not abate any of their opposition to the proposed League of Nations in 1918.

Isolationism: A policy which advocates avoidance of commitments or responsibilities in regard to international politics, symbolized by American failure to join the League of Nations, and in our attempts to maintain neutrality before we were drawn into World War I and II.

itemic veto: Particularly in appropriation bills the President may be presented with one item which some group has demanded as a concession for approval of the whole measure; yet under the present veto arrangement there is no practical way to eliminate the annoying item—either the President must accept the whole measure or throw it all out. If he vetoes it as a whole it may cause great hardship to thousands of government employees, for money can be paid out only on the authority of Congress. An "item veto" would allow the President to strike out the objectionable item while at the same time approving the bill as a whole. The Legislative Reorganization Act (q.v.) contained a provision prohibiting "riders" (q.v.) but they continue to be a problem.

Ives-Quinn Anti-Discrimination Law (1945): This is a law in effect in New York State providing for a permanent commission for the purpose of eliminating discrimination in employment, because of race, color, creed, or national origins, and providing for severe penalties for deliberate violation; but which works hard at smoothing out misunderstandings and difficulties first.

"ivory tower": To live in an ivory tower means to be out of contact with the realities of the world, to be sheltered from any of the conditions that make politics likely to be called "dirty."

J

Jacksonian Democracy: With the election of Andrew Jackson as president in 1829 a change of emphasis was noticeable in the program of the party in the sense that more importance was laid upon the common man. The development of the frontier had led to demands for universal suffrage, popular election of all officials and a curb on monopoly. The Nominating Convention had just come into use for the nomination of the president. Probably the strongest point to be advocated by the Jacksonians was their liking for "rotation in office" (q.v.) and their idea that any man was capable of holding any office. The attack upon the Second United States Bank was another important plank in their program. While they placed less emphasis upon the value of an education they did proclaim all men equal under any circumstances.

"Jim Crow" laws: These are state laws providing for racial segregation in such places as railroads, busses, hotels, theatres, parks and schools. Though upheld by the Supreme Court in 1896 on the basis that segregation does not of itself involve inequality, strong dissent has been voiced that discrimination is involved. Recent decisions have required full equality in regard to educational opportunities in universities, and full participation in the jury system and property ownership.

jingoism: A program supporting an aggressive foreign policy based upon "superpatriotism" rather than a well thought out approval based upon loyalty to the true ideals of Americanism.

joint resolution: A resolution passed by both houses of a state legislature which may have the effect of law when approved by the governor in some states. Congress, too, may pass such a resolution in regard to foreign policy by merely a majority vote rather than the two-thirds vote required in the Senate for the full formal approval of a treaty. Hawaii and Texas were admitted by joint resolutions.

joint session: The meeting together of both houses of a legislature. The Congress meets as one body when assembled to count the electoral votes and when being addressed by some outstanding personality.

"joker": The insertion of an obscure provision in the body of a bill for the purpose of weakening an unwanted provision, or of altering the original intention of those introducing the bill.

Journal of the House of Representatives: The record that contains the minutes of the daily proceedings, reports of committees, motions and votes (all the activity of the House except the verbatim record of the speeches) and which is read each day at the opening of the session unless dispensed with.

judge advocate: An officer in the United States Army usually of the Judge Advocate General's department, appointed to act as a prosecutor at a court martial. He acts as a representative of the government and may act as counsel for the accused if he has none.

judge-made law: The judge may be considered to have "made" the law where there are no legal precedents to draw upon, no statutes in effect to judge by, and no common law involved.

judicial councils: A program initiated in Ohio in 1923, for creating advisory groups to improve a state judicial system. Now in use in thirty states to improve the judicial organization and administration by means of collecting statistics, and general judicial research for the purpose of making recommendations to the courts.

judicial review: *See* APPELLATE JURISDICTION.

"judicial spoils": Office holders have it within their power to award many lucrative positions to lawyers "affiliated" with the party in power. Such positions as: masters in chancery, receiver, trusteeships and other judicial functionaries involving very large fees make such appointments extremely desirable to the legal lights of the political machine.

junior college: A new trend in higher education in which a two-year course is established for those who finish high school too young to go into business, but who do not want to take the traditional four-year college course toward a degree. Emphasis in many such schools is laid on education for civic responsibility and for understanding modern political and economic problems.

junior high school: A recent trend in education which operates on the so-called 6,3,3 year level in contrast to the 8 year elementary and four year senior high school span of the more traditional type. The junior high starts with the seventh and eighth grade of the grammar school and adds the first year of the regular high school. One group of educators feel this arrangement makes the transition to the senior high school more gradual and that it introduces some of the high school subjects earlier, a benefit for those who may leave school at the minimum age, and they feel it gives more attention to the "teen" age problems. Others are equally opposed to the program, considering it time-wasting and uneconomical.

junkets, legislative: Literally a junket is a banquet or an excursion at government expense but recently the term has been applied to the trips of Congressmen either home or around their districts for the purpose of "mending fences," that is, preparing for reelection, but doing it while the legislature may be in session and on their government expense accounts.

jurisdiction: 1) The authority of a court to hear and decide cases concerning certain individuals or subjects. One court may send the case to another or a superior court and order a lower court to refrain from exercising jurisdiction over some specific aspect of a case before it (writ of prohibition). 2) Another aspect of the word refers to the extent or limit within which the authority of the government may be applied.

jurisdictional strikes: When a dispute arises between two unions over the right to control certain types of work, workers or areas of work a jurisdictional strike may result, though under the Taft-Hartley Law this practice is restricted. Another possibility of conflict may arise over the situation due to the extension of the program of industrial unionization as advocated by the Congress of Industrial Organization, which may find that in attempting a "vertical" organization of an entire industry it runs into conflict with a number of "horizontal," craft unions members of the American Federation of Labor. In the choice of bargaining agent for such a newly constituted group great care has to be exercised to avoid jurisdictional strain.

jury: The body of men or women, usually twelve, who are officially concerned with determining the guilt or innocence of an accused person in a civil or criminal trial. They are selected by lot from among those called for a particular case.

just compensation: The full value paid by a government agency for property taken by eminent domain.

justice of the peace: A minor county, or township official elected usually for two years and often without formal legal training who has jurisdiction in both petty and civil suits, and for minor infraction of the law, and to hold preliminary examinations preparatory to handing the case over to the grand jury. He may perform marriages or administer an oath and is compensated by the fees he collects.

juvenile courts: So great has been the increase in crimes by young people that special courts have had to be established in many communities to handle such cases, usually with the cooperation of local social welfare agencies who recognize the serious social problems involved in these delinquencies. Under their jurisdiction falls usually the case of the dependent or neglected child whether involved with the law or not.

juvenile delinquency: Under this category are included offenses against the law committed by young people under eighteen years of age. Many of these are very serious, but other cases cover misdemeanors which only for young people are classed as delinquencies.

K

kangaroo court: A practice in some jails which allows previously committed prisoners to regulate the treatment of prisoners newly admitted in regard to petty indignities imposed upon the new arrivals.

Keating-Owens Act of 1916: An act of Congress forbidding the transportation in interstate commerce of products made in factories in which children under fourteen were employed; or in which children between 14-16 had worked more than eight hours or six days a week or at night. Similar prohibitions applied to the products of mines in which children under sixteen were employed. These provisions were found unconstitutional because they were held to apply to the production or manufacture of goods, not to merely the transportation of goods which would have been within the scope of the Federal government's power; but control of manufacturing within the state was a residual power resting with the states. Ultimately regulation was obtained through wage and hour minimums. See CHILD LABOR LAWS.

keynote speech: The address delivered by the temporary chairman of a National Nominating Convention which in flamboyant style reviews the political situation, attempts to heal discords, and urges the gathering on to greater efforts for victory. General Douglas MacArthur's address at the Republican National Convention aroused much discussion in the summer of 1952.

kickback: A payment by a worker to his employer or foreman, or to an unscrupulous union official in order to obtain a job.

"Kick the rascals out": The classic cry of those who desire to overthrow the party in power.

Kid-glove politics: Politicians may play a careful game when a wave of reform is leading to many attacks against their program or candidate. Instead of making it a "free for all" and battling out the issue, reformers will be handled with kid gloves; that is, with great care to preserve their dignity and to try to prevent their going any further with their criticism.

"kill in committee": A bill already introduced into a legislature must be referred to its appropriate committee. If this group decides against recommending the bill to the whole legislature, it will never be brought to their attention and will therefore be considered to have been killed in committee.

Knights of Labor: An organization which reached its highest membership, 700,000, in 1886 in its efforts to form "one big union" including everyone regardless of craft, skill, creed, sex or color. Even employers joined for the brotherhood of man was a cardinal principle and their quarrel only with the "money power." They aimed to eliminate private banking, favored an eight hour day, abolition of child labor. All were to be obtained by uplift movements. They lost out to the newly created American Federation of Labor (q.v.) which was offering more concrete gains for a homogeneous grouping of craft workers.

L

labor leader: One who devotes his full time and energies to union activities as a paid official.

labor legislation: Laws having to do with hours, wages and conditions of work, providing for compensation or requiring certain educational standards. All these are residual powers coming under intrastate regulations. Federal regulations in regard to labor operate only when interstate commerce is involved.

Labor Management Act (Taft-Hartley Law) of 1947: A measure passed by Congress to supplement the Wagner Labor Relations Act continuing in existence, but enlarging the National Labor Relations Board (q.v.). The earlier provisions for ensuring unfair labor practices by employers are matched by a number of restrictions imposed upon the unions, such as the possibility of being sued for breach of contract, of publication of the union constitution; the requirement that the union file affidavits that they have no members in the Communist Party, and have made no direct or indirect contribution to a political party; that no excessive dues be collected or "featherbedding" (q.v.) practiced. On the other hand some parts of the earlier law are reversed as the outlawing of the closed shop (q.v.), the right of jurisdictional strikes (q.v.) prohibited, and permission granted to employers to express their views to their workers without being accused of unfair practices.

labor spies: Undercover agents, or detectives hired by employers to report to management concerning the attitudes of workers, matters discussed at union meetings or related materials. In a period of unstable labor relations they sometimes become "agents provocateur," and have led to disturbances that have caused the management to appeal for state or federal authority. With the passage of the Wagner Act and the more accurate definition of unfair business practices toward labor and the institution of collective bargaining it was felt the use of such individuals would come to an end.

labor turn-over: Changes in workers due to leaving employment because of lay-offs, discharge, or resignation. It is usually expressed by a percentage based on the average number of positions during a certain time interval. A high percentage is not looked upon favorably as regards the condition of labor in that plant or industry.

labor union: A voluntary association of employees which may act as a collective bargaining agent for a group of workers when so elected, and which is concerned about such basic matters as wages and hours and conditions of work, but which may also provide many recreational and welfare services. *See* COLLECTIVE BARGAINING, INDUSTRIAL UNION, CRAFT UNION.

Labor's League for Political Action: An organization of the American Federation of Labor to arouse the interest of its members in political affairs usually with some attempt to maintain a non-partisan basis but very definitely stressing the support of the candidate with a good record from Labor's point of view. It was created in 1947.

laissez-faire: A policy popularized by Adam Smith in his "Wealth of Nations" published in 1776 which originally advocated the removal of all the irksome government regulations established under the policy of "Mercantilism" or under the remaining guild controls. The phrase meant literally "let one do as one will." Gradually after the Industrial Revolution the idea was extended to mean that all business was to be free of government regulation. The expression today seems to imply a contrast to the "Welfare State" (q.v.) encroachments and to symbolize "rugged individualism."

"lame duck": An expression used to indicate a former office holder who was not reelected, but who remains in the legislature "limping" along though repudiated by the voters until the new session meets. Because for Congressmen this interval might be as long as fourteen months, the Twentieth Amendment was added to the constitution in 1933. It states that each new session of Congress must meet on January the third. Thus, the maximum length of time a modern lame duck can remain in Congress can only be from the November election until the January session of Congress.

land-grant colleges: Under the Morrill Act of 1862 the federal government was permitted to help certain educational institutions by the distribution of public land. This policy has been continued through money allowances to divisions of state universities or to independent agricultural and mechanical colleges that have courses for teacher training, scientific agricultural courses, and engineering.

land poor: A term used to refer to the condition of a person who may own much land, but finds that it is insufficiently productive to meet the taxes or other indebtedness on it, or to repay the owner adequately if intensive cultivation is undertaken.

landslide: If a candidate in a popular election receives an overwhelmingly large vote it may be likened to a landslide.

larceny: The unlawful taking of property with the intent to deprive the owner of its possession. Grand larceny is distinguished from petty on the basis of the amount involved.

League of Women Voters: An organization founded in 1918 to win the support of women in political affairs by providing interested groups with organizational help in the form of bulletins and research assistance, setting up study groups, suggesting vital speakers, and holding conferences. The work is kept on a nonpartisan basis to give it a broad appeal but with a strong emphasis on the understanding and appreciation of the complexity of government with an alertness to any form of corruption. As the training becomes effective some leaders resign to take up duties in party organizations.

"leave to print": A congressman who did not have an opportunity to speak, or did not say all he intended may request the right to have his speech printed in the Congressional Record for that day regardless of what was actually said. He may then have copies of the page bearing his speech printed in large quantities and through his franking privilege (q.v.) have it sent to all his constituents at public expense. Some criticism has arisen where "leave to print" as a privilege has been abused, but so far the voter is the only one with ability to curb such excesses.

"leftists": A term used to indicate those persons who are radical, or extreme in their political views. The expression originated from the practice in foreign parliaments for the conservative parties to sit on the right of the meeting place and the more progressive groups on the left. The degree of "leftness" may represent all shades of political opinion, but the range to the left will be from mildly socialistic, to socialist, communist to anarchist.

Legal-Aid Bureaus: A recent trend to help the poor in legal difficulties favors the establishment of "public defender" (q.v.), and "small claims" (q.v.) courts, but also recommends the creation of Legal-Aid Bureaus as a supplement though not as a part of the judicial system. Local law schools, or progressive law associations, or charitable organizations may provide such foundations which usually give legal advice in civil cases, and outside of court since many of those giving such services may still be students in law school.

legal tender: Money which the law requires creditors to accept when offered in payment; however, the seller is under no compulsion to complete the sale if he does not want to.

Legislative Councils: These are permanent research committees established to assist legislators in their work. They usually consist of leading legislators appointed by the houses themselves to give continuous study to the legislative problems of the state, with an appropriation provided, and a research staff and adequate headquarters. Started in 1933 by Kansas, the movement has been spreading rapidly. The more thorough and objective the work of such a group becomes the less the opportunity for partisan pressure and the better will be the final law evolved.

Legislative Reference Service: With the great extension of the number of fields in which a Congressman is now expected to be not only familiar, but an expert on many occasions, the job of helping him obtain this additional knowledge has grown greatly also. In 1946 the funds made available to this Service were enlarged so that the personnel increased in numbers and in professional training to render aid to the representatives and senators in a more effective fashion. Congress could always have information directly from any government agency, but it was felt wise to improve the scope of such a group as this Service in order to obtain a possibly more impartial or neutral view.

Legislative Reorganization Act of 1946: Despite some degree of opposition a bill embodying many of the reforms advocated by the Joint Committee on the Organization of Congress was started through Congress by Senator La Follette and Representative Monroney. The number of standing Committees (q.v.) in Congress was greatly reduced, with more equal distribution of the legislative burden, and members of the House and Senate were limited to one such committee in most cases. On the other hand, there has been a great increase in the number of sub-committees (146 in 1950). Great increase in research facilities has arisen. The Legislative Reference Service (q.v.) has provided expert assistance. Registration of "lobbyists" was required. "Riders" were restricted in their use. The problem of seniority as a basis for promotion on committees and filibustering were ignored.

Lend-Lease Act: An Act of Congress March, 1941, which allowed the president to sell, exchange, lease or lend, or otherwise dispose of whatever article of defense he saw fit to any state he wished whose defense he considered vital to the United States. This measure cancelled the "cash and carry" (q.v.) provisions of the Neutrality Act of 1937, virtually restoring the "freedom of the seas" which had been more or less suspended by our previous attempts to stay neutral by restricting closely our trade with the world.

libel: A defamatory statement which imputes to a person the commission of a criminal act or tends to injure a person's trade or profession, or holds a person up to ridicule. Though entitled to freedom of speech and press under the First Amendment of the Constitution, if one publishes information simply because one dislikes someone and is prompted by spiteful or malicious motives one become subject to a damage suit, whether the information is true or not, and may find that the action has constituted a crime. Calling a person in a magazine article a "Stalinist busybody" resulted in a fine of $1500. A Congressman is free from any suit for libel for what he says on the floor of Congress.

liberal: A believer in liberalism, in a philosophy which proposes that the individual be accorded the fullest freedom compatible with the rights of others. It follows that this can usually be accomplished by favoring reforms and in breaking from the orthodox or conservative position; and in doing all this by gradual, legal means won through majority approval. It is a support of a "middle way" between standing pat and radicalism and is thus often many things to many people. The liberal of the Nineteenth Century might be the Conservative of the present.

Liberal-Republicans: A term first used for a group of Republicans interested in reform, especially in civil service reform, but also in regard to the tariff. They included some of the great liberals of their day such as Horace Greeley and Charles Francis Adams. Strong on ideals but weak in politics, they were joined by Carl Schurz, George Curtis and William Cullen Bryant. The assassination of Garfield gave great impetus to their program and the first civil service reform measure was passed in 1883. (See PENDLETON ACT.)

Liberty Party: A minor political party active in the elections of 1840-1844, important as a precursor of the Republican Party (q.v.). It was for the abolition of slavery everywhere in the United States in contrast to the Free Soil Party, which only wanted to limit slavery in the newly organized territories; and it stood for the equality of rights among all men. Though polling only two percent of the vote in 1844 they drew enough votes from Clay, the Whig candidate in New York, to throw the presidency to the Democrat, Polk.

lien: A legal right to keep control or enforce a claim against another's property or earnings for the satisfaction of a debt or claim. It does not give the right to sell the goods involved.

lieutenant-governor: The official who presides over a state legislature and acts in the absence of the governor and succeeds to that position if it becomes vacant.

life expectancy: The average length of life of all the people in a given place. In 1910 in the United States this was estimated at about fifty years, but by 1940 it was approaching sixty-five. The goal for 1960 is optimistically estimated as being within reason seventy years. Women have had a favorable margin of four years with the likelihood of gaining more. On the other hand other parts of the world have a far less hopeful trend, with the Middle East and India hardly attaining an expectancy of forty years.

limited voting: A method of voting for boards in city or state government so that a minority group has some opportunity of representation. An individual may vote for four members of a seven-man board. The seven candidates with the largest vote are declared elected.

Lindbergh Law: This law passed in 1934 provided for imprisonment or the death penalty for those accused of transporting across a state line a person who had been kidnapped and held for ransom.

line departments in the city government: Line departments are administrative units of the city which render services to the inhabitants. They have direct contact with the public, as with the police, health, sanitation, and public works departments. They are in contrast to the staff departments which are the "tool" departments performing the services necessary for the operation of the line. These duties may include purchasing and financing.

liquidate: To discharge or pay off an indebtedness, or to determine the amount of the debt and apportion the liabilities, and distribute assets so as to wind up a business. Used also to indicate the disposal of an individual whose interests are found opposed to a totalitarian regime.

liquor regulation: With the passage of the Twenty-first Amendment, the Eighteenth Amendment was repealed so that there was no longer any Federal restriction on the transportation or possession of intoxicating liquor; but several states have retained some form of regulation. Mississippi and Oklahoma have prohibition. Twenty-eight others depend on a licensing system whereby all activities incidental to manufacturing, distribution and sale of liquor are handled by individuals licensed by the state. In Wyoming state stores monopolize all wholesale transactions while sixteen other states monopolize all retail outlets. Federal permits are required of all importers of liquor and of all distillers, rectifiers and wholesalers; but not of brewers and retail distributors. Except for the fact that alcoholic beverages constitute a luxury item and as such are heavily taxed the Federal government has sponsored no temperance control.

list system: A method of proportional representation more commonly used in European countries in which open recognition is given to political parties permitting them to put up slates of candidates which appear on the ballot. Each party is rewarded with seats on the basis of the percent of votes polled. A party polling 25% of the votes would receive five positions if 20 candidates were to be elected.

literacy test: A qualification for voting having limited application and used in only about one third of the states. Much argument has been expended as to whether such a requirement is really appropriate in a democracy especially since its use in seven southern states falls more heavily on the Negro. However, with the present widespread practice of compulsory education, the case for some sort of educational test is being strengthened, particularly where it is administered by school authorities on a non-partisan basis.

litigant: A party to a law suit.

Little Assembly of the United Nations (also called the Interim Assembly): An unofficial meeting of the General Assembly set up in November 1947. Because the delegates of the Soviet Union had been exercising the veto so frequently in the Security Council, an interim meeting of this body was arranged where the vote was by majority vote and the stalemate encountered in the official Security Council could be partially circumvented. This body also attempts to make preliminary studies of critical situations and may call a special session of the General Assembly. Naturally it has been attacked as illegal by the Soviet and satellite countries.

Little Steel: A group of independent companies, such as Bethlehem, Republic, Inland, Jones and Laughlin, whose smaller production makes for different problems than the "Big Steel" organizations, particularly United States Steel Corporation.

Lobby Regulation: A Federal Lobby Control Law was enacted in 1946 which requires each person hired to influence the passage or defeat of legislation in Congress to register with the Clerk of the House of Representatives and disclose by whom he was hired and how much he was paid. Every organization whose principal purpose is to influence legislation must keep a detailed record of all expenditures and contributions for Congressional inspection.

local: A branch or basic administrative unit of a labor union.

localism: A policy or interest with an emphasis on the affairs of the immediate community at the expense of any concern with national or international activities.

localization of labor: The tendency for skilled and semi-skilled workers to become centered in certain areas favoring a particular trade or industry, as cattle raising in the West or mining in Pennsylvania.

local option: The vote held in a community by which a decision is rendered as to whether or not saloons or bars may be licensed to sell liquor within their limits.

local relief: Any type of assistance given to needy persons by a local agency, village, or social service agency, in contrast to assistance provided under Social Security grants of the Federal Government.

lockout: The exclusion of workers from their place of employment usually to forestall a strike or force acceptance of the employer's conditions.

log rolling: A cooperative venture by which member A of a legislative body gains the support of member B for an appropriation beneficial to A's district by promising to vote for an appropriation beneficial to B's district. Needless extravagance results for no member wants to return empty-handed (without "pork") to his own constituency. *See* PORK BARREL.

London Economic Conference 1933: This was an attempt to improve the world economic situation in the depth of the depression by stabilizing national currencies. Its failure was charged against Franklin D. Roosevelt because of his major concern with his internal economic reorganization in the field of banking reforms, extension of credit, and an extensive program of public works in America.

London Naval Conference 1930: A meeting of Great Britain, United States and Japan, intended to supplement the work of the Washington Conference of 1922 in an effort to limit the tonnage of cruisers, destroyers, and curb the construction of capital ships completely. France and Italy would not sign the agreement, so that an "escalator clause" was inserted which permitted the sign-ers to increase their armaments if other nations menaced their security.

long ballot: A rather unusual way to express the situation which existed before the reform of the short ballot (q.v.) was introduced, when there were a great many state and local officials to be chosen at each election, and the voter found it practically impossible to know much about each individual candidate, and therefore made control by the machine fairly reliable.

long-term borrowing: A practice of all state governments, and the United States, of selling bonds with a life period of from five to thirty years to finance a program of long lasting duration. For the opposite program *see* SHORT-TERM BORROWING.

loose interpretation of the Constitution: Also called "loose construction." By means of the "necessary and proper" clause in the eighteenth power assigned to Congress, a great many "implied powers" have been derived. Such activities as subsidizing railroads, steamship companies and airways are implied as being "necessary" because of the power to regulate post roads. The right to create the United States Bank was derived from the original provision "to coin money and regulate the value thereof."

lottery: A scheme for the distribution of prizes by lot or chance. It has been proposed as a means of providing income for some municipalities, as a painless way of raising money for some special project, but with a sufficient share of the fund to be awarded certain lucky individuals, to induce widespread participation. On the other hand, some states have made such undertakings unconstitutional.

low-rent housing: Decent, safe and sanitary housing provided especially for the low-income families by a government agency, or by the payment of subsidies by the government to make up the difference in rent between what the individuals, legally allowed to live in such projects, can afford to pay, and the rent that would have to be charged at the present day high cost of building and maintenance.

Loyalty Review Board: After much publicity in regard to the problem of the possibility of subversive activity on the part of federal government employees, a special board was established in March 1947 to investigate persons held to be poor risks for critical positions. There are also local loyalty boards in each of the separate agencies.

"lunatic fringe": A term originally applied by Theodore Roosevelt to those reformers who agitated and annoyed Congress to produce improvements faster than the government found reasonable or possible.

lynching: Execution, often by hanging, of a person by means of mob action without legal trial and in deliberate defiance of the law.

M

machine: An organization controlled by a political boss who "pulls the wires" with such uniformity and with so little consideration of right or wrong, or of the needs of the people that the whole arrangement has been likened to a piece of mechanism automatically and blindly operating for the interests of a few.

made-work: Public works whose primary purpose is to provide for employment in contrast to work contributing permanent values to the community. It was a means frequently used in the 1930's to avoid the "dole" or relief contributions for able-bodied workers. *See* BOONDAGLING.

majority floor leader: Except for the Speaker of the House of Representatives, the floor leader of the majority party is the most important party leader in the House. He must be a clever speaker, quick to see the weakness in the opposition's arguments, ingratiating in personality, and an able organizer. To help him advance the party's program, he may select a number of assistants, the party whips (q.v.); he also must work well with the minority floor leader in planning their strategy. Successful accomplishment of these diverse duties may win him the Speakership in time.

majority rule: The principle that the policies of a country should be determined by the views of the greater number, as expressed by the voters in their choice of candidates for office, or by the members of law-making bodies in their passing of laws.

make-work fallacy: The false assumption that deliberate construction, or inefficient production is beneficial to the worker in the sense of insuring employment or of continuing employment. The surplus luxuries of the rich, or the process of slowing down on the job also comes under the "make-work fallacy," which economists easily refute by showing a reduction in the supply of worthwhile production is a loss to all.

"mala prohibita": Things wrong because prohibited by law.

Some of these actions prohibited may not in themselves be wrong, but for some far-sighted purpose may be held harmful by a law-making body.

"malefactors of great wealth": An expression created by Theodore Roosevelt to refer to the rich and powerful business interests or leaders, who he considered were acting against the public interests in forming ruthless monopolies or performing unfair business actions, or controlling the extension of easy credit facilities to the common people, and whom he attacked vigorously in his "trust busting" program.

malfeasance: The performance of an illegal act on the part of a public official.

managed currency: A controlled currency whose volume in circulation, or the backing of which, may be changed as the government desires. In order to keep business conditions stable, an unchanging price level may thus be maintained, by means of encouraging inflation or deflation, as required. Some proposals would use "index numbers" to manage this stabilization, others have even mentioned a "commodity" dollar which would attempt to use some reliable average of commodity prices in order to eliminate the evils of fluctuating price levels.

mandamus: (Latin for "we order"). A court order commanding an official, or a corporation or a lower court, to perform an act that is its clear legal duty.

mandatory powers: Those powers that are compulsory; that is, expressed in a positive fashion for a legislature or an office holder to carry out, are mandatory. They may be stated in a constitution or in specific laws and are to be contrasted with "permissive powers" which only represent what these officials may do, but are not required to do.

Manifest Destiny: An expression of the views of many who felt that it was predestined that the United States would ultimately extend from ocean to ocean. It came into use about the time we had annexed Texas (1845) and were acquiring California and land in the Mexican Cession.

manifesto: A formal announcement of a program as of a political party.

Maritime Commission of the United States: This commission was established in 1936 to take over the functions of the Shipping Board, to create an adequate and well-balanced merchant fleet, and to administer construction and operating subsidies. Because American shipbuilders and operators were severely handicapped in competition with foreign shipping interests, due to the high wages and better arrangements for hours for American seamen (LaFollette Act) and the higher costs of labor and equipment in the United States, and because it was felt that a merchant marine was a valuable adjunct to the country in case of war, provisions were made to overcome the advantages enjoyed by foreign merchant ships. The Maritime Commission was authorized by Congress to award to American operators a differential between what it would have cost him to have had his vessel built abroad and what it really cost him to have it built in the United States. A similar "parity" was given for the difference in operating costs. This policy continued on a larger scale during World War II.

maritime law: The law and usages concerned with peaceful commercial undertakings on the sea. It may regulate licensing, contracts, salvage operations, treatment of seamen and forfeiture of ships as determined by international agreements, or in accord with local judicial codes.

marshal (United States): The marshal is one of the assistants in the federal district courts who helps to maintain order, guard prisoners, serve court orders and carry into effect court judgments as far as can be done. They are appointed by the President for four years and have deputies to assist them. It has been suggested that they be selected on a merit system rather than through party influence.

Marshall Plan (European Recovery Program): A program initiated by Secretary of State George Marshall in an address at Harvard on June 5, 1947. Over sixteen European states having pooled their resources and estimated their needs, received over two billion dollars in aid to help them along the road to economic stability so as to speed up rehabilitation and to prevent the spread of Communism in distressed areas. Complicated exchange procedures attempted to meet the dollar shortages handicapping recovery in Europe. *See* COUNTERPART FUNDS.

martial law: Rules and regulations issued by a military commander but not military law since these regulations apply to the civilian population. The federal government may declare martial law, but it may also be declared under state authority when it is proclaimed by the governor at the time of a disaster, or emergency, or when civil disorder is threatened. The writ of habeas corpus is suspended (q.v.).

Mason and Dixon's Line: The boundary between Pennsylvania and Maryland was surveyed by Charles Mason and Jeremiah Dixon from 1763-1767. Because slavery developed in Maryland and was not allowed in Pennsylvania, the Line became a symbol of the division of the country on the slavery issue.

mass media: An expression referring to the influence of various cultural forces through the moving pictures, television shows, radio, records, or the theater where large groups of people are exposed to influences tending to produce standardized or uniform reactions.

mass production: Large scale production characterized by the manufacture of standardized commodities. Such production commonly utilizing an assembly line makes possible a very large volume of production at low cost per unit due to increased efficiency and adequate use of division of labor. It also makes necessary large scale distribution and transportation to reach the nationwide market essential to disposing of such large production.

Massachusetts Ballot: This type of ballot used by about eighteen states places the names of the candidates opposite the office for which they are running.

maverick: A non-conformist. This meaning has developed from the practice of a Sam Maverick who did not brand his cattle.

mayor: Chief executive of a municipal corporation. He may be of the weak type that has little authority, may make few appointments, and can have his veto easily over-ridden and has little control over the group of independent offices that really "run" the city. Or he may be of the strong type, as the mayor of New York City, Boston, or Detroit, with substantial appointive and removal powers, considerable veto power, and broad administrative control. The trend has been more toward the latter type with the voters holding the executive responsible for the full conduct of his administration.

Mayor-Council type of city government: This type of city government is still the commonest, though council-manager and commission types are growing in popularity (qq.v.). The council carries out the law-making duties of a city under a variety of names, and is sometimes elected by wards or districts, and sometimes at large, and even by both means at once. The numbers range from five to thirty and the term is usually two years. The laws passed are called ordinances and the duties depend upon those assigned in the city charter as approved by the state legislature. The mayor may be a "strong" or "weak" type depending on the power given or withheld by the charter. He usually has a group of executive departments under his supervision. *See* MAYOR.

mediation: A form of settling conflicts in which an outside agency acts as a go-between for the disputing parties. The emphasis is on the giving of counsel and advice.

medical examiner: A government official, usually appointed, whose functions are to make a post-mortem examination of persons dead from violence, suicide or under some other unusual circumstance. There is an overlapping in some communities with the duties of the coroner, whose duty it is to hold an inquest in the same circumstances.

megalopolitan: Matters having to do with a very large city.

mending fences: The pre-election activities of a candidate for office in making certain that the party machinery is in good working order.

Mental Health Act of 1949: According to this act the federal government provides funds for a preventive program contributing to the enlarging of work already under way in existing clinics, but not for care and treatment in mental institutions. Annual appropriations of $3½ million are considered slight but show recognition of a difficult problem.

Merit System: A means of obtaining a government position through competitive examinations based upon necessary qualifications without regard to political favor. *See* PENDLETON ACT on the national level.

meter versus flat rates for water fees: Because of the considerable expense involved in the installation of meters, most communities determine the water tax by some form of estimated figure based either on "frontage," the width of the building, or upon the number of faucets in the building. For industrial users of water the meter system is well worth the expense of installation to the city, besides being a factor in preventing waste. Many modern air-cooling devices use enormous quantities of water. Americans have been most extravagant in this respect so that efforts in the future will surely be directed to curbing the very large amount of wastage that will become a very serious problem as more and more cities begin to reach the point of limit of supplies.

methods of voting in Congress: The simplest device for determining the views of the members of Congress is that of "viva voce" vote. The presiding officer decides from the volume of sound of those voting yea, and those crying nay, which he thinks has the majority. The second method is by "division." The yeas stand and are counted. The nays likewise. The third way depends upon the use of tellers. The members pass between the tellers and are counted, the yeas first and the nays following. The last method is the most time-consuming. The roll is called and the individual member's vote is recorded. This is repeated as a check.

metropolitan area: A large city and its surrounding suburbs, sometimes to an extent of twenty miles or more, make up such an area. The biggest problem connected with such a unit is to coordinate the activities of a number of the local governments. Frequently the suburban communities are incorporated into a "greater city" as in Philadelphia. The Metropolitan District of Hartford includes seven communities. It has complete control of highways, sewage, and water supply with resulting economy and efficiency.

migrants: Workers not specifically attached to any industry or to any particular locality, and who must move from place to place to keep pace with the seasonal requirements of agricultural workers. The question of an education and a better future for the children of these workers is becoming a conscious social issue in some of the communities affected.

mileage: An allowance for traveling expenses of members of a legislature for official trips from their homes to the session. Congressmen were given a twenty cents a mile allowance.

militarism: The doctrine that cultivation of the arts of war makes a nation strong, and that national prestige is best served by the maintenance of a large army and navy. It is used to indicate the substitution of military for civilian institutions and ideals.

military government: Military government is directly related to the successful operation of the armed forces; but its immediate purpose is to assist in the carrying on of a war by relieving the tactical forces of many problems concerned with the civilian population, such as keeping them out of the way of the tactical activities, and securing resources available in occupied territories, and after hostilities have ceased providing a temporary civil administration. Military government does not operate the government itself but attempts to use whatever incumbent officials are available, amply provided with military government advisors. Removals are made where necessary and laws modified through the orders of the Supreme Commander. These methods have evolved through experience during the Mexican and Spanish Wars, but especially during World War I when a report on the situation in Germany was made, known as the Hunt Report, which served as a basis for much subsequent activity in World War II.

Military Staff Committee: A subordinate organization of the Security Council, consisting of the Chiefs of Staff of the Big Five nations, to give advice on all military questions.

militia: The able-bodied male population of a state which may be called out by the state for the defense and preservation of order in emergencies. The national government may provide for their organization, arming and disciplining, and call them out, as was the National Guard, into national service in time of war. The Second Amendment to the Constitution of the United States provides: A well regulated militia, being necessary to the security of a free State, the right of the people to keep and bear arms shall not be infringed.

Miller-Tydings Law, 1937 (Fair Trades Act): Permits the manufacturer of branded and trade-marked articles destined for interstate commerce to fix minimum retail prices in about forty states already allowing this in intrastate business. This practice of making price-maintenance resale contracts would have been an unfair business practice under the terms of the Sherman Antitrust Law, if this measure had not specifically exempted this action under certain conditions. This law, derisively called the Unfair Trades Act, was actively opposed by the National Grange, and some big department stores on the grounds that it would increase prices to the consumer. Retail druggists and some small businesses claimed that the law would protect them from competition with big organizations able to reduce prices through the effectiveness of large scale production. There seems to be general agreement among economists that such "fair" trade legislation is a monopolistic measure which is incompatible with the support of the policy of competition.

Minimum Wage Law of New York State (1937): The control of labor is one of the residual powers that the Federal Constitution permits to fall within the state's exclusive control. This law is typical of what the legislature of a highly industrialized state concerned about the welfare of its citizens would enforce. The New York State Labor Department requires that there be no discrimination in rates of pay because of sex. It provides that women and minors especially should receive wages sufficient to promote adequate maintenance and to protect health in all fields of employment except domestic service and farm labor. A wage board composed of three employers, three representatives of labor, and three disinterested members acting for the public should hold hearings to determine a fair wage. Violation of their orders is a misdemeanor. An individual may recover what is due him if underpaid by a civil action. Over one million workers in the state are protected.

minimum wage legislation: Laws establishing a scale of wages below which payments would be illegal in certain industries. These laws were finally found constitutional under the "police power" of the various governments involved. The Federal Wage and Hour Law has made seventy-five cents an hour the minimum in interstate commerce for full time work. *See also* PUBLIC CONTRACTS ACT (Walsh-Healey Law).

minority: A group of individuals who are numerically less than others in the city, state, or nation, whose interests require safeguarding despite democracy's support of majority rule. The minority may be in the field of religion, or of economic position or racial or national origin, or even of progressive, or reactionary views.

minority presidents: To win a presidential election a candidate must obtain one over half the electoral vote. He may satisfy this requirement and still not be the choice of the majority of the voters. On a few occasions such "minority presidents" have been elected. Both Lincoln and Wilson were elected in this fashion for their first terms. In each case the popular vote was only about forty percent of the vote cast. In each case this situation arose because of a split in the opposition so that more than fifty percent of the votes were against the successful candidates, but they were scattered among a number of candidates. In 1888 Harrison had a popular vote 100,000 less than the defeated Cleveland.

minority report: The position taken by the group not subscribing to the general or majority position.

minority representation: The group gaining representation in a legislature through a special type of voting such as preferential voting (q.v.), or proportional voting which allows "splinter" or diverse groups to express their preference and thus give representation to varied opinions.

mints: Metal coins of the United States are manufactured by the mints located in Philadelphia, Denver and San Francisco.

misdemeanor: A minor violation of the law as contrasted with a felony which is the name for high crimes. The distinction is vague in some circumstances, though usually the length of sentence indicates the more serious crime. Those carrying a sentence of more than one year are usually felonies and the others may involve only a small fine.

mobilization: The readying of a nation's manpower and physical resources for military action. This will usually include conscription of soldiers and the conversion of industry to production of war materials.

monopoly: The ability to so control the supply of an article by artificial means or by exclusive possession of the natural sources (geographical areas, or natural talents), or by privileges extended by the government (patents and copyrights) that the price can be maintained at a high level without recourse to the normal operation of the laws of supply and demand.

moderator: Presiding officer of a town meeting originally, used also for its modern counterpart—the "Town Meeting of the Air."

Moral Re-Armament: A program which had been known for many years as the Oxford Movement, founded by Frank Buckman, was revived in 1938 under this new title. By 1952 it had over a thousand full time workers, with an international headquarters and officers in many large cities in the United States. Their aim is to get people to become "changed" by a dedication to Christian principles so that everyone will stop being quarrelsome and dishonest and permit peace to really have a chance. One of the movement's many activities consists of the Senate Breakfast Group, which meets on Wednesdays at 8:30 in the capital to try to solve some of the world's problems with guidance from God.

morals court: The difficult problem of handling the arrested prostitute, so that society, the girls themselves, and justice can all be served properly, has resulted in some large cities setting up special courts, where judges of the best type can try to keep politics or favoritism out of the situation, where for the young recruit at least a constructive decision may be rendered.

moral turpitude: Guilty of depravity and baseness, a situation sufficiently serious to prevent a person from being allowed to enter the United States.

moratorium: A period during which ordinary operations are temporarily held up. The Hoover Moratorium of 1931 was supposed to be only a temporary suspension of payment of European war debts to the United States, but became permanent without any official recognition.

mortgage moratorium: *See* FRAZIER-LEMKE ACT.

muckraker: A term created by Theodore Roosevelt borrowed from "Pilgrim's Progress" to designate certain journalists of his day who were active in exposing evil conditions in a variety of fields. Upton Sinclair in "The Jungle" revealed the horrors of the meat packing industry. Lincoln Steffens wrote of boss-ridden cities all across the United States. Ida Tarbell described some not too idealistic conditions in the rise of the Standard Oil Company.

mudslinging: An unfortunate practice which develops in some campaigns when a candidate makes insulting remarks about his opponent.

"Mugwumps": A term used to describe those reformers favoring Cleveland, a Democrat, in the 1880's, and primarily drawn from the independent Republican ranks and resented especially by the party regulars (the Stalwarts q.v.). One story has it that the term was created in derision because they had their "mugs" in one party and their "wumps" in the other.

municipal corporation: A subordinate government unit such as a city, town or township created by a state legislature, as an agent of public administration to operate only in the public interest and in accord with its charter.

Municipal Indebtedness Moratorium legislation: *See* CHANDLER ACT.

municipal government, types of: The degree of independence of a municipal corporation depends on the type of charter issued by the legislature of the state in which it is located. A *Special Charter System* provides for a specific, individual charter tailored for a particular city's needs. A *General Charter System* sets up a uniform, model charter with a state-wide municipal code that makes no allowance for unique characteristics of a municipality. A *Classification* System combines the two preceding in that a series of uniform charters are prepared but are applied to the cities coming within specified classes. A *Home-Rule System* is the one gaining most in popularity, now in use in twenty-one states, and the system used in fifteen of the thirty largest cities in the United States, and in 600 other cities. Under home-rule a state legislature grants the city most generous terms for governing itself. The last, but most recently proposed plan is the *Optional* Plan which provides the greatest variety in permitting the city to select either city-manager, commission, or council-manager (q.q.v.) or any type of mayor-council plan.

municipal liability: The city as a creature of the state is not to be sued for damages or other claims that come under its government functions. It may be sued for responsibilities in connection with its proprietary functions (q.v.). Political scientists recognize that if every type of claim made against a city were legally acknowledged it would be a considerable drain on the city's resources, and thus against the public's interest in the collective sense; but they feel that the rights of the individuals involved in many of the prohibited suits should be given consideration also, and that some compromise solution will probably have to be worked out in the future.

Muscle Shoals: The acquisition of this original site on the Tennessee River by the United States during World War I finally led to the great modern Tennessee Valley Authority (q.v.) of the present though there was little activity there until 1931 when from 2,300 acres the project grew to over 41,000.

N

National Association of Manufacturers: An organization established in 1895 to "maintain a mutual and cooperative organization of American manufacturers to foster trade, business and financial interests, to reform abuses therein, to secure freedom from unlawful and unjust exactions, to diffuse accurate and reliable information . . . for the mutual benefit of its members." It is now composed of over 15,000 manufacturers from all over the United States.

national banks: Under the National Banking Act of 1863 national banks could be chartered under certain definite conditions. These banks were authorized to issue National Bank Notes upon depositing government bonds with the Comptroller of the Currency, which would provide a safe, uniform currency to replace the state bank notes, many of which were counterfeit or issued by banks without adequate backing.

National Committee: A standing executive committee of each of the two major parties established to carry on the work of the Democrats or Republicans during the four-year interval between the elections. Each is federally constituted with an equal number of members from each state and territory, one man and one woman, elected by the previous national convention, and in some cases nominated by party primaries.

National Convention: A meeting of the official delegates of each major party for the purpose of nominating the presidential and vice-presidential candidates. After the appropriate National Committee (q.v.) has issued the "call" (the announcement of time and place of the meeting) the complicated procedure for determining the number of delegates is started. Each party has a somewhat different arrangement but the basic plan rests upon the selection of a minimum of four delegates from each state and then increasing that number according to the size of the previous district vote for president. The Republicans give three additional votes for a state going for them and the Democrats give four. An equal number of alternate members are chosen. When all assemble in some vast auditorium noisy demonstrations often take up much time. Reports are heard and and the platform determined after much discussion. Frequently the candidate for president wins on the first few ballots taken, but on occasion it has taken as many as forty or fifty ballots to agree and once in 1924 it took 103 ballots before a compromise was reached. Then the balloting for Vice-President is held with an attempt to balance the ticket geographically.

National Farmers Union: A private agricultural organization founded in 1902 with some 400,000 present members, concerned especially with the small family-type farm, and stressing the establishment of rural cooperatives, and wielding considerable influence in regard to political action in the thirty-two states where it has organizations, but being especially active in Washington, D. C.

National Industrial Recovery Act: A measure to "assure a reasonable profit to industry and a living wage to labor with the elimination of piratical methods, and practices which have not only harassed honest business but also contributed to the ills of labor," said President Roosevelt in 1933 when he approved it. "Codes of Fair Competition" were established in all industries. Child labor was limited, shorter hours and minimum wages were arranged, and collective bargaining provided for. The "Blue Eagle" was a coveted award for full compliance with this program. A unanimous vote of the Supreme Court in May 1935 found the law unconstitutional because the regulations involved represented an invalid transfer of legislative power from Congress to the President.

nationalism: This belief is upheld by the theory that a people of a particular nationality should be independent, if possible, or at least be given fair representation as a minority. However, this term has come to have a different application in American history where Americanization wiped out the need for consideration of nationality; but where a unique situation arose, in that national issues became those associated with a strong federal government, and the opposite of nationalism was sectionalism, or an emphasis on States' Rights (q.v.).

nationalization of gold: An order provided for in the Gold Reserve Act of 1934, gave the United States Treasury title to all the gold owned by the Federal Reserve Banks which had previously required all gold coins to be turned in by all persons in the United States. All these coins were melted down into bullion which the Treasury stored away and for which it issued a new paper money not redeemable in gold.

National Labor Relations Board: An agency created by the National Labor Relations Act of 1935 (Wagner Act) to promote equality of bargaining power between employers and employees, and to diminish the causes of labor disputes. Since collective bargaining (q.v.) was made compulsory the Board had to see to it that every business enterprise elected their bargaining agent fairly, and that union activities were not interfered with. With the extension of its powers under the Taft-Hartley Law not only does it investigate the unfair practices of employers, but there are limitations upon the unions themselves to insure democratic conduct. The Board also has to settle disputes between rival unions of the A. F. of L. and the C. I. O., and such jurisdictional disputes as may arise, or order payment of back wages where an employer has lost his case, or the reinstatement of workmen, or the suspension of some union activity it has banned.

National Municipal League: A private, professional organization with headquarters in New York City, especially concerned with the improvement of governmental and administrative units of the state and city. It operates by making surveys, collecting facts, and even appointing trained members to advise legislators and administrators so that the best information on social activities, education and financial security, and new vocational methods and techniques will be available, ultimately for the public's interest. It publishes the *National Municipal Review*.

National Origins Act: A new immigration law which went into effect in 1929. Some Asiatics and all Europeans are placed on a quota basis. The national origins idea was carried out by the provision that a quota was to be determined for every country by means of a ratio, which was to be a proportion between the estimated number of people of that national group in the United States, and the population of the whole country in 1920. Every country was given a minimum quota of 100. All persons of the American countries (western hemisphere) are admitted without numerical restriction. The total immigration for one year, exclusive of this latter group, was to be 150,000 persons.

National-Republicans: The name taken over by those members of the Democratic-Republican Party (q.v.) who were supporting Adams and Clay in 1832, and who were opposed to President Jackson. The remnants of the old Federalist Party assembled with them and by 1834 they took the name of the "Whigs" (q.v.).

National Security Council: A council including the President, Secretaries of State, Defense, Army, Navy, and Air, and the head of the National Security Resources Board (q.v.) which coordinates the program of all national defense by presenting the collective advice of all the appropriate officers and agencies of the executive branch.

National Security Resources Board: A board to investigate and plan for the correlation of foreign and military policy with natural resources and economic capacity. It is composed of the Secretaries of State, Treasury, Defense, Interior, Agriculture and Labor. Its advice may range from recommendations for strategic relocation of industries, stockpiling of critical materials, to considerations of potential manpower. It parallels the work of the War Production Board of World War II.

nationals: In international law "nationals" in a general way denotes all persons identified with a nation, but not necessarily citizens. For example, while the Philippines were part of the United States, Filipinos were nationals but not citizens.

Native American Party (Know Nothing Party): A party existing in the 1850's opposed to the increasing tide of immigration and directed against minority religious and racial groups.

nativism: Partiality in favor of native-born citizens in preference to foreign-born.

naturalization: Congress holds that naturalization is the conferring of the nationality of a state after birth. To be obtained individually the applicant must be eighteen, have entered the

United States lawfully, passed satisfactory tests of literacy and residence, and shown that he does not advocate the overthrow of the government by force and violence, and is a good moral character. There are three distinct steps involved, the declaration of intention, the filing of a petition before a judge two to seven years later, and a final hearing before a judge concluded by an oath to support the Constitution, and to renounce all fidelity to any other country, and to swear allegiance to the United States.

Collective citizenship is bestowed upon inhabitants of ceded territories usually at the time of cession or soon thereafter: In 1900 on the Hawaiians, in 1917 Puerto Ricans, and in 1927 the Virgin Islanders.

natural rights: These are the rights belonging to a man by his very nature, and independent of human institutions. One of the earliest expressions of this idea was that of Locke in the 17th century, when he proposed such a philosophical doctrine in opposition to lack of individual rights under the divine right monarchies of that day. Jefferson was influenced by him in proclaiming "life, liberty, and the pursuit of happiness" as the natural rights of man.

"necessary and proper clause" of the Constitution: *See* ELASTIC CLAUSE or IMPLIED POWERS CLAUSE.

Negro suffrage: The right of the Negro to vote was won on paper after the Civil War by the Fifteenth Amendment (q.v.), but in actuality it was attained only in the North and only very recently in some parts of the South on any large scale. Various devices were introduced in the Southern States after the bitter period of the "Reconstruction Era" to keep the Negro from voting. The use of a "grandfather clause" (q.v.), of literacy tests, poll taxes, and other forms of discrimination made voting difficult if not well nigh impossible. With more recent trends such as the curb on the "white primary" comes hope that all restrictions will be reduced in time.

neighborhood associations: These local organizations usually exert their greatest influence to prevent certain types of businesses from "spoiling" a neighborhood, or push efforts to have improvements, such as parks or other public works, constructed in their area first. Examples of such organizations in New York

City would include: Park Avenue Association, Fifth Avenue Association.

neophyte: A recent convert or a novice. The term comes into political use in reference to campaign managers and supporters of political candidates who are quite inexperienced and who, though looked down upon by the seasoned veterans, often prove very successful because of their very naïveté and simplicity.

neutrality: A situation in which a nation abstains from taking sides in a conflict and maintains its impartiality toward the belligerents. The Swiss have traditionally maintained this position for centuries. Ireland, Sweden, and Spain, though all neutral in World War II, did maintain different degrees of "impartiality." The United States by legislation originating in 1935, and renewed in 1937 and 1939, attempted to enforce laws which would have kept us neutral if we had not violated the spirit of it ourselves in such actions as the "destroyer deal" (q.v.) or by Lend-Lease or had it broken for us as at Pearl Harbor, December 1941.

New Deal: A phrase used by F. D. Roosevelt in his acceptance speech in 1932, and later applied to his whole program of economic and social reform in which he sponsored currency reform, wage and hour regulation, flood control, and banking reform.

"New Freedom": The program of Woodrow Wilson to adjust the inequalities of our society and provide reforms of benefit to the common people. During his first term in office (1913-1917) he favored the introduction and passage of the Federal Reserve Act (q.v.) to reform the banking system in the interest of the small investor, the Underwood Tariff to reduce duties so as to lower the cost of living, and the Clayton Antitrust Law (q.v.) to curb the evils of "Big Business" and check monopolies.

New Jersey Plan: The plan proposed in the Constitutional Convention (q.v.) by William Paterson in the form of nine resolutions to protect the interests of the small states, and carried out in a compromise form in the provision for a Senate having an equal number of delegates from each state regardless of size. *See* VIRGINIA PLAN.

Newlands Act of 1902: A federal law providing for extensive reclamation work and for irrigation projects in the Far West. Money spent for this purpose was recovered by the sale of the improved land to settlers, and thus a revolving fund was provided for continuous service.

"New South": This term has been used to describe the states of the deep South that were so badly devastated by the Civil War, and adversely affected by the Reconstruction Era (q.v.) so that they made little economic recovery during the 19th century. However, industrialization is now making a start, many textile plants are being built in the South. The Tennessee Valley Authority (q.v.) is providing cheap electricity to encourage new industry. Mechanization in agriculture is progressing as in the use of the "cotton picker" and with the greater diversification of crops to produce plastics and materials for paint and like projects a "New South" is rising economically. *See* CHEMURGY.

"nine old men": A reference to the Supreme Court in the New Deal days. *See* COURT PACKING PROPOSALS.

Nineteenth Amendment: An amendment to the Constitution of the United States ratified in August 1920 which stated: "The right of citizens of the United States to vote shall not be denied or abridged by the United States or by any State on account of sex." *See* WOMAN'S SUFFRAGE

"noble experiment": A sarcastic allusion to the attempts to enforce the Eighteenth (Prohibition) Amendment.

noncombatant: A civilian, or also a member of the military or naval services, whose duties do not include fighting.

non-communists-left: A designation used for a group of radicals who, though firmly opposed to reactionary ideas, would not subscribe to any Communist principles, or go along with the fellow-travelers in Communist front organizations. They claim their liberalism to be founded on the maintenance of individual liberty and in democratic control of economic life, so that no man should be entrusted with absolute power either public or private. This group finds itself in a very exposed position, since the "center" is suspicious of them for their radicalism and the communist left would either use them or besmirch their motives.

non-conforming uses: If a person lives in a restricted area of a city and attempts to make his property over into some sort of commercial enterprise such as a cafe, he may be found guilty of converting to "non-conforming use" and of breaking the zoning laws established to protect other home owners from a use of property in the community which would depreciate the value of their investment and not be conforming, that is, acceptable to the majority view.

nonpartisan: Not supporting any political party, usually implying a position in which consideration is given to a program that would be of benefit to all and be above petty political bickering.

Nonpartisan League: An organization which was started in North Dakota in 1915 to benefit farmers, gained control of several Western state legislatures and pushed a program advocating state-owned flour mills and terminal grain elevators, a state-owned and operated bank, and government authorized loans to home owners.

non-quota immigrant: The National Origins Law does not apply to those entering the United States from the Western Hemisphere or under eighteen years of age, therefore they are not subject to the usual quota regulations.

non-tax revenue: Money paid to the Federal government through Federal enterprises returns large sums to the Treasury, but little profit is found after deducting operating expenses of such activities as the Post Office, Panama Canal, the Inland Waterway Commission, or the Maritime Commission. Small amounts are obtained by the sale of public lands, and rental privileges (such as grazing in National Parks). Over forty million dollars was made by the Bureau of the Mint due to the difference between the amount spent for metal for coins and the face value of the coins when minted and put into circulation. State and city governments may obtain non-tax revenue also through granting franchises, from rentals and other services rendered.

Norris-LaGuardia Act of 1932: An act passed by the Federal Government limiting the use of the injunction. The courts might issue injunctions in labor disputes after hearing the testimony of witnesses in open court with opportunity for cross examination, but, in general, were under regulation which would prevent their arbitrary use, as in the prevention of picketing or to restrain workers from persuading their fellow workers to violate yellow-dog contracts (q.v.). The law also stated that those found in contempt of court by one judge for disobeying the injunction he had issued should have another judge for their trial and have a jury in addition. This is, of course, a national law but over half the states of the United States have passed similar measures.

North Atlantic Treaty Organization: The creation of NATO in 1949 provided for a regional organization which in the beginning consisted of the United States and Canada associated with Great Britain, France, Norway, Belgium, Denmark and Luxembourg. The general aim was not only for military cooperation but specified that the "parties will contribute toward the further development of peaceful and friendly international relations by strengthening their free institutions . . . and they will seek to eliminate conflict in their international economic policies." In 1952 Greece and Turkey were added to the Organization and under General Eisenhower considerable advance was made in the actual creation of the planned for European army. Problems in regard to the possible military contributions of West Germany required considerable discussion in the light of the French fear of a strong, revived Germany.

Northwest Ordinance: A measure passed by Congress under the Articles of the Confederation and repassed under the new Congress of the United States (1789). It established the extremely important practice of the admission of the new territories as states on an equal basis with the thirteen original states, thus precluding any possibility of developing any colonial dependencies. It also established a bill of rights for the protection of the individuals in the new territories, and forbade slavery.

Oath of Allegiance: Following is the oath which must be sworn to by the alien as part of the process of his naturalization. "I hereby declare on oath, that I absolutely and entirely renounce and abjure all allegiance and fidelity to any foreign prince, potentate, state or sovereignty, and particularly to (name of sovereign of country) of whom I have heretofore been a subject; and that I will support and defend the Constitution and laws of the United States of America against all enemies, foreign and domestic, and I will bear true faith and allegiance to the same."

oath of inauguration: The President-elect on January 20th (*see* TWENTIETH AMENDMENT) takes the oath administered by the Chief Justice. "I do solemnly swear that I will faithfully execute the office of President of the United States, and will to the best of my ability preserve, protect and defend the Constitution of the United States."

oath of office: An oath taken by persons upon assuming public office in which they swear to uphold the Constitution, and to perform their public duties faithfully.

obiter dictum: An incidental or extra-judicial opinion given by a judge on some point that was only indirectly related to the case. Chief Justice Taney in the Dred Scott Decision stated as his obiter dictum the opinion that Congress could not control slavery in the territories. Encouraged by this view, Southerners found all laws limiting slavery in the territories null.

occupational disease: A disease traceable to specific conditions arising from a particular industry or occupational activity. These may include abnormal changes in air pressure, dampness, radiation, excess dust or lint, or poisons. Some of these diseases may include silicosis, tuberculosis, arsenic poisoning or anthrax. Many preventives and cures are becoming available; however, Workmen's Compensation must cover many cases where workers have proof of industry responsibility and where the states make such provision.

occupation money: Funds issued for expenditure in occupied territories by military forces. The United States issued a special currency in North Africa in 1942, and also later in Japan.

occupation tax: A fee exacted through the licensing power of the state or city government, imposed upon the individual in special professions or callings. It might also be called a privilege tax. There is considerable difference of opinion as to the value of the 1951 Federal tax on bookmakers which was paid by very few.

office: A government position held through election or appointment. Part of the title of several administrative establishments, see under title of agency. (Office of Land Utilization.)

Office of Education of the United States: Now a subdivision of the Federal Security Agency, this office has been in existence since 1867 as an advisory and information center. It now administers grants-in-aid under such acts as the Morrill Act (q.v.), Smith-Hughes, and Bankhead-Jones Act for promoting vocational training in agriculture, home economics, and trade and industry.

Office of Price Stabilization: A federal office created as a result of the Korean situation (1951) to administer controls on prices, and authorized to direct rationing of goods if it becomes necessary.

Oil Scandal: This situation arose because oil was sold to a private company from the national government's Elk Hills reservation, after a "bribe" had been given to Secretary of the Interior Fall to permit Doheny to act for the private interests at the public's expense. Criminal suits were brought against each man, but Fall alone was convicted, the only cabinet member in American history to have so suffered.

Old Age and Security Insurance: *See* SOCIAL SECURITY ACT.

Old Guard: A term used to refer particularly to the conservative part of the Republican Party in the 1880's but often used to designate the conservative, or "Big Business" element of the party at any time.

old law tenement: Multiple dwellings built under the New

York Law of 1879 which did not require more than 600 cubic feet of space for an adult, and did not require that every room have its own access to outside air.

oligarchy: Government by the few who presumably have seized power and rule by means of military, social or financial influence.

Open Market Committee: A committee of the Federal Reserve Board composed of all the members of the Board of Governors and five members of the Reserve Banks, who may act to stabilize the general credit situation by the purchase or sale of government obligations, or any other securities being offered on the open market. The original purpose was to "thaw" out frozen credit by buying stocks and bonds so as to put more money into circulation; now the prospects would more likely be to offer more government bonds and stocks for sale in order to absorb some of the inflationary money in circulation.

open shop: A plant where union and non-union workers may be employed, in contrast to a closed shop where only union workers may be employed.

opportunity to be heard: In every criminal or civil case, the interested parties must be given an opportunity to present their evidence. Pertinent facts cannot be refused admission nor can such a brief period of time be allotted that it is out of the question to present the defense.

optional primary: This is a primary that may be held at the pleasure of the governing authorities, though other means of nominating candidates would also be tolerated. On the other hand some states have made the holding of primary elections mandatory. *See* DIRECT PRIMARY.

ordinance: A local by-law passed by a city council through the authority of the state legislature.

organic act: An act providing for the creation of a territory. The Organic Act of 1909 provided for the governing of Hawaii. The Organic Act of 1917 extended citizenship to Puerto Ricans.

original jurisdiction: The power of a court to have a case start in that court. The United States Supreme Court has only two types of such jurisdiction: those affecting ambassadors, consuls, and public ministers, and those concerned with suits arising between the states.

original-package doctrine: Until an import has lost its distinctive character, that is, has been removed from its original package, it may not be taxed by a state, for then a tax on it would be plainly an import duty, and that the states are not allowed to do according to the Constitution. Congress has made exceptions to this doctrine in regard to liquor, oleomargarine and prison-made goods.

orthodoxy: Probably applying more frequently in the religious field where it would mean sound and correct in opinion of doctrine, the term has been frequently used in regard to party loyalty, referring in the narrowest sense to blind allegiance to party directives, and in the widest application to a general sympathy with the broader principles of the party without complete subservience.

"outlawing war": The Kellogg Briand Peace Pact signed in Paris in 1928 outlawed war "as an instrument of national policy," making war illegal but providing no way to implement this statement of policy.

Oxford Movement: *See* MORAL REARMAMENT.

P

"package" deal: A term which has recently come into usage to indicate an accumulation of agreements or concessions. A collective bargaining agreement may contain such a "package" providing for pension benefits, welfare contributions and a small wage increase. The mayor of New York City looked for such a "package" from the state legislature which was to permit the city to raise its debt limit, increase state aid for education, and allow other arrangements to help the city's financial situation, but it fell through.

Pacific Island Trust Territory: The area containing the Marshalls, Marianas, Carolines and Gilbert Islands which as former mandates of the Japanese were turned over to the Trusteeship Council (q.v.), were awarded to the United States April 1947 to administer as a trust territory (q.v.).

pairing: In a legislature when a member must be absent at the time a vote is going to be taken, he will try to arrange to have his vote "paired" with that of another absentee member who has planned to vote in the opposite way from that which the first member had intended. In this way they cancel one another out, and may prevent some unexpected developments from arising.

panacea: Literally a panacea is a remedy supposedly able to cure any and all diseases. Especially in the field of city administration has the American public suffered from the danger of panaceas offered as simple reforms able to remake all the government on an ideal scale in a short time. Emotional fervor pushes forward a reform which the proponents will swear will overcome all difficulties. Superficial reforms have been glamorized in the public eye where interest in the less spectacular, but fundamental improvements have been overlooked.

Panama Canal Zone: A strip of territory five miles wide on either side of the Panama Canal, leased in perpetuity from the

Republic of Panama as a result of a treaty signed in 1903 (Hay-Bunau Treaty). These arrangements were agreed to after Panama, a province of Colombia, had revolted because she had been fearful lest Colombia's attempt to force the United States to pay a large "fee" for the same privileges from her, might have driven the United States to build the Canal in Nicaragua. The population of the Zone has reached 52,000 (1950) and it is under Army control because of its strategic importance.

Pan Americanism: A movement to unite the nations of the Western Hemisphere in regard to economic, cultural and political activities. Such a program is vitally aided by the Pan America Union which prepares material for publication, arranges conferences of journalists, jurists, scientists, and educators and others in its aims to develop commerce, friendly intercourse and understanding to advance peace. Because of some unfriendly overtones connected with the term Pan Americanism, the movement is now referred to as Inter-American cooperation (q.v.). The new administrative agency of the Union, as part of a similar reform, is the Organization of American States. The position of the United States in this new secretariat indicates a significant change in American foreign policy from what had been formerly attacked as "Yankee Imperialism" (q.v.) to the much more admired "Good Neighbor Policy." The crowning symbol of this new Latin American cooperation is the Act of Chapultepec of 1945 providing for Western Hemisphere solidarity. *See* CHAPULTEPEC.

paper money: Documents issued by the government in place of coins to circulate as money. In most cases the paper money serves as a substitute for the specie by which it is fully backed, and is used only for convenience; however, there is a temptation to issue "printing press" money, that is, paper money without any security behind it. At present the United States issues silver certificates and Treasury Notes secured by silver bullion held by the government. The most common paper money in circulation is the Federal Reserve Note. These Notes are backed by 40% of gold held by the Federal Reserve Banks, formerly 25%, and by 60% commercial paper. Since these credit instruments represent loans to business men to meet their increased needs of business, this currency provides the elasticity our economy requires.

National Bank Notes and gold certificates are now being called in.

pardon: To absolve from the consequences of. The pardon may be granted before or after conviction, conditionally, or absolutely. To pardon on a large scale *see* AMNESTY.

parity: After the depression an attempt was made to bring to the farm population some of the benefits the New Deal (q.v.) was bringing to other classes of the population. This aim was based on the idea of providing equality of purchasing power, that is, the farm income should be on a parity with that of the industrial worker. This was first undertaken by the A.A.A. of 1933 (q.v.), and then that of 1938. The aim was further attempted during the post war period by a steadily growing list of subsidized farm products. The continuance of this attempt at creating parity for the farmer was much discussed in considering the case for the Brannan Plan (q.v.). Some farm leaders were recommending the return to "rugged individualism," with the Department of Agriculture continuing all its advisory services but letting the laws of supply and demand operate in regard to the determination of farm prices. However, the Aiken Act was passed in 1948 which continued supports on some nineteen agricultural commodities on a sliding scale depending on supply, 60% of parity payment if a very large supply, 75% if normal, and 90% if below normal, as a means of discouraging production in fields of surplus production and providing an incentive to production of commodities in short supply. *See* AIKEN ACT.

parochial schools: A local educational institution conducted by an ecclesiastical organization, Catholic, Jewish or Protestant. Much discussion arose in 1950 in connection with the administration of certain parts of the federal aid program, whether certain benefits in regard to the health program were to be administered for *all* children or just for those in the so-called public schools; a like question was brought up in connection with the controversy over the use of city-owned school busses for any handicapped children, whether in public or parochial schools.

parole: Release from a penal institution under certain conditions in an attempt to observe the effect of freedom upon an individual who has not yet completed his full sentence and who is required to continue to report to the authorities. For the Federal government this may be carried out by the Parole Board of the Department of Justice.

partisan: A supporter of a political party usually implying unreasoning devotion regardless of the right or logic involved.

party: An organization concerned with nominating and electing their own candidates so as to control personnel and policy in the government. For American political parties *see* FEDERALISTS, DEMOCRATIC-REPUBLICANS, NATIONAL REPUBLICANS, WHIGS, FREE SOIL, LIBERTY, and REPUBLICANS up to the Civil War; and for minor parties thereafter, GREENBACK, POPULISTS, PROGRESSIVES, SOCIALISTS, FARMER-LABOR, and STATES-RIGHTS DEMOCRATS.

party circle: A circle (or square) at the top of the columns in a party column or Indiana type ballot in which the voter may place an x, thus voting for all the candidates of that party and no one else.

party conference: Because the word caucus (q.v.) has such an unpleasant connotation in the public mind, reference to such a meeting is now more frequently made by the expression "party conference."

"party line": An expression usually employed in regard to the Communist Party, meaning following blindly the instructions determined by the party leadership, often with the result that there may be complete reversals of position. For example, the party line was much opposed to American preparation to aid the enemies of Hitler, but as soon as Germany had attacked the Soviet Union in 1941, the line reversed itself and came all out for full American military support for Britain and Russia.

passing a dividend: When a firm fails to pay a share of the profits to a stockholder at the time required, it may have passed the dividend as a matter of policy to retain the profits to plow back into the business, or because business was so poor that there were no profits to distribute.

patent: An exclusive privilege which the government grants to an inventor to control the manufacture, commercial processing, sale and use of his invention or discovery for a term of seventeen years.

paternalism: A term referring to a large degree of regulation of those individuals needing welfare benefits. Application of the term has also been made to some business enterprises which initiate benefits for their workers in the form of disability payments, hospitalization, and similar advantages, in the hope of weakening the appeals of union organizers. *See* STATE SOCIALISM, WELFARE CAPITALISM.

patrolman: A policeman assigned to a certain area as part of his regular duty of supervision.

patronage: A term commonly applied to the awarding of governmental appointments on the basis of party loyalty where the right to fill the position is not limited by Civil Service restrictions or other administrative regulations. The awards thus distributed by mayor, governor or president have become important factors in the winning of party support. It may also include the "honest graft" (q.v.) of awarding contracts to favored companies, granting of franchises to privileged companies, and similar accommodations within the power of a governing group.

Patrons of Husbandry: *See* GRANGER MOVEMENT.

pauper's oath: An oath taken by an applicant for public aid in which he swears that he is completely destitute and has no means of support. Though required in some states as a means of preventing abuses in regard to the administration of the relief program, it is being used less and less since it is looked upon by welfare workers as being unnecessarily severe and humiliating.

"pay as you go" policy: When a city or state government arranges to pay for capital expenditures for long term improvements out of current income, it is "paying as it goes"; that is, avoiding the necessity of accumulating large sums for payment at some future date. It requires careful planning to select those items whose expenses can be met in a single year and which the community needs most, and to set aside a portion of the taxes for these purposes, together with all the other budget arrangements. The great advantage resulting from this policy is that a city does not run into heavy debt and maintains a credit rating which is good when a real emergency arises.

pay roll tax (Social Security Act): *See* EMPLOYMENT TAX.

Peace Observation Commission: The General Assembly in its efforts to maintain the peace may in a tense situation use its newly created Peace Observation Committee to conduct on the spot investigations, provided the approval of the state into which the committee is to go approves.

peccancy: An act of sinfulness or offensiveness. Used in regard to the suspicion of corruption brought out in many of the Congressional investigations.

peculation: The stealing of funds entrusted to one's care.

peer: An equal. Trial by one's peers was originally guaranteed by the Magna Carta in 1215. A peer in England also means a member of the nobility.

penalty wage rates: Wage payments for overtime. They usually amount to one and a half times the regular rate for hours worked over the maximum allowed (forty hours in interstate commerce), and double the rate for work on Sundays or holidays.

peonage: A situation where a person is bound to perform a service in order to pay off a debt. In some cases he was "farmed" out by prison authorities to work off a fine, but often struggled deeper into debt because he was charged for his room and board. Such action is illegal under the Thirteenth Amendment (q.v.) as involuntary slavery.

per capita: A term used to indicate what part of the calculation is allotted to each individual person. If the per capita wealth in the United States for 1953 were to be estimated at $2,000, each "head" in the United States might claim that much as his average share of a three billion dollar total.

perjury: Deliberate lying while under oath to tell the truth.

permanent registration: One of the recommended reforms in election procedure is for permanent registration to qualify for voting. Some states require it every two, four, or six years while New York State has it for every election. It is felt much time and expense could be saved by maintaining a permanent record which would need only to be brought up to date as appropriate. Data is assembled through cooperation of moving companies, reports from public utility companies, tax offices and death notices, but above all it is maintained by a vigilant community effort of interested citizens who through house-to-house canvasses or "spot checks" get out and reach those who might otherwise neglect their opportunity, thus providing a challenge to the performance of good citizenship by all. Some communities make a special ceremony of the registration of the new twenty-one-year-old voters.

perquisite: A profit from one's employment in addition to the regular salary provided. Congressmen get a twenty-cent a mile travel allowance, the services of an administrative assistant (at $8,400 a year), generous provision for secretarial assistance, and a $500 allowance for telephone and telegraph expenses.

person: Legally an individual is a "natural person" but a corporation is an "artificial person," enjoying all the rights of a natural person such as to sue and be sued, and full protection under the law, but not the right to vote.

personation: The act of deception in which a person other than the one actually registered votes in an election.

personnel: The body of persons employed by a private organization or in the public service. Civil Service Boards classify specific positions in carefully determined grades of experience and salary level.

petition: To make a formal written supplication to any branch of government. Guaranteed in regard to the federal government by the First Amendment (q.v.) of the United States Constitution.

Philippines: An archipelago of hundreds of islands extending eleven hundred miles north and south off the southeast coast of Asia. They were ceded to the United States in 1899 by the Treaty of Paris after the Spanish-American War. After going through various stages toward self-government the Tydings-McDuffie Act of 1934 provided for complete independence in 1946. Attacked by the Japanese in 1941, they were liberated in 1944. A Commonwealth was reestablished by Sergio Osmena, who succeeded President Quezon. On July 4, 1946, full independence was accorded the country with General Roxas the first President. Much assistance has been rendered by the United States and a mutual defense treaty was signed in August 1951.

picketing: Patrolling the entrance of a place of business in order to prevent persons from carrying on normal business activity. Peaceful picketing is usually held to be legal and to be protected under the provision for freedom of speech. However, by means of "police power" (q.v.) picketing may be curbed. Picketing may also be limited if it is found to be "in restraint of trade" as described in the antitrust laws.

pigeonhole: To put aside indefinitely, especially applied to legislative committees who do not report out of their committees bills which they have decided to "kill," prevent from reaching the main body.

pivotal states: When a president is under consideration for nomination by the National Convention, a candidate from a pivotal state will be more likely to get the preference. However, what makes a state "pivotal" is a little more open to debate. Those states which are quite "safe" in their party's column are certainly not pivotal. The South, before 1948, would be considered safely in the Democratic column because of long standing party loyalty and therefore not pivotal. However, a populous state where the party vote is fairly evenly divided qualifies as a pivotal state, that is, one where a little encouragement like having a native son as a candidate might bring in a large electoral vote. New York and Ohio represent this condition ideally and show an impressive number of candidates for the White House and successful occupants.

plaintiff: The person who makes the complaint, who starts a suit in a court of law in a civil procedure. The state, or federal government, is always the plaintiff in a criminal case depending on whether a state or federal law has been broken.

plank: A statement of belief or program to be supported in the platform of a political party.

planned economy: A system where a government authority is given the power to deliberately set goals and limitations for production in the expectation of attaining greater production in the long run and eliminate waste and reduce the chance of extremes of boom and bust in the business cycle. *See* ECONOMIC PLANNING.

platform: A document containing the principles and policies of a political party or of a particular candidate. The major parties prepare an elaborate statement of their aims at their National Conventions, which may later be distributed as handbooks to the party leaders in the various districts throughout the United States. Since most issues are decided on the basis of compromise, the position stated often fails to satisfy anyone. Detailed study of such campaign literature usually results in the discovery of very little basic difference between the rival parties.

plebiscite: Submitting a question to a popular vote. This is different from a referendum (q.v.) which provides for the enacting of a law, not just for an expression of an opinion.

pledge of allegiance: A pledge used in saluting the flag as a reminder of one's loyalty to one's country. "I pledge allegiance to the flag of the United States and to the Republic for which it stands; one Nation indivisible, with liberty and justice for all." See OATH OF ALLEGIANCE.

plurality: The number of votes received by one voter over those for another. In the case of three or more candidates the candidate with the largest number of votes when none has a majority is said to have a plurality.

plutocracy: A government controlled by men of wealth, or ruled by them.

pocket veto: A means of preventing a bill from becoming a law because the chief executive failed to sign it before the legislature adjourned. In other words, merely by keeping the bill in his pocket it is vetoed without the necessity of his presenting his reasons. The adjournment has also prevented the passing of the bill over his veto so that it is effectively "killed."

"Point Four Program": In his inaugural address January 1949 President Truman announced the United States would extend technical assistance to the underdeveloped areas of the world in order to help the free people to help themselves by producing more food, clothing, more material for housing and more mechanical power. This was to be one of the four major pillars of United States foreign policy. On June 5, 1950, the President signed a bill authorizing the expenditure of $35 million for the first year of the program. Fifty nations of the United Nations pledged an additional $20 million for the International Development Fund.

police power: The power of the state to regulate matters relating to health, comfort, safety and morals in emergencies where no authorized measures are adequate to the situation. These powers may be assumed on the state, national or municipal level.

police state: A state which is governed not by law but by the ruthless power of its secret police.

police strike 1919: Dissatisfied with wages and conditions of work, the police in Boston went on strike with some degree of violence resulting. The governor, Calvin Coolidge, finally intervened, breaking the strike and restoring order. The nation-wide reputation won under these circumstances is supposed to have contributed to his nomination as Vice-President with Harding in the 1920 election.

Policy Committee: In the Senate both the major parties have such a committee. It attends to the formulation of an overall legislative policy which its special staff has assisted in determining through analysis and research on the problems involved in policy making. The membership is the same as that of the Steering Committee including the floor leader and the party whip plus two other advisors.

Political Action Committee: Originally set up by the Congress of Industrial Organization under the leadership of Sidney Hillman, this Committee announced its intention to back a program which would advance the welfare of labor and promote reform as vigorously as possible. It raised over half a million dollars in 1944 to elect state and national candidates favorable to labor. In 1945 it sponsored a National Citizen's Political Action Committee attempting to obtain on a non-partisan basis the support of those outside of the labor movement, such as farmers, business and professional people. In thirty-four states, 73 of the 318 Congressional candidates backed by the P.A.C. were elected. Five of the twenty-six Senators supported were successful. This work continued with a program favoring increased minimum wages, support for a Fair Employment Practices Commission and an extended Social Security program. Though temporarily absorbed in Wallace's Progressive Party in 1948, the C.I.O. has continued to maintain an aggressive political program under its original name. Many consider its most useful work to have been the stress on full registration and the need for full participation in political responsibility.

political clubs: Political clubs are common in large cities. They may claim to be distinct from political organizations but will usually have some indirect contacts. They have permanent headquarters and take a large interest in the city life with political issues seemingly nonpartisan, and bosses carefully concealed. Such clubs were very prominent during prohibition, providing an alternate meeting place, perhaps, for the poor man's club (the saloon), but have declined since 1933. New York City once had more than six hundred. Colorful names adorned these organizations; the Democrats seem to favor Indian names, but some groups would select the names of famous Americans or of national groupings. Their greatest activity was usually the annual outing for which tickets would be sold and which was usually the only source of financial support.

political machine: A method of referring to a political organization which dominates in a particular locality with such accurate precision that comparison with a machine is not too far fetched. Ability to provide for the party faithful and, well "oiled" with funds contributed by those expecting favors in return, the machine ultimately finds a reform movement bitter in attacking for a time, then back comes the machine into power again unless the electorate remains constantly on the alert.

political morality: Political morality is made up of many elements, including honesty, reliability, responsibility, lack of corruption, vice or spoils. The standards unfortunately vary with different areas. The consensus would probably be today that there is certainly some improvement to be noticed. The "scandals" of the present day do not seem to be on the same scale as they were in the 1870's and 1880's.

political refugee: One who has fled for safety from his own country, or as a displaced person, after a war, fears to return to his native land because of political changes there. This problem has been growing since 1945 because of the increasing number of countries "disappearing" behind the "Iron Curtain," that is, succumbing to political changes engineered on the part of minority Communist groups as in the case of Czechoslovakia and Poland.

poll tax: A direct tax, or head tax, often used as a requirement for voting, though the number of states so using it has been reduced to seven (1948). The House of Representatives has attempted to pass a law outlawing the tax as restricting the right to vote in national elections because it discriminates heavily against the Negro. Such a measure has been defeated five times in the Senate. Some, however, question its constitutionality since the states have the sole power to determine the qualifications of voting, and would prefer to see the remedy come through the states themselves.

poll watcher: The individual selected by the party to be present at the voting place to report any illegal action. Each major party has its representative.

pool: A combination of interests, or an agreement between competing companies to the mutual advantage of all, usually by eliminating competition, to fix prices, or assign sales areas, or share profits. Such actions on the part of railroad companies at the expense of the small shippers led to the creation of the Interstate Commerce Commission in 1887, which made pools illegal in order to force competition and lead to lower freight rates.

popular election of Senators: *See* SEVENTEENTH AMENDMENT.

population density: The number of individuals per square mile of territory determines the density of the population for that area and represents a figure used for purposes of comparison. For example the density for Puerto Rico is 640 per square mile, and that of the state of Nevada one per square mile.

Populists: In 1892 the Populists accumulated the backing of many discontented groups, especially of the debtor classes, and many farm and labor groups resenting the growing power of the "Big Business" (q.v.) interests. They actually took over the Democratic Party in 1896 when William J. Bryan fought his epic campaign on the issue of free coinage of silver at the ratio of sixteen to one, which was expected to produce an inflated currency and higher prices for farm products. Though defeated by McKinley, the advocacy of many reforms such as popular election of senators, antitrust legislation and government regulation of business ultimately had its effect. *See* FREE COINAGE.

pork-barrel legislation: The voting of appropriations for any purpose must have the approval of the majority of the legislature. In order to obtain enough votes for an appropriation for some local project a legislator may make arrangements for other members to vote for his favorite scheme, if he in turn votes for theirs. This is delicately expressed as "If you scratch my back I'll scratch yours." The pieces of "pork" obtained by these raids on the "pork barrel" (the state or federal treasury) may be appropriations for post offices, veterans' hospitals, highways, irrigation or other types of construction not always critically needed but hardly ever questioned for fear that by retaliation the critic may find he is the one forced to return to his constituents empty-handed. Reform movements often question the extravagance, duplication and waste in such legislation, but until the taxpayer actually revolts the system goes right on working. *See* LOG-ROLLING.

portal to portal pay: Payment for the time spent by the worker in traveling from the gate of the mine or of the plant grounds to the point at which activity actually begins. It became an issue after the passage of the Fair Labor Standards Act (q.v.) and was settled by a Supreme Court decision.

Port of New York Authority: An organization created under an interstate compact approved by Congress in 1921 between New York and New Jersey to improve the transportation facilities of the metropolitan area. A Board of Commissioners (six from New York and six from New Jersey) supervises the widespread activities necessary in the construction and maintenance of the George Washington Bridge, the Lincoln and Holland Tunnels, bus terminals and airports of considerable extent and importance.

posse comitatus: "The power of the county," that is, the whole body of male persons over fifteen which a sheriff may summon to assist him in law enforcement.

possessions of the United States: *See* ALASKA, GUAM, HAWAII, PANAMA CANAL ZONE, PUERTO RICO, SAMOA, VIRGIN ISLANDS. Additional areas in the mid-Pacific consist of Howland and Baker, occupied in 1936 as meteorologists' stations, and Midway, Wake, Jarvis and Palmyra Islands.

Postmaster General: The head of the Post Office Department. Usually the president just elected will appoint to his cabinet as

Postmaster the man who has been most useful in obtaining his election, the National Chairman. However, President Truman broke the tradition by appointing a career man of the post office with many years of practical experience to that post.

Potsdam Conference: A conference attended by President Truman, Prime Minister Atlee of Great Britain and Stalin during July and August of 1945, at which the Council of Foreign Ministers was established to draft treaties with Italy, Roumania, Bulgaria and Finland (a job they completed in 1947) and to make further arrangements about the occupation of Germany, with some provision for local self-government. Plans were also made to take action against Nazi war criminals.

powers of Congress: *See* ENUMERATED POWERS, LOOSE INTERPRETATION OF THE CONSTITUTION.

"power of the purse": Control of the finances. The House of Representatives has the right to initiate financial bills and no program can go into effect until an appropriation has been first approved by them, thus this power to authorize spending of funds does become the "power of the purse."

preamble: Preface—literally that which walks before. Perhaps the most famous preamble is that to the Constitution of the United States. "We, the people of the United States, in order to form a more perfect union, establish justice, insure domestic tranquillity, provide for the common defense, promote the general welfare, and secure the blessings of liberty to ourselves and our posterity, do ordain and establish this Constitution for the United States of America."

precinct: The basic unit in electoral processes, and in party organization. It is based on the number of voters, usually 300, but urban units may be twice that size. Precinct committeemen are felt to be the key to the whole political setup in the United States.

prefabricated houses: A method of construction inaugurated to satisfy the needs for low-cost housing, whereby structural panels or sections are built on the assembly line in factories, shipped to the site and put together by relatively unskilled labor. While this new method is not intended to replace the conventional ways of building, its proponents believe they can build houses for low-income groups in quantities that will surpass all other methods, an important consideration in connection with the current housing shortage.

Site prefabrication is a related development and refers to construction where whole blocks or neighborhoods are built at one time. An outdoor factory shapes and assembles the parts through mechanized labor operations. Henry Kaiser used such a method in building housing for his 35,000 shipbuilders in ninety days.

preferential trade agreements: Arrangements made between governments having to do with matters of trade. Starting in 1922, the members of British Commonwealth of Nations were considering giving one another special privileges in reduction of tariff duties and other related benefits.

preferential voting: Preferential and proportional voting have been devised to give sizeable minorities an opportunity to express their wishes at the polls. A voter in preferential voting may list his first, second and third choices. The candidate having a majority of the first choices wins.

presentment: When the evidence has not warranted an actual indictment (q.v.) the grand jury can bring a presentment or formal accusation calling attention to a particular evil. This may be done especially where the grand jury considers that the law enforcement authorities have not investigated a source of potential crime sufficiently.

President of the United States: The Chief Executive of the United States has the power to appoint his cabinet and to fill all the high administrative, judicial, and diplomatic posts with the consent of the Senate. He may seek advice but need not follow it since he alone is responsible for the determination of policy. He has judicial power in regard to issuing pardons or granting amnesty. His legislative power consists of his authority to approve or veto (q.v.) a bill passed by both houses of Congress. He may allow a measure to become a law without his signature if he does not return it to the House from which it originated within ten days. He also may exercise a "pocket veto" (q.v.) if he retains a bill after the adjournment of Congress. He may influence legislation indirectly by calling a special session for a specific purpose, or by his recommendations in his annual "State of the

Union" message (q.v.) or by "fireside" chats, or by radio or other forms of speech-making. In all he may well be the most powerful executive in the world if he exercises all his powers on the basis that he may do anything he is not specifically denied.

President-elect: The candidate successfully elected President in the November election but not yet sworn into office. The date for this official act has been moved up from that of March fourth to January twentieth by the Twentieth Amendment (q.v.), which also provides for replacement of the President-elect in case of death or failure to qualify, a condition not previously provided for under the Constitution.

presidential elector: It has only been since 1845 that a federal law has required that every state determine the presidential electors for that state by popular election. Even now there is considerable diversity as to whether they are chosen "at large," or from each congressional district, and as to whether their individual names appear on the presidential ballots. As soon as the popular vote is determined the whole slate of electors of the party having the majority is notified. The number of such electors is the sum of the number of representatives and senators that state has in Congress. Ultimately their individual votes will be sent to the Senate for the official count. *See* ELECTORAL COLLEGE.

presidential primary: Several states have provided for a primary for the purpose of electing the delegates to the National Conventions (q.v.) held for the nominating of presidential candidates as was first introduced in Wisconsin in 1905. Other states went even farther after 1910, with preference primaries, which, after popular expression of opinion, bound the delegates to vote for the particular choice of their district. Over twenty states for a time sent these "pledged" delegates to the National Conventions. However, enthusiasm lapsed, the expense amounted to a second election, the public seemed apathetic in some areas and the practice lapsed in many states. Fourteen states still use some method of popular election of the delegates, though the remainder send their delegates as the choice of the state or district party conventions.

Presidential succession: The Congress has provided through the Presidential Succession Act of 1947 that the order of succession upon the death or incapacity of the President and Vice-President shall be first, the Speaker of the House of Representatives, second, President Pro Tem of the Senate, third, the cabinet starting with the Secretary of State, and then of Treasury, Defense and on down the list. *See* CABINET.

presidential timber: An expression meaning that a person has potential qualities that might make him available for nomination for president because of the part of the country he represented or for the special group for whom he was spokesman.

president pro tempore: A member of the Senate chosen by that body to preside over its sessions when the Vice-President is absent or serving as President. He stands fourth in the order of succession to the Presidency under the Act of 1947.

pressure groups: The common term for organized special interests that exert influence on government. This is done by paid lobbying or by threat of political punishment at the next election. Not always does the interest come from the outside. Some members of Congress have acted of their own accord in the "interests" of certain groups. Cotton, Tobacco, Iron, Sheep-raisers have had their defenders. Half a century ago "Oil" or "Railroad" or "Silver" senators were commonly spoken of.

previous question: A basic motion in legislative procedure. To move the previous question requires an immediate vote. If it is supported by a majority vote debate ends at once, and the bill is brought to a final vote. If the previous question is defeated the debate continues.

price-fixing: The legal determination of prices by a government, as in World War II by the Office of Price Administration, and in the renewal of such control by the Office of Price Stabilization after the Korean Crisis of 1950. Price-fixing for monopolistic purposes is illegal.

price support: Action by the government to maintain a certain minimum price usually by some system of making up the difference between the market price and the price fixed by a governmental agency as in farm parities.

"price war": A form of cutthroat competition in which one business cuts its prices in order to undersell a neighbor, and the practice spreads to other businesses in the community, until a whole series of enterprises are fighting one another into bankruptcy.

primary election: *See* DIRECT PRIMARY, PRESIDENTIAL PRIMARY.

priority: Precedence. During the war the Office of Production Management gave certain enterprises priority over others in obtaining certain scarce commodities.

private bill: In earlier American history a certain day was set aside when members of Congress could present measures which were for the individual benefit of their constituents. Since the passage of the Reorganization Act of 1946 Congress may not pass any such bills. Matters which have to do with pension, which formerly were a large percentage of the private bills introduced, are to be handled by the Veterans Administration. Others having a wrong to be redressed by the United States will, if the sum involved is under $1,000, turn to the government agency involved, or if over that amount bring suit in the federal district courts.

probate court: A court especially concerned with the supervision of estates or trust funds, and the acceptance of wills. Because of its guardianship of minors it is sometimes called the "Orphans' Court."

probation: Many courts in an effort to deal leniently with youthful offenders will provide an alternative to their being put on trial and facing the possibility of imprisonment with hardened criminals. Certain individuals felt capable of improvement will be placed on probation. During this period of from one to two years under the close supervision of a probation officer, an attempt at rehabilitation is carefully carried out. A job, new environment, good counseling, and someone with faith in their ability to keep out of trouble have effected lasting changes in many incipient criminals. These boys and girls upon the completion of the probationary period satisfactorily may have their previous records wiped out.

processing tax: A tax such as that levied under the terms of the Agricultural Adjustment Act of 1933 (q.v.) upon millers, meat packers, and other converters of agricultural commodities. From this fund was to be obtained the money to pay the compensation to those farmers reducing their acreage. The Supreme Court found this tax unconstitutional.

Production and Marketing Administration: An important agency in the United States Department of Agriculture created in 1945 to supervise the Commodity Credit Corporation (q.v.), the Federal Crop Insurance Corporation (q.v.) and other agricultural agencies.

profits, undistributed: The profits which a corporation has decided not to divide among the stockholders as dividends. This may be due to a desire to apply the surplus to improving the business with the expectation of greater ultimate profit in time.

proletariat: The working class. Frequently contrasted with the highest social class, the very wealthy, and the middle group, the bourgeoisie.

Progressive Party: Originally the Progressives represented the reform element in the Republican Party. They advocated government regulation of Big Business, the direct primary, popular election of Senators, and the initiative, referendum and recall (q.q.v.). As an insurgent group they were influential in bringing on the "Revolution of 1910," a situation which considerably reduced the great power held by the Speaker of the House (q.v.). In 1912 this radical group turned from the support of Taft who had just won the regular Republican nomination and offered to back up "Fighting Bob" La Follette, the organizer of the "Progressive Party." Theodore Roosevelt who had just broken with Taft and lost a chance to win the Republican nomination indicated he was willing to accept the Progressives' nomination instead. Though loyal to La Follette the Progressives felt it was too good an opportunity to miss, to have such a dynamic candidate as Roosevelt available, so they campaigned strongly for him. This split in the Republican party threw the election to Wilson, because of Roosevelt's inability to win the Eastern support as a Progressive candidate.

In 1924 the Progressives tried hard again, their candidate, La Follette, winning Socialist backing as well as the support of the American Federation of Labor, and the Farmer-Labor Party. In an election where their efforts were much the most active they still won so few votes as practically to eliminate them as a formal party, though they might claim that their influence had led to the introduction by the older parties of many reforms originally sponsored by the Progressives.

progressive taxation: This is taxation in which the amount of the percent to be paid increases sharply as the income received by the individual paying the tax increases. This tax is enforced on the basis that the burden should increase with the ability to pay.

Prohibition: The name used for the period during which the Eighteenth Amendment (q.v.) was in force forbidding the manufacture, sale or transportation of intoxicating liquor anywhere in the United States, except for medicinal or scientific purposes. *See* LIQUOR LEGISLATION, TWENTY-FIRST AMENDMENT (for repeal).

promulgate: The proclamation of an executive of a law when it is put into effect.

propaganda: A means of influencing the public mind with respect to certain issues, specific or general, short term or long. It may further the general welfare, or be narrow and selfish. It may be spoken, written, pictorial or musical. In totalitarian regimes it is not to be distinguished from education, or even from governmental activities.

property tax: The property tax is a tax imposed by the state governments and is fourth in importance as a source of income after the income tax, the corporation tax, and the sales tax. It is poorly administered on the whole, for some property escapes listing for tax purposes, some is incorrectly assessed. The tax is not collected in accord with the ability to pay: a poor family with a large house may be paying property taxes higher than a prosperous firm making large profits on a small piece of land. The states have relinquished to local authorities most of the privileges of collection which constitutes for the cities virtually their entire income—over six billion dollars a year.

Proportional Representation: The Hare System is the more commonly followed system of proportional representation in the United States. Rather than emphasize political parties it encourages voting on the basis of economic, social and racial types of interest. Each voter has one vote, but this vote is transferable. If the first choices of the ballots counted are enough to reach the quota determined ahead of time, that candidate is declared elected. Then the second choices are assembled until another candidate has attained the quota. The third choices are distributed until still another candidate has been determined. This continues until all the members have been chosen. The quota is arrived at by dividing the total number of valid ballots by the number of members on the Council to be elected plus one. The commonest criticism has been of the tendency to create "splinter" parties with over-representation for radical groups and the consequent delay in coming to agreement on necessary measures. The method of counting also may take many days and is expensive.

proprietary functions of cities: These are functions that have been assumed by many city governments which are scarcely to be distinguished from governmental functions, but which legally present a different character. They are not performed by the cities as agents of the states, but are permitted rather than required. Some say they arise from the invasion of private business, but this is not always so. Among such functions are: furnishing of electricity and gas, running of street cars and buses, operation of theatres, roller or ice-skating rinks, and bath houses. The city is held liable for its actions in these undertakings though it may refuse to assume liability for its strictly governmental operations.

proprietor: The sole owner of a business to whom may be paid the full amount of the profits, but who also assumes all the risks. If his business is not incorporated, he has unlimited liabilities and may be sued for his personal as well as his business wealth. A partnership represents two or more proprietors bound together by a legal arrangement.

prorogation: The act of proroguing or adjourning a session of a legislative body. If the executive uses this privilege, meant to be used in case of deadlock, he fixes the time of reconvening, otherwise the legislators themselves determine the date for their next session.

prospectus: A preliminary statement of an enterprise about to start or extend a business undertaking, giving advance information calculated to arouse interest. If this program is to be financed by a stock issue the prospectus must be approved by the Security Exchange Commission.

protective tariff: A tax placed on goods imported into the United States. The first protective tariff was passed in 1816 and served much the same purpose in those days as today. The duty imposed on the import raises the selling price of that commodity in this country and therefore may eleminate the possibility of foreign competition with the domestic product.

pro tempore: Literal meaning is for the time being. It is an expression used especially for the presiding officer in the Senate when the Vice-President is not available or has become President. The President pro tempore is next in line after the Speaker of the House of Representatives who follows the Vice President in the succession to the Presidency.

protest vote: A vote cast for a minor or less popular candidate in order to show a voter's dislike of a program or individual of his own party. On occasion votes have been cast for the Socialist candidate when voters have been dissatisfied with both the major candidates, especially in 1912 and 1920.

protocol: (1) Diplomatic etiquette involving correct form of address, seating according to proper rank and related matters. (2) Negotiation on a diplomatic level leading to the ratification of a convention or a treaty.

prototype: An original pattern or model. Politically, the establishment of the British Parliament has served as a prototype for many modern law-making bodies.

proxy: A document by means of which a stockholder signs over authority to someone else to vote in his place at the annual stockholders' meeting. This leads to what some consider the outstanding weakness of the corporation—absentee ownership. A small group may by means of obtaining enough of these proxies control the policies of the corporation at the possible expense of the interests of the larger number. Cooperatives (q.v.) have tried to overcome this problem by assigning one vote to each member holding any stock regardless of the number of shares sold.

Public Contracts Act (Walsh-Healey Act): An act of Congress, 1936, later amended which requires that where a government supply contract involves sums over $10,000, the minimum prevailing wage as determined by the Secretary of Labor must be paid by the firms concerned and a basic eight-hour day or forty-hour week with the rate of time and a half for overtime with basic safety standards, and restrictions on child and convict labor must be observed.

public debt: The total indebtedness of a government, a state or one of its subdivisions. After World War I the public debt of the United States reached 25½ billion dollars, by 1930 it was down to 16 billion, rising to 40 billion in 1939, 54 billion in 1945 but reaching 252 billion as a result of World War II expenditures.

public defender: A lawyer designated by the court to provide for the defense of indigent persons accused of criminal offenses. In Los Angeles this is an official government position.

public domain: The public land owned by the United States. At one time or another one and a half billion acres or 80% of continental United States has been such land. Some was given to the states so that the income would help in the work of education, or to the railroad companies as incentives in transcontinental railroad construction; other parts were disposed of under homesteading agreements. Allotment to private individuals was suspended in 1935, but was resumed in 1946. Different regulations exist for different kinds of land: desert land, timber land, and mining areas represent some types.

public enterprise: The production or sale of goods and services by the government itself. These may range from municipalities which take charge of water supply, garbage disposal, and street transportation to service projects of the federal government, such as the work of the Post Office, the Government Printing Office, or the Tennessee Valley Authority; or projects involving great capital outlays like the building and operation of the Panama Canal or the Atomic Energy Projects. The state governments may also participate in similar cases of public enterprise in regard to the construction of highways, bridges and tunnels.

Public Health Service: An agency in the Federal Security

Agency whose functions include inspection of ships and planes to prevent the introduction of disease from abroad. It makes valuable recommendations to the states which are followed in a large part of the nation in regard to restaurant standards of health, milk ordinances, water pollution and control. It has waged continuous battle to forestall disease through cooperation with local agencies. Since 1938 the mortality from syphilis has been cut in half with the campaign sparked by the Public Health Service through a federal appropriation for all its work of over $200 million a year.

"**public power**": An expression referring to the fact that government agencies have been embarking upon the field of production of electricity for power. Government-owned municipal plants are estimated as producing three million kilowatts and the federal projects thirteen million kilowatts when all the plants at the Tennessee Valley Authority, Bonneville, Fort Peck and Central Valley projects are completed.

Public Roads, Bureau of: Now an agency in the General Services Administration, this Bureau sees to the integration of the most elaborate system of highways in the entire world, and through grants-in-aid has encouraged the states to construct such highways with the National Treasury paying one-half the expense, or in special areas the whole expense must be assumed. Appropriations for these purposes run to half a billion dollars a year.

public service franchise: *See* FRANCHISE.

public use: Private property devoted by its owner to a public use becomes subject in various ways to government regulation. This is particularly true of public utilities where competition would be socially undesirable as in such natural monopolies as telephone companies, gas, water or electricity distribution. The controls may be by state agencies, as the Public Service Commissions in regard to bus or trolley lines, or on the federal level through the Federal Power Commission, or the Securities Exchange Commission. Railroads constitute a special category under this grouping and are closely supervised by the Interstate Commerce Commission.

public utility: An enterprise privately owned but whose operation is not only essential to the public, but likely to constitute a natural monopoly so that it is necessary to subject it to many types of special regulation. The States usually require a special franchise for its operation, and when its "products" such as power, electricity, gas and pipe lines extend to other states the Federal Power Commission (q.v.) regulates wholesale rates of electricity, requires uniform accounting methods and related activities, and the Securities and Exchange Commission regulates its stock issue and must authorize its program of expansion. The Public Utility Holding Company Act of 1935 provides further regulation in regard to restricting the transfer of trust certificates or other security transactions, or the making of loans and contracts that might weaken the provision that no "secondary" holding companies may exist.

public works: Construction jobs undertaken by city, state or nation for public use at public expense may include such items as schools, housing projects, dams and highways. A Public Works Administration was created as part of the New Deal in 1933 to carry out work of this type.

Puerto Rico: An unincorporated territory in the West Indies acquired by the United States at the close of the Spanish American War. The Organic Act of 1917 extended some self-government and made the inhabitants citizens of the United States. Nationalism became a strong influence which coupled with the economic backwardness of the island led some extremists to demand independence, though most of the discontent seems to be focused on the desire for statehood. Both political parties have promised to satisfy this hope "eventually," but an attempt at compromise was carried out in the concession introduced in 1947 of a popularly elected governor. *See* INSULAR CASES.

"puffing": In advertising some companies make extravagant claims about their products. The Federal Trade Commission has allowed some of this on the ground that it was "innocent puffing." If however any of the claims are definitely misleading or contain any ingredients that might do an individual any harm, an injunction would be issued ordering the firm to stop selling such an article or to stop making such false claims.

pull: A hold or means of influencing those in power, through undue or illegitimate means.

pump priming: Term applied to the period of the New Deal after 1932 when in order to restore purchasing power to the great number of unemployed, the federal government authorized great expenditures on such items as the Works Progress Administration, the Civilian Conservation Corps, and on the Public Works Administration.

pusher: A slang term for a narcotics peddler who has success reaching the underprivileged because they are seeking escape from their sordid lives. Fantastic profits are reaped because of the frightful craving involved. Difficulty of curbing such action arises because of the seeming inability to stop the flow of unlawful narcotics into this country.

"pussyfooting": The action by which a candidate avoids taking an absolute stand on some critical, or significant question on which he is expected to make up his mind. By ambiguous remarks many politicians may avoid losing votes which they might do if they took an unequivocal position. The term was used quite frequently about those candidates who could only find the attempt to enforce prohibition a "noble experiment."

Q

qualifications: Requirements such as those of age, citizenship, residence, character, or education which an individual must satisfy before he may be in a position to run for office.

quantity discount: If the manufacturer can show savings in costs passed on to the purchaser of large quantities, the reduction in price is valid. The burden of proof rests on the manufacturer to prove that the full amount of the discount was based on an actual saving, otherwise it may be considered by the Federal Trade Commission as an unfair business practice in the sense that it is discriminatory to the large business interests at the expense of the small who would then be unable to compete or survive.

quarantine: The isolation of persons having or suspected of having been in contact with a person having a contagious disease. The policy may be enforced by either State or federal government.

quasi-judicial: Partially resembling a judicial action, and partly the work of an administrative agency given authority to make decisions affecting individuals under the specific controls with which they are concerned. The Federal Trade Commission (q.v.) accomplishes a great deal before final recourse to the courts becomes necessary. The decisions of these agencies are on the same level as those of the federal district courts and may reach the circuit court of appeal on much the same basis.

quid pro quo: Latin meaning something for something. In politics a basis for bargaining put more crudely as "you scratch my back and I will scratch yours." In government, well illustrated in the provisions for the federal government to match funds raised under standards established under federal requirements, as grants-in-aid for child welfare or agricultural education.

quorum: The number required legally to carry on legislative business. For Congress the quorum is fixed by the Constitution as a majority in each house. These figures, 49 for the Senate, and 218 for the House are not maintained constantly as members come and go; however, the quorum must be present when a vote is taken to render it effective.

quota: The quota of a particular country is the number of persons able to enter the United States. This is a proportion of the 150,000 persons admitted under the National Origins Law (q.v.).

quo warranto, a writ of: A writ issued on the behalf of a state to inquire into the title by which a person holds an office, or a public corporation its franchise, as the first steps in legal proceedings to vacate the office or franchise. This is not a commonly used writ today but does serve a purpose in checking upon an administrative action.

R

rabble rouser: A politician or so-called social reformer who seeks support for his program by means of high pressure salesmanship filled with oratorical and emotional fervor, but without sound moral or ethical foundation, and intended instead to serve the selfish purposes of the speaker or his own group.

racism: An assumption of inherent superiority by certain races, also a doctrine or program of racial domination based on such an assumption.

racket-buster: A term that has come into usage in the same fashion as that of "trust-buster" in Theodore Roosevelt's time, as a popular way of referring to a local, or state law enforcement official who makes special efforts to disrupt organized crime where certain criminal elements have attempted to systematically extort money from legitimate business men, who want to obtain "protection" against further damage or further intimidation. Thomas Dewey and William O'Dwyer made reputations through their efforts as "racket-busters."

racketeer: A new type of criminal who extorts bribes from certain types of legal and illegal business men through promise of "protection." A labor racketeer is curbed by the Hobbs Act, a measure passed by Congress in 1947 which imposes penalties on those found guilty of robbery or extortion when these acts have the effect of obstructing, delaying, or otherwise interfering with interstate commerce. Companies were being forced to hire an additional driver when certain trucks were being taken into the city, and this law was to check such "racketeering."

radical: In popular usage radical means one who advocates thoroughgoing and speedy changes in laws and methods of governing which would probably be considered left of center or to some degree socialistic. However, in the 1900's it might have been applied to those advocating women's suffrage, free compulsory education for all, and government ownership of railroads. The term in the 1860's was used in still another sense, being applied to those Republicans who were avid abolitionists before the Civil War and who as bitter opponents of any lenient program toward the Southern political leaders forced the passage of the Reconstruction Act providing military occupation of the South.

raid on the treasury: A large appropriation of public funds for the benefit of a locality.

rally: A mass meeting which may be for a political purpose as when certain candidates are campaigning for office, or when the opposition has called a demonstration in regard to some administration program.

ranking member: The member next below the chairman of a Congressional committee who has the greatest seniority in the committee.

rate making: Determination of the amount to be charged as in either freight or electricity rates. This has become a particularly difficult task as far as the government agencies assigned such duties are concerned; as for example the Interstate Commerce Commission for the railroads, because of the difficulty in fixing a fair rate that will provide sufficient income to permit adequate wages, and which will also provide profits to meet the desire of the stockholders for increased dividends, and which will also serve to keep the rates themselves low enough not to force those producing the goods to pass on the increase to the consuming public. For the railroads still another problem arises in regard to the problem of joint costs, a situation in which it is impossible for the rate makers to distinguish between the expenses incurred in carrying freight or in carrying passengers.

ratification: The giving of approval, as in the case of the Senate which may ratify a treaty by means of a two-thirds vote, or the approval extended to a Constitution when ratified by a Constitutional Convention.

rationing: A method of providing for a fairer distribution of scarce goods by limiting the amount available to an individual and providing some means of enforcing the arrangement, as the ration books of World War II which contained a certain number of coupons which could be used for the purchase of designated items from shoes, coffee, canned goods to gasoline.

raw materials: Natural or semi-manufactured goods that are essential to further industrial production, or may be immediately consumed as food stuffs. With the introduction of large scale production and the assembly line method the necessity of providing a continuous flow of raw material is particularly important.

reactionary: A person desirous of returning to an earlier, more conservative program. After the overthrow of Napoleon the reactionaries who had supported Louis XVIII in exile were able to return to power.

reading: The essential steps in the passage of a law in a legislative body are referred to by the term "reading," though this includes a great deal more than its literal interpretation. In the Congress of the United States the first reading is by title only, after which the proposed measure is sent on to the appropriate committee. If approved it will in time come up for a second reading when reached on the appropriate calendar. The third reading is by title only as a matter of form when the measure is finally approved in the House in which it originated. The same process is repeated in the other House to advance the bill to the last hurdle, presidential acceptance.

reapportionment: Reallotment or reassignment, as of members of a legislative body. Following every taking of the federal census when the population figure for each state has been determined, Congress may find it necessary to rearrange the number of representatives each state is entitled to have in the House of Representatives. Since the total number is fixed at 435, shifts of population may cause one state to lose some representatives and others to have more reapportioned to them. As the result of the 1950 census, California was supposed to gain eight additional members and New York and several other states were to lose one or two. By 1950 also the unit of representation had risen to over one representative to 330,000 people.

rebates: These refunds represent a sum of money returned to a shipper after having already agreed upon a higher payment originally. Before the passage of the Interstate Commerce Act in 1887 such practices on the part of many railroads permitted a form of discrimination which was very distressing to many small farmers who paid the published railroad rates, and then discovered that some big shippers were receiving rebates that substantially lowered their costs, and made cutthroat competition at the expense of the small business men possible. Such rebates are now illegal unless they are awarded uniformly to all dealers as, for example, incentives for large orders.

rebuttal: Counter-arguments in a discussion as a defendant's answer to the plaintiff's reply to a previous rejoinder.

recall: The method by which a public official may be removed from office by the vote of the people. It is usually considered in connection with two other examples of "direct legislation," the initiative (q.v.) and the referendum (q.v.). The required percentage of voters varies from ten to thirty percent in the different states. Although incompetence and misconduct are the most common cause for removal, personal animosities have been the basis for removal of some judges and a comparatively small number of states have made provision for its use, about one quarter for removal of executive officers and one sixth for removal of judges.

"recapture clause": A provision of a law making it possible to take a portion of the profits of a company above a certain minimum. It was applied to the railroads by the Transportation Act of 1920; but few lines had profits over the six percent permitted to contribute to the "pool" which was to be assembled in order to make loans to the less successful lines.

receiver: A person appointed by the court to manage the affairs of a bankrupt firm.

recess appointment: When the Senate is not in session the President may make an appointment, but it expires on the last day of the succeeding session of the Senate.

recidivists: A youthful offender placed on probation who relapses to his former criminal activities and therefore must stand trial. *See* PROBATION.

reciprocal trade agreements: Arrangements for mutual benefits in regard to the reduction of tariff duties between two countries within certain limits. The United States in particular has allowed the lowering of tariff duties by fifty percent through the Reciprocal Tariff Agreements Act of 1934 and its later amendments. In return for the lowering of tariff duties on certain items that the United States would like to send to their countries, the United States lowers its duties on certain goods coming to this country. The consumer gains in each case through the possible reduction in price of the goods thus admitted, but "protected" industries are resentful.

reclamation: A program for recovery of land otherwise lost to use. By draining swamps and marshes or by irrigating deserts and by the construction of dams for flood control, both state and federal governments have helped in this vital work. *See* NEWLANDS ACT.

recognition: Acknowledgment of one state by another represents the official acceptance of that state's existence. The United States has usually insisted that recognition be based on "de jure" grounds, that is, that the change has come about by legal means, but has acted in regard to the de facto (revolutionary) creation of a new government in some cases. The recognition of Panama was immediately offered in her break from Colombia, but the Soviet Union was not recognized until the period of the New Deal (1933).

recognizance: A bond recorded with a magistrate guaranteeing the appearance of a person in court under penalty of forfeiting the bond; also a promise to carry out the same program.

recommittal: To send a bill back to the committee from which it originated.

reconstruction: Though possible of application to any situation where a nation needs to be rebuilt, the usual use is in regard to the period following the Civil War (1867-1877) when the Reconstruction Act was passed by Congress which divided the South into military districts, delayed the readmission of the states of the Confederacy into the Union and allowed the application of martial law (q.v.). This severe program, advocated by the Radical Republicans (q.v.) was a reversal of the lenient position taken by Abraham Lincoln and accounts for much of the bitterness long active among the Southerners. It also explains the political phenomena of the "Solid South" (q.v.) and accounts partially for the Southern attitude toward the Negro.

Reconstruction Finance Corporation: This government-owned corporation was chartered in 1932, and is managed by a Board of five Directors appointed by the president. The purpose of the agency was to "make temporary advances upon proper securities to established industries, railways, and financial institutions, which cannot otherwise secure credit, and where such advances will protect the credit structure and stimulate employment." The original two billion dollars of loans undoubtedly saved many banks, insurance, and railroad companies from bankruptcy and thus did keep many people employed and savings safe; however, there would be those who would question whether its functions were as valuable in the 1940's. It has loaned over twenty billion during its existence, but recent legislation has reduced its loaning capacity to one and a half billion with the expectation of ultimate dissolution.

recruiting: Getting individuals to join the armed services through voluntary enlistments. Also applied to the full process for obtaining a competent staff of public employees by means of the work of the Civil Service Commission.

"red-baiting": Criticism of Communists with the expectation that they will "growl" in return and perhaps inadvertently reveal information usable for the anticommunists' purposes.

rediscounting: A system of advancing money on a promissory note before it matures by taking out the interest in advance. In usual banking practice, a local bank may discount a loan made to an individual and then send the note, with other commercial paper, to the Federal Reserve Bank of that district to be rediscounted, that is, to have an additional "fee" deducted so that the local bank may "thaw out" the credit it has extended. This is an attractive opportunity because the local bank then has additional funds to make further loans, at a discount which is its profit. The ability to do this provides the "elastic currency" (q.v.) which is the primary asset of the Federal Reserve System (q.v.).

redistricting: The creation of new districts following the reapportionment of Representatives in Congress according to which a state may be divided into a larger or smaller number of Congressional districts. The same process may apply to state senatorial, or assembly or judicial districts that have to be redrawn.

redress of grievances: *See* RIGHT OF ASSEMBLY.

red tape: Rigid observation of official routine. The term probably originated from the practice of tying up official paper with a piece of red tape.

refer to committee: Bills after being officially introduced into a legislature are then referred to the appropriate committee. For the Congress of the United States this is not always an easy task. Many bills may possibly be considered by more than one committee and the possible reception that might be accorded the bill there might influence the referral. Occasionally the bill may be recalled from one committee and be re-referred to another.

referee: An official or umpire appointed by the court to report regarding some legal controversy.

referendum: In an effort to extend the participation of the voter in the legislative process, many states require that there be a popular vote on a bill already passed by the legislature. Practically every state requires such a vote on a constitutional amendment; many require it also to authorize a new bond issue, or for salary increases of government officials.

reformatory: A penal institution for imprisonment and rehabilitation of young or first offenders or those not found impossible to correct.

refund: A repayment of a portion of a tax to an individual who had paid in excess, or return of a contractual obligation paid in excess also.

regimentation: A characteristic of a totalitarian regime or of state socialism where education, cultural activities, and political life is forced to conform to narrow patterns under a central authority.

regionalism: An administrative program geared to an in-between level between that of the national government and the local, municipal or state level. This level has developed with the increasing complexity of government, and the need for broader cooperation, and the carefully integrated planning of large projects which usually represent a bigger issue than sectionalism. The Tennessee Valley Authority would be an example, but the rise of the so-called "metropolitan areas" (q.v.) illustrates another aspect of the program.

"regional pacts": Agreements binding certain areas to mutual aid, as in the North Atlantic Treaty Organization (q.v.), or the Act of Chapultepec (q.v.).

register of deeds: An administrative county official who records all deeds, mortgages, and land contracts, and any other matters relating to title of land.

registry: The listing or record of a ship regulated by a particular country.

regressive tax: A tax which puts a heavier burden on a low income group. This may be accomplished through a sales tax or a uniform income tax, because either will be taking a bigger proportion of the small income available to the low income group than of those earning more.

rehabilitation: The work of preparing crippled and disabled persons to earn a living. The National Rehabilitation Act of 1920 provides for federal funds to match state endeavors along this line, with the Veterans Administration doing a tremendous job since World War II.

relocation centers: After the Japanese attack of December 7, 1941, thousands of aliens of Japanese ancestry and their American-born children were evacuated from the West Coast and detained in interior areas called relocation centers. Many were forced to get rid of their businesses and though some were able to obtain part time employment at the various centers to which they were assigned many suffered considerable financial loss as well as physical inconvenience. Under the War Relocation Authority loyal Americans were eventually released upon investigation.

remand: Return to custody as an accused person.

"Remember Pearl Harbor": An American slogan used during World War II to remind the public of the unexpected attack made by the Japanese upon Pearl Harbor, the United States naval base in the Hawaiian Islands, on December 7, 1941, while peaceful negotiations were going on in Washington between Japanese and American high officials.

"Remember the Alamo": The battle-cry of the Texans in their struggle for independence from Mexico in 1836. In a preliminary fight a garrison of Texans had been massacred in defending themselves in the Alamo, a mission of San Antonio.

"Remember the Maine": An American battle-cry of the Spanish American War. The explosion of the battleship "Maine" in the harbor of Havana, though for a long time not fully explained, fanned into flame the resentment of American and Cuban patriots over the treatment accorded those seeking a more democratic government for Cuba in 1898.

remission: Suspension of all or part of a fine or penalty.

removal from office: The possibility of dismissal from office varies with the position of the individual concerned. Elected executive and legislative office holders may be removed by impeachment (q.v.). Cabinet members are subject to removal by the President because he is held responsible for the carrying out of the work of the executive departments, it is assumed he must have the right of removal of those with whom he is not satisfied. He may not, however, remove members of quasi-judicial or quasi-legislative boards like the Federal Trade Commission, or judges who hold office during good behavior. With these exceptions, and those officials holding office under the Merit System (q.v.), the President may remove any civil officer at any time and for any reason without explanation.

rent control: *See* HOUSING EXPEDITER.

reparations: Money or payments in kind (as lumber, coal, iron) demanded of a defeated power for damages done during a war. *See* DAWES PLAN.

repatriation: The opportunity to regain one's citizenship.

"reported out": When a committee has approved a bill sent to it after the first or perfunctory reading in the legislature, and it is ready to be considered by that body it is then said to be "reported out," that is ready for discussion.

Representative-at-large: When a state legislature fails to provide for redistricting after additional seats have been apportioned to it, one or more Representative-at-large is assigned to it. Each voter in that state therefore votes in his own district for his own Representative and then casts an additional ballot for the candidate at large, who serves the regular two-year term. This condition continues until the state is finally redistricted.

reprieve: Suspension of the execution of a sentence. An action that may be performed by a chief executive.

reproduction cost: The money required to purchase new equipment to replace old or worn out parts at the current prices. The determination of such costs has played an important part in the fixing of railroad rates, where a very large fixed overhead cost is involved and where "original" costs were quite low, partly due to allowances made to some lines to meet the heavy expenses of transcontinental building in the late 1860's, and where the states donated tracts of land for the right of way. The issue actually reached the Supreme Court in the O'Fallon case in 1929. A question arose as to the value of the property of the St. Louis and O'Fallon Railroad which the company claimed had been found too low because reproductive costs were not calculated at the current rates. The Court agreed that due consideration had to be given to the current costs in determining the "reproductive" costs.

Republican Party: With the slavery issue splitting the two political parties of the late 1850's, Northern Democrats and Northern Whigs joined with the Free Soilers (q.v.) and abolitionists to establish the Republican Party, whose first Presidential candidate, Abraham Lincoln, won in 1860 because of the split in the opposition. The Party became in the 1890's the representative of the rising business interests of the East, of the sound money supporters, and of those who favored the benefits of a protective tariff; the same interests who chose to follow a "Back to Normalcy" program under Harding, and a "chicken in every pot" slogan under Hoover in 1928. Since then as an opposition party they have advocated less government in business, and fewer curbs on business, particularly wanting to limit the extension of the New Deal and Fair Deal (q.v.) programs of the Democrats.

repudiation: Refusal to honor an obligation. A political candidate may attempt to repudiate the support of certain groups. For many liberals support by the Communists is looked upon as the "kiss of death."

requisition: An order or request, as for supplies by a government agency or department; also the right assumed by a belligerent to seize enemy property upon the demand of a commander of an invading force.

rescind: To make void or repeal as of a law.

reservation: A condition or qualification. The Senate in 1926 listed a series of reservations under which it would join the World Court, which were rejected as constituting too much favoritism toward the United States.

Reserve Officers Training Corps (ROTC): A student organization for college men to provide military training financed by federal funds.

reserve ratio: The amount of cash which a bank keeps on hand in proportion to the amount of deposits it has on hand at the same time. This proportion is expressed by a percentage determined by cash divided by deposits. The amount of this percentage must be high enough to cover expected withdrawals by depositors and low enough to permit the bank the maximum amount of funds to invest. It is fixed for national banks by the Federal Reserve Board and has been as high as 26%, and may vary with state banks in accord with their local practices.

Resettlement Administration: This agency whose work is now done by the Federal Department of Agriculture functioned independently during a period of crisis from 1935 to 1937 in order to provide relief for farmers suffering from devastation in the "Dust Bowl" (q.v.) area. Its primary job involved the removal of destitute or low-income families from "rural slums" such as shacks located on deserted hillsides, in cut-over timber areas, and in areas ravaged by flood or erosion. This rehabilitation included establishment of several model towns, built to provide employment, but also to indicate how slum clearance could lead to amazing improvement in the area. Greenbelt, Washington, Greenhills, Cincinnati, and Greendale, Milwaukee, were started as such government projects, though now largely privately owned through government loans and grants. Large residential blocks, five times as large as a city square, have been established, with the center a small park and a network of paths and underpasses, make a safe and healthy area.

residual powers: Also called residuary powers, these include all the powers not specifically granted to Congress by the United

States Constitution, or prohibited to the States, and are specifically reserved to the States by the Tenth Amendment. By the loose interpretation of the Constitution (q.v.) the power of the Federal government seems to have been expanded at the expense of the States by means of the interstate commerce and conservation provisions particularly. However, it is interesting to note that the States have very carefully retained the right to administer such laws as the "welfare" provisions of the Social Security Law (q.v.), which only permits grants-in-aid to be paid under certain circumstances, if the States desire to satisfy them. Also the Unemployment provisions of that same law are administered exclusively through the States. In many other fields the States have jealously protected their residual rights, as in education, though willing to accept grants for agricultural and vocational education.

"restraining orders": Orders to stop an employer or a union from performing some action which the National Labor Relations Board (q.v.) has held to be an unfair practice.

restricted area: A portion of the country to which there is limited access by the general public. Areas surrounding centers of atomic research are subjected to varying degrees of restriction. In local matters there may also be reference to a district which is restricted by zoning regulations as to the types of business that may be carried out there.

Resumption Act: A measure written to go into effect by 1879 by which the greenbacks issued to finance the Civil War and without any backing, were to have a fund provided to change them from fiat (q.v.) money to "sound" money. Though over a hundred million dollars was to be set aside to redeem the greenbacks, and though greenbacks were in circulation in excess of that amount, so great was public confidence in them that none were offered for redemption.

retrenchment: The cutting down on expenses or on the number of officers in a bureau or a government agency in order to save money.

retroactive legislation: Laws made to apply to situations which were not considered criminal when they were originally committed. They are contrary to the Federal Constitution. Retroactive pay may be authorized under some circumstances as when an arrangement is made with a union under which a pay increase is made effective as of an earlier date, usually the date on which a former contract expired.

"Return to Normalcy": An expression used to refer to the period of the Harding administration (1920-1921) meaning the readjustments to be made in the period following World War I, and probably to some extent referring to the return to the conservatism of the Republican business interests in contrast to the Democratic "New Freedom" of the Wilson administration.

revolving fund: A special fund accumulated for some definite purpose which is self-liquidating; for example the fund originally loaned by the Federal government for irrigation purposes which was returned as the land became fertile and profitable.

"rider": A supplementary measure which is attached to a more important piece of legislation, usually of unrelated subject matter. Since the Reorganization Act of 1946 riders may not be attached to appropriation bills, a practice which had been popular in the past, for it was usually imperative to have the money bill passed and the rider was accepted with it, even though there might be widespread disagreement with it.

rigged market: A term used in regard to stock market operations meaning that certain investors have arranged by the release of rumors or false information to have certain stocks rise or fall in price as they desire. Such practices are more or less impossible today under the Securities Exchange supervision.

right of assembly and petition: The First Amendment of the Federal Constitution guarantees the right of people to peaceably assemble to petition for redress of grievances. This principle is based on old English law which provided for relief from injustice imposed by government.

right of entry: An assessor may enter upon real property at any reasonable time to ascertain the character of the property for tax purposes; fire department officials may also enter upon the property in order to carry out their functions properly.

right of way: A right to pass over land owned by another. It may be obtained by the state's exercise of eminent domain.

Robinson-Patman Act of 1926: This law was passed in order to impose a curb upon the preferential treatment which was being given to the large chain store buyers, by those supplying them, in relation to the prices paid by independent merchants. The supporters of the measure in Congress felt the financially large wholesalers had been discriminating in setting higher prices for small retail merchants than those charged to large concerns, even allowing for price reductions based on economies due to greater efficiency in large scale production. It was felt the lower rates were obtained not as a matter of justice, but because they were able "to throw their weight around," and to introduce subterfuges such as false brokerage and fraudulent advertising allowances as means of price discrimination. They claimed that quantity discounts (q.v.) must be regulated so that concerns of tremendous purchasing power may not drive out of business everyone in the same line of business as himself.

rotation in office: Jackson particularly supported the idea that long continuance in office often caused men to become careless and corrupt and therefore to change those in office frequently was a cornerstone of Jacksonian democracy (q.v.), which claimed that the duties of public office should be simple and all citizens should have an equal right to hold office. The view of the opposition at that time was that this procedure was really a phase of the "Spoils System" (q.v.), because after Jackson's election as president in 1828 he speedily turned out his opponents from office to place his victorious followers.

rubber stamp, to be a: This means that one performs certain actions without questioning the value of the act, or to follow blindly a leader whose authority one does not challenge.

"rugged individualism": An expression used to indicate the right of an individual in a capitalistic society to start a new enterprise without government interference, and to express his personal opinions or convictions in whatever field of activity he pleases without fear of reprisals or of government censorship.

"rule of reason": This expression refers to a modification in the application of the federal government's antitrust program, so that a combination in restraint of trade would not be curbed for merely being big—but for the unfair practices in which it engaged. That is, the law would be interpreted to apply to "unreasonable restraint" rather than just "combinations in restraint of trade" as stated in the original Sherman Antitrust Law (q.v.). Even with the introduction of the "rule of reason" there were uncertainties remaining in the enforcement of the curbs on monopoly so that the Clayton Antitrust Law was passed in 1914 to further make clear the exact unfair practices prohibited; and the Federal Trade Commission (q.v.) was created to go still further in protecting the public from harmful practices or monopoly.

Rules Committee: This committee is one of the nineteen standing committees of the House of Representatives and plays an important part in directing its activity by giving precedence to particular measures, by limiting time for debate, or by fixing the number of amendments, or just keeping a measure bottled up if no "rule" (or green light) is given. Even an attempt to stop such "stalling" by the Rules Committee by means of a House vote in 1949, when a limit of twenty-one days was put in effect, was later rescinded in 1951, and this committee's power remains undisputed. As the matter now stands, the chairman of a committee can force action after the Committee on Rules has delayed for twenty-one days, *if* he can get the Speaker to recognize him.

run-off primaries: When there have been more than three candidates nominated in a primary, in order to insure one of them gaining a sufficient number of votes to obtain a majority many states require a second primary vote to be held. In this "run-off" primary the two candidates who had the highest and next highest vote are the only competitors. This type of primary is more common in the Southern states where there is practically a one-party system and success in gaining the nomination assures one of the election.

Rural Electrification Authority: Since 1936 under various acts the federal government has attempted to promote construction of electric lines to serve the farm population. Loans are made at very low interest rates and allowed to run for thirty-five years. Loans are also made for wiring farm homes and for the purchase of electrical appliances and telephones. By 1949 over one and a half billion dollars had been loaned to bring electricity to some three million rural dwellings.

"rural slums": It was discovered that bad housing conditions could exist as well in country areas as in the cities, and in recognition of this fact a Farm Housing Act was passed in 1949 which arranged for loans for home building under generous terms requiring thirty-three years for repayment at only four percent interest.

rurban centers: In the discussion of community subdivisions, a new term has come into use to describe an area which is somewhere between the agricultural village with a farm-centered population and a small city. It combines the least arduous aspects of rural life with some of the attractions of urban living with some industrial activity with a population range of from four to twenty thousand.

S

sabotage: Deliberate destruction, more commonly in an attempt to interfere with industrial production, as part of a program of radical labor groups, or as a result of personal resentment. Sabotage was also used by secret underground groups as part of their campaign against the enemy in enemy-occupied territories. The term came into use in the early stages of the Industrial Revolution from the action of some of the peasants, who, fearful of being thrown out of work by the newly introduced machines, tossed their wooden shoes (sabots) into the newly invented machinery in order to wreck it, thus naïvely hoping to hold back industrial progress.

safe districts: An election district where a candidate is quite sure of reelection, with the result that the candidate may conduct his campaign with rather close regard for the national party issues. However, if the district is not a "safe" one then the candidate must trim his sails to the program of the special groups he wants to win over, making concessions to labor or industry as the case may require. As a result of all this temporizing the successful candidate, when he reaches Congress, may not respond well to party leadership and be subjected to some disciplinary action such as threats of the loss of some patronage benefits.

safety education: A program now being carried out in many schools, plants, clubs, and similar organizations, to make clear the dangers involved in certain situations and how they may be minimized, stressing the reason why accidents arise, so that they may be more easily avoided.

St. Lawrence Waterway: One result of the creation of the proposed St. Lawrence Waterway besides the extensive power production planned would be the making of the river navigable to Great Lake ports for large ocean-going vessels. Congress, recognizing perhaps the effect on Atlantic ports like New York, has never seen fit to appropriate the money for our share of the construction costs. Whether the Canadian announcement in the summer of 1952 that she would start construction alone will bring action on the part of the United States is very problematical. With the "War" in Korea still on, and the need to assist in the rearming of Europe still competing for scarce materials, there is also a basis for postponement in the claim that such construction should be kept for a period of unemployment.

sales tax: A general tax on specified commodities, it has been in use since 1921, the use increasing rather widely following the depression of 1929. Few states have adopted it since 1937. Twenty-seven were using it up to 1950. It has proved highly productive, yielding in 1948 over a billion and a quarter dollars.

Samoa: The American portion of Samoa was obtained as a protectorate for the United States by an Anglo-German-American Agreement in 1899; full recognition was not accorded until 1929. The group is located about 5,000 miles southwest of California and consists of five islands including Tutuila representing 76 square miles of territory with a population of 18,000 (1950). They are valuable as naval and air stations and are administered by the Navy.

sanctions: Penalties applied against those who break the law. More specifically, the term is associated with the means provided through the League of Nations to curb the action of an aggressor. Article XVI of the Covenant stated that sanctions could be imposed against member states resorting to war without submitting their case to arbitration. All member states in the League were to sever all trade and financial relations with the offending country. This program was partially attempted against Italy in 1935 but proved quite inadequate. The United Nations Charter has provision (Chapter Eight) for the use of sanctions in a similar manner in like circumstances.

sanitary code: This list of laws defines the duties of citizens in matters of health and sanitation in such cases as waste disposal, food inspection, quarantine and related subjects.

satellite: A small nation wholly dominated by a large power. The term has been used particularly in regard to nations under the domination of the Soviet Union such as Bulgaria, Hungary or Czechoslovakia. The Soviet officials counter this reference by finding the Latin American satellites of the United States.

savings bank: A bank which carries out only one of the usual functions of a bank, that of receiving deposits. These deposits are usually subject to some form of regulation. New York State limits the amount in any one account to $10,000 and restricts the type of investment the banks may make with such funds and the amount of cash reserves to be kept available typical of the type of supervision imposed by most state authorities.

scalawag: A Southerner who took advantage of the confusion of the "Reconstruction Era" to act with the carpetbagger of the North to exploit conditions for his advangtage in the new state legislatures. *See* RECONSTRUCTION.

scape-goating: A device used by propagandists in which an individual, group or race is cited as the reason for the frustrations of those to whom the propaganda is addressed. Hitler could use the Jews in Germany with a double effectiveness, though with much inconsistency by attacking them as being communists and urging the overthrow of capitalism, while at the same time attacking them for the large business interests they controlled, particularly in international banking fields.

school lunch program: The Federal Government contributes money and surplus commodities to the schools of the nation as part of the grant-in-aid program to provide hot and nourishing lunches, where in so many cases it was found to be the only really adequate meals some children received.

Scientific Management: The effort of industrial engineers and managers to apply methods of science to the production of commodities. They stress that rules-of-thumb should be superseded by investigation and analysis with the development of standards based upon research. Frederick Taylor advocated this program both for the interest of the workman as well as of the employer, though labor resented at first the various "efficiency" devices.

Seabury Committee: An investigating committee appointed by Franklin D. Roosevelt while still Governor of New York State in 1932 to look into the question of maladministration in New York City government, as the result of which Mayor James J. Walker resigned. The influence of Tammany Hall was lessened and finally a new city charter was proposed whose eventual ratification did a great deal to reform the government in the city. Former Judge Seabury was the chairman.

search warrant: Documentary evidence of the right to enter and search a man's home or place of business, provided the warrant has been properly authorized and bears the name and address of the individual involved, with a statement of the purpose for entering and a description of the material to be removed. A warrant is not required if an officer sees or knows that a crime is being committed or is in "hot pursuit" of one who has just committed a crime.

seasonal employment: Employment dependent upon the condition of the weather as in the building trades, or canning of produce, or in the preparation of certain clothing. Attempts are being made to combine activities to provide a more equal degree of employment, as coal miner doing some farming at appropriate times. *See* SUBSISTENCE FARMING.

secondary boycott: A refusal of workers in one plant to handle work or goods produced by an outside employer who is involved in a labor dispute already. The effect of this curtailment is to limit the amount of work done in an establishment that has no direct labor grievance with its workers and therefore it has been held an unfair labor practice under the Taft-Hartley Law.

Secretariat (United Nations): Under the leadership of the Secretary General, this agency represents the force that does the routine clerical work, carries on the correspondence and does the necessary research, and performs much administrative detail to keep so active an international organization working properly. Drawn from the sixty or more nations members of various organizations of the United Nations, these employees constitute the equivalent of an "international civil service."

Secretary of State of New York: An appointed official now but one who was elected when New York was burdened with a long ballot; he has charge of the records and papers of the state and issues charters to corporations.

sectarianism: Though basically referring only to the actual existence of a religious group with peculiarities of faith and practice and representing a significant aspect of American culture, the connotation of this term implies some degree of bigotry and isolationism because many religious minorities retain their separate identities.

Sectionalism: Excessive devotion to a particular geographical area or state at the expense of national interest. Regionalism would be the equivalent situation in a European district, but in the United States the practice developed especially after the War of 1812, when a temporary wave of Nationalism subsided and left the sections, East, West, and South, severely divided over the tariff question, the United States Bank, internal improvements at federal expense, and led finally to the greatest cleavage of all, on the slavery issue to the Civil War.

Securities Exchange Commission: An independent, quasi-judicial agency of the United States government created by the Securities and Exchange Act in 1934, to protect the interests of the public and investors from unfair practices, such as misleading information about stock issues, or the offering for sale of valueless stock.

Security Council: The Security Council is one of the major agencies of the United Nations consisting of eleven members five of whom are the permanent members, United States, United Kingdom, Union of Socialist Soviet Republics, France and China. The six non-permanent members are elected for two years with three chosen each year. The Council's primary job is to curb aggression by proposing arbitration or by the threat of using sanctions against the aggressor nation. On strategic matters the vote must include the affirmative of all five of the permanent members. It is here that the USSR has asserted its influence most by its ability to block proposed action by means of the veto. For a method of trying to get around this situation *see* LITTLE ASSEMBLY.

sedition: Sedition, publishing, or uttering words deemed to encourage resistance to law or disrespect for the government, though closely related to treason (q.v.), is not so closely limited by definition in the Constitution, and Congress may decide what acts it considers seditious and what sort of punishment it wishes to impose. By the Act of 1798 severe penalties were imposed upon those who wrote or printed false or malicious statements concerning the President, or Congress. However, in many cases editors were imprisoned because they criticized the partisan activities of the President or Congress rather than the government in general. A great reaction to these arrests resulted in the defeat of the Federalists in 1800, and the repeal of the law was speedily carried out by Jefferson, who also released the unfortunate editors.

The Sedition Law of 1918 led to many arrests of mere "crackpots" who thoughtlessly sounded off about some action of the government in war time. The test of guilt in World War II was usually based on the answer to the question, "Did the accused write or utter a statement that was able to cause direct and serious interference with the conduct of the war?" In 1950 the Alien Registration is looked upon by some as equivalent to a "Sedition" Law in its restrictions on free expression lest one be held "subversive."

segregation: Though the word means cutting off of one group from another it has been generally accepted in the United States as referring to racial segregation, that is the cutting off of Negroes from freely mingling with white persons in schools, waiting rooms, theatres or transportation facilities. Supreme Court decisions have held some of these actions not to be discriminatory if equal provision is made for white and colored groups; but public opinion is probably ahead of the courts in feeling that segregation is out of line with full democratic practice. An interesting trend might be noticed in the fact that the legitimate theatres in Washington, D. C., reopened in 1952 without segregation after having been closed for many years because the unions involved would not permit their members to perform where segregation was observed.

Selective Service: A renewal of the war time act which expired in 1947 was passed by Congress in 1948. Those eligible were all males from 18-26 though various exemptions were established: those students still in high school had until they were twenty to finish, and college students who took certain qualifying examinations could remain in college as long as their work was satisfactory.

selectmen: New England towns are governed by a group of officials among whom are usually three selectmen elected for from one to three years. They have general supervisory powers and financial duties at which they are assisted by other town officials, such as the tax collector, the assessors, or the treasurer. See TOWN MEETING.

self-liquidating project: A government undertaking for which fees may be charged which will in time not only pay for the operating expenses but cover the cost of construction, so that ultimately the services will be free to the public. Bridges, irrigation projects, or highways may qualify under these arrangements.

Senate: The upper house of the United States Congress, which consists of two members from each state with a total membership of ninety-six since the admission of Arizona as the 48th state of the Union. Members were chosen by the state legislature until the Seventeenth Amendment (q.v.) was passed in 1913 which provided for popular election. The term is for six years. Vacancies may be filled by temporary appointment or by special elections. The vice-president presides when available but in his absence, or upon his accession to the presidency, a president pro tempore (q.v.) is elected. The Senate has special duties in approving presidential appointments, ratifying treaties, and conducting the trial in impeachment proceedings, all by means of a two-thirds vote. It also may determine the vice-president in case of a failure on the part of the electoral college. In other respects its duties are coequal with the House in the passing of laws, proposing amendments and similar duties.

"Senatorial courtesy": A custom has developed according to usage that no nomination of any official will be confirmed in the Senate unless the nominee is satisfactory to the Senators (from the President's party) from the state in which the office is to be filled.

seniority in standing committees of Congress: Chairmanship of the committees of Congress goes automatically to the member of the House or Senate who has held office longest regardless of ability, reputation, or leadership, in the party. A much regretted situation arose when Senator Reynolds, by seniority, became head of the Military Affairs Committee despite the fact that he had openly opposed the national defense program and had voted against extending the Selective Service Act in 1941.

separation of church and state: At the time of the American Revolution there was some reason to fear that the Established Church of England was to have a stronger hold in the New World when the other economic and political controls had been successfully tightened. With this background in mind, the Constitutional Convention in 1787 made very clear in the resulting Constitution that there was to be no tie-up, direct or indirect, between the state and any particular church. No government funds were to be paid to any privileged institution. Religious tests were not to be imposed to hold office. So great has been the fear that this policy might be encroached upon that schools have been challenged for compulsory Bible reading, or for the use of prayers in the assembly program. A bitter controversy arose as to whether parochial school children were entitled to the same privileges accorded other school children who were crippled in the use of school city-owned busses or should receive the benefits of the school health program established by federal grants-in-aid.

separation of powers: The recognition that the Constitution of the United States has created three distinct branches of government: executive, legislative, and judicial. Though each has separate identity and need make no attempt to dominate the other, they are not fully separated in practice. There are exceptions where there is an overlapping of powers for the President's appointing power, as chief executive, requires legislative confirmation by means of a senate approval; and laws passed by Congress may be declared unconstitutional by "judicial review" (q.v.). The system of checks and balances is sometimes confused with the separation of powers, but they are different; checks may operate exclusively within one branch of the government, as the House serving as a check upon the Senate. Though the idea of separation of powers originated from European sources, Montesquieu advocated it in his "Spirit of Laws" in the middle of the eighteenth century, European governments do not observe the practice. The British Parliament not only has legislative functions, but with the requirement that the cabinet be selected from those elected to Parliament, it attains executive authority, and through its ability to try certain cases and pardon has judicial functions also. This was looked upon with disfavor by those writing the Constitution of the United States, so an attempt at separation was undertaken particularly with the provision that American cabinet members must not be members of Congress.

sergeant at arms: An officer but not a member of Congress. A police officer who attends continually all sessions to maintain order and decorum. He disburses the pay of members and accounts for their mileage allowances. He may arrest absent members on warrants from the Speaker. He may bring any person to Congress if so ordered. The mace is his symbol of authority.

seriatim: One after another in connected order serially.

service rating: A record of the proficiency, qualifications, rights, and other pertinent material of a Civil Service employee usually retained in the Service Records of the Civil Service Commission. A like record is kept of a member of the armed forces.

settlement houses: Buildings through which a program intended to bring some relief to the dwellers of slum areas was organized. A few of the most famous include Hull House, founded by Jane Adams in Chicago, and the Henry Street Settlement of New York City with which Lillian Wald was associated, besides Kingsley House in New Orleans, and Hiram House in Cleveland. Club activities, social-service work, child care, courses in home economics, represent a few of the fields of activity undertaken in these places in an attempt to do something to improve the conditions in the neighborhood for the children whose homes often have so little to offer.

Seventeenth Amendment: An amendment to the Constitution of the United States ratified in February 1913 which provides for the election of two United States Senators from each state for the six-year term. Those entitled to vote are those who were previously qualified to vote for the most numerous house of the State legislatures. It further provides that when vacancies occur in the Senate "the executive authority of such State shall issue writs of election to fill such vacancies: Provided, That the legislature of any State may empower the executive thereof to make temporary appointments, until the people fill the vacancies by election as the legislature may direct." The demand for such a change from permitting the State legislatures to do the selecting of the Senators had been an often repeated demand of Populists (q.v.) and illustrates the way in which a Third Party program becomes accepted by the major parties in time.

Seventh Amendment: One of the first ten amendments to the Constitution of the United States added as part of the "Bill of Rights" in 1791. In suits at common law, where the value in controversy shall exceed twenty dollars, the right of trial by jury shall be preserved, and no fact tried by a jury shall be otherwise re-examined in any court of the United States, than according to the rules of the common law.

severance tax: A tax placed upon natural resources such as timber when cut, or coal when mined. The purpose of the tax is to prevent waste of our natural resources and as a means to regulate output. Some states exempt forest land from taxation as long as timber remains standing on it. Others make the tax less where natural resources are protected, but in most cases they will impose this severance tax when the natural resource is removed, thus indirectly assisting in the Conservation Movement.

shake down: The paying of what amounts to a bribe on the part of a business man or householder to a minor official of a local government, or of a union usually to avoid the consequences of petty annoyances for infractions of city ordinances, or for fear of more serious reprisals for "non-cooperation."

share cropper: An agricultural worker, usually in the South, who received for his labor on a given piece of land a share of the crop. Against this allowance was deducted the credit extended to him during the raising and marketing of the crop, and other debits such as fertilizers, or ginning expenses, if, as was usual, the crop was cotton. Under this system the worker had a very small cash return. The soil was given little care and a "money" crop was produced with frequent surpluses and consequent drop in price. The remedy proposed was the Bankhead-Jones Farm Tenant Act which arranged for reliable individuals to buy land on generous terms with forty years to pay and low interest rates. Better preservation of the land and diversified farming has brought a higher standard of living and better purchasing power has aided industry also.

share-the-wealth program: The program sponsored by Huey Long to "make every man a king" by means of equalizing the distribution of wealth by heavy inheritance taxes, higher wages and shorter working hours. So great was the popular appeal of this program that the Long machine had no difficulty electing their boss to the United States Senate and was aiming for considerable influence in the Democratic Party when checked by the death of their leader.

Sherman Antitrust Act: By 1890 public opinion was so aroused over the question of monopolistic practices that remedial legislation was demanded. This was afforded to some extent by the Sherman Antitrust Act. It contains the statement that "Every contract, combination or conspiracy in restraint of trade or commerce among the several States is hereby declared illegal." Fine or imprisonment were provided for violation of these prohibitions. Good as the intentions of the law makers were, the government won no suits against any "combination" until 1902, and it took a rewriting of the law in 1914 to provide a more effective measure of regulation under the Clayton Act (q.v.).

short ballot: A short ballot is one where only a few names appear on the list such as governor, lieutenant-governor, comptroller or auditor, attorney-general, State Senator, and a member of the lower house of the state legislature. All the remaining positions would either be filled by Civil Service or by executive appointments. The argument for the short ballot rests on the point that only those officers should be elected who are important enough to attract and deserve public examination, and that very few offices should be filled by election at any one time in order to permit adequate and unconfused public examination.

short-term borrowing: This represents a practice of city or state or national governments desirous of temporary financing for short periods of time by using notes, bills, and certificates of indebtedness which run for thirty or sixty days to a year or two.

shyster lawyer: A lawyer who will resort to any trick to enrich himself and take advantage of his poor or helpless clients earns the title of shyster. Some such lawyers may bribe the police to notify them when arrests are made, or pay jailers a fee for every case they can get for these unscrupulous but often poorly trained lawyers. "Ambulance-chasers" give them information about accident cases, which they may then take up in return for a promise of one-half of any award won for the victim. The most notorious of these men may be expelled from the bar but many are too clever for that but skirt so close to the edge that they retain practically no standards of professional ethics.

silk-stocking district: A way of referring to an election district containing a large number of wealthy voters.

sinecure: A well paid job that requires little work, the type formerly awarded to active party men for services rendered.

sine die: Without fixing a day for reassembly. Congress may adjourn sine die, but it need cause no concern, for the Twentieth Amendment provides that Congress shall meet once a year on January third.

single tax: A name used to describe a program originally introduced by Henry George about the 1880's, by which a payment resembling rent would be paid by the owner of land to the government in lieu of any other form of taxation. This payment it was assumed would be adequate to meet all the necessary activities of the government, and would be owed because the increased value of the land was in most cases not due to the individual efforts of the owner, but to the growth of the community that had made his land more valuable. The supporters of this program are still active in its behalf, recommending particularly the point that it would discourage the withholding of land from unproductive use, while waiting for it to enhance in value, because of the universal application of the "rent" requirement (tax) to be paid by the owner he could not afford to not use it; also the Georgists feel that their program is a very good defense against the spread of socialism.

sinking fund: When a city or state government has borrowed money by selling its bonds it must arrange to have enough money to cover them when they mature, therefore some funds from the yearly tax collections are set aside in the sinking fund which will be available to redeem the bonds.

sit-down strike: A type of strike originating in the rubber and automobile industries in 1937 where the workers did not leave the plant but remained at their places and refused to work. The question of legality arose on the basis of the possibility of being accused of trespassing, but the issue was not settled though the practice fell into disuse because of adverse public opinion.

Sixteenth Amendment to the United States Constitution: *See* INCOME TAX AMENDMENT.

Sixth Amendment: One of the first ten amendments added to the Constitution as the Bill of Rights in 1791. "In all criminal prosecutions, the accused shall enjoy the right to a speedy and public trial, by an impartial jury of the State and district wherein the crime shall have been committed, which district shall have been previously ascertained by law, and to be informed of the nature and the cause of the accusation; to be confronted with the witnesses against him; to have compulsory process for obtaining witnesses in his favor, and to have the assistance of counsel for his defense."

"slow down strike": A strike not formally called or authorized but used in cases of labor disagreements, so that the workers may most meticulously observe every letter of the regulations and thus, though actually working, take twice as long to do a specific job. "Going by the book," it is sometimes called, meaning the book of regulations.

slum area: A residential area in which the housing has deteriorated through age and mistreatment, or because of original substandard provision for adequate construction of hygienic equipment, or where narrow streets, or overcrowding of buildings, or where overshadowing warehouses or dumps or swamps exist.

slush fund: Money paid for the purpose of bribing opponents or improperly influencing public opinion.

small-claims courts: An increasing number of states are establishing inferior courts in municipalities where suits for small sums of money may be easily settled without need for expensive litigation, usually only a small fee being charged to bring the claim (as a rule for sums less than one hundred or less than fifty dollars) before the court, which ordinarily makes provision for enforcements of judgments.

Smith-Lever Act (1914): A law which established the Agricultural Extension Service which organizes educational, demonstrational and technical programs for reaching the farm population. Federal funds are supplied to the States for this purpose.

snow under: Political slang for a situation where a candidate has obtained a great quantity of votes at his opponent's expense.

soap box: To get on one's soap box means to make an impassioned speech, to harangue on political matters.

social agencies: Organizations, public or private, concerned with social welfare because the problem of helping the unfortunate has now become far greater than neighbors and relatives can handle. Examples of such agencies include: Salvation Army, YWCA, YMCA, Catholic Welfare League, Humane Society, and various old people's homes.

Socialism: Socialism in so far as it relates to government stands for a modification of the system of private ownership of property rather than its complete abandonment. Governments are vested with the ownership of important natural resources, such as coal deposits, iron mines, oil wells, utilities, telephone and electric companies. Socialism may also extend government ownership to certain key industries such as steel, cement, credit, banking, and insurance. Other property, farm land, residential areas, retail and wholesale markets and intangibles may remain in private hands. Herbert Morrison, speaking for British Socialism, stated that 20% of the field of business enterprise was covered by government ownership and it was expected the other 80% would remain private property.

Socialist Labor Party: A minor political party first created in 1877 through the activities of Daniel De Leon, a more doctrinaire, more dogmatic and more rigidly Marxian group than the Socialist Party with which it has never affiliated though advocating the abolition of the capitalist system and urging political organization of workers. It has always had a very small following.

Socialist Party: Originally a Social Democratic Party whose membership after suffering many schisms adopted the name Socialist in 1900. Groups had disagreed about opposition to war and on their attitude toward the Russian Revolution. They nominated Eugene V. Debs five successive times for the presidency of the United States. In 1912 and in 1920 he polled over 900,000 votes. In 1924 they supported Robert La Follette and have since nominated Norman Thomas six successive times. In recent times the more extreme "left wing" group wanting to have full government ownership of the means of production has lost some of its membership to the Communists, while the liberal group has lost some of its supporters to the New Deal program (q.v.) because of its attempts to extend social security, government power production, and its so-called welfare state (q.v.) proposals.

Social Security Act of 1939 and 1947: There are four major divisions under which the Social Security Act functions. By 1938 all the states had passed the necessary legislation to enable them to participate in the first part of the program, federal grants-in-aid for old age assistance. Each state may have a different system, but certain minority requirements are as follows: a person must be over sixty-five, and have insufficient means to support himself. The federal government contributes two-thirds of the first fifteen dollars paid by the state, and one-half up to the maximum of forty-five dollars (thirty dollars originally). The average payment to an individual is about forty-five dollars, though the range may vary from twenty to eighty dollars. Recipients make no contribution.

II. The other part of the program is handled directly by the federal government. A fund is built up by a payroll tax (q.v.) which started at one percent and now is 1½% on that part of the employee's salary up to $3600, and paid by both employer and employee. Coverage applies to all with the exception of those engaged in agriculture, government service, or employed by educational institutions, reaching it was estimated 35 million persons. Since 1950 legislation has been enacted to bring in another 10 million. Permanently located agricultural workers, household help, certain self-employed individuals are now eligible. Under this "Old Age and Survivors Insurance System" annuity payments may start at the age of 65. To obtain the maximum payment of $85 a person must have contributed for forty years at an annual wage of $3000. Since 1950 he might obtain as a family allowance $150 per month.

III. The other phase of the program is unemployment insurance (q.v.).

IV. The final phase of the Act provides for Child Welfare and is supervised by the state according to Federal Security Agency standards with the federal government assuming half the cost. The average monthly family payment is approximately $45. Aid for the blind and the handicapped is provided for under much the same terms.

Social Security Administration (United States): This agency administers the Social Security Law (q.v.), approves state plans for unemployment compensation and other types of state aid to social dependents and certifies grants-in-aid for this purpose. With the ever increasing scope of this law the Administration has assumed new and broader power.

socialized medicine: A phase of the social security program which would provide for medical and hospital services for all citizens under compulsory insurance. Much opposition has arisen in the United States for such a program largely because of the compulsion involved with some question as to the quality of the service under government administration. Full need for additional medical care has been conceded in most cases but stress is laid on the growth of voluntary methods of medical insurance under private supervision. *See* HEALTH INSURANCE PLAN.

Soil Conservation and Domestic Allotment Act: After the first Agricultural Adjustment Act (q.v.) of 1933 was found unconstitutional the need for benefits for the farm population was still felt to be as great as ever, therefore another measure for that purpose was introduced but to make sure of its constitutionality the emphasis was to be on conservation, since that side of the program had already been found constitutional under the general welfare provision of the Constitution. This measure was the S.C.A.D.A. of 1936 which provided for the payment of bounties for curtailed output which would incidentally raise prices but which more importantly shifts land from soil-depleting crops such as corn, cotton, tobacco, and wheat, to soil-conserving crops such as alfalfa, or clover, or to pasturage, or legumes. The goal of

SOCIAL CONSERVATION SERVICE 246

reducing the surpluses was not attained, it took the A.A.A. of 1938 (q.v.) to help further in that, but conservation made a good start, and farm income was raised somewhat.

Soil Conservation Service: This division of the Department of Agriculture has currently had over 2,000 soil conservation districts organized for demonstration purposes covering over a billion acres and concerned with over four million farms. The experts connected with this work find that much farm land has been "mined" not farmed and is good for little but planting trees or shrubs. From 1895-1930 they estimated that a full million acres of top soil was lost every year at a valuation of four billion dollars annually. Through these demonstration centers and other services of the Department, the rate of erosion has been considered to have been cut in half, but much more remains to be done.

Solicitor General: Attached to the Department of Justice is the office of the Solicitor General which is primarily concerned with representing the federal government in the Supreme Court. In order to present a case to support the constitutionality of some far-reaching law, marked ability and ingenuity are required. The Solicitor must also represent the interests of the United States in a State court where needed.

Solid South: An expression used to show that the South after the Reconstruction Period (1865-1875) turned away from the Republican Party completely and remained firmly in the Democratic column.

"South Carolina Plan": In a program to avoid the possibility of the application of the Federal Constitution to nominations as well as to the right of the individual to vote, this "Plan" has been suggested by which the states would rescind all laws for control of primaries, so as to transform political parties into private clubs to avoid any accusation of discrimination.

sovereignty: The supreme power of an independent government. It has been the fear of the loss of some of this power which has caused hesitation on the part of some nations to consent to possible diminution of it, by joining in collective security agreements or in other international organizations, where the nation would find itself committed to a program without having had a chance to vote for participation through their own legislatures.

In the monarchies the ruler is "sovereign" in name only, and in the democracies the sovereignty of the people is exercised for them by their elected representatives.

Speaker of the House: The Speaker of the House of Representatives is chosen by the majority party caucus (q.v.) and his election follows automatically in the House. He is a partisan officer and is replaced as soon as his party loses its party majority. His duties include the calling of the meeting together, the preserving of order and decorum, the signing of all official documents, and the acting as arbitrator on all points of parliamentary procedure, and most frequently the one who recognizes those who rise to speak.

special assessment: An additional tax paid by those real estate owners benefiting from a major, local public improvement and not collected from all land owners generally.

"special districts": More than two-thirds (over 100,000) of all government units in the nation are special districts. The Bureau of the Census lists seventeen functions that they may perform from fire protection, weed control, drainage, diking, navigation, sewers, cemeteries, to water supply. These special districts may be created for a single purpose, such as a school district, or they may be combined for a number of purposes. A board or commission, either elected or appointed, usually heads such districts, often including highly skilled members such as sanitary engineers, and may appoint their subordinate employees and raise their own operating funds. Critics of municipal and state governments often criticize the multiplicity of these districts considering that if the local units were properly consolidated much duplication and overlapping would be avoided.

specialization: A term often used as equal to "division of labor" recognizing a period in our economic development when certain craftsmen limited their production to a specific commodity while others "specialized" in other production, leading at first to the rise of the shoemaker, the tailor, the pottery maker and, today, to even more technical subdivisions.

special session: *See* EXTRA SESSION.

speech of acceptance: Formerly, the presidential nominee made his speech of acceptance when a month after the National

Convention had adjourned he was formally notified of his nomination. However, since Franklin D. Roosevelt in 1932 went before the Convention to give immediate acceptance that has been the procedure for Thomas E. Dewey and Harry S. Truman. In this speech the candidate customarily gives his views on the issues of the campaign and may stress or modify portions of the newly prepared platform.

spellbinder: A convention or campaign speaker who is most bombastic in his speech making, prone to make many oratorical flights of fancy and to hold a huge audience in the palm of his hand. William Jennings Bryan was supposed to have been able thus to spellbind his audience, especially with his famous "Cross of Gold" speech in the 1896 election campaign.

"split" primary: Some Southern states, in order to avoid a suit over the unconstitutionality of their practice of conducting "white" primaries, provide that the Negro may vote in the primaries to nominate federal office holders, but cannot vote in the other, or split primary which nominates the local and state officials. This practice was based on a Supreme Court decision that seemed to acknowledge that a political party was a private organization and could conduct its primaries as it pleased. Recently there has been some question as to whether the federal government may not regulate the system of nominations for the welfare of the individual as well as the elections.

split ticket: A ballot on which a voter has voted for candidates of more than one party. The opposite of a "straight" ticket (q.v.) so highly recommended by partisan politicians.

spoils system: A system of awarding office to party followers regardless of their ability to hold the job, but considering only their obligation to the party. To make room for the party appointee the holder of the position would be removed without consideration of service or efficiency. Many measures today having to do with Civil Service Reform (q.v.) have made such wholesale removals after a change of party impossible.

Square Deal: A slogan used to describe the program favored by Theodore Roosevelt who as a progressive Republican was favoring legislation to benefit the common man in his attack on the "malefactors of great wealth," in his "trust busting" campaign, in his stress on conservation and his defense of the Monroe Doctrine.

"Stab in the Back": President Roosevelt's reference to the action ordered by Mussolini for Italy to make war on France in the period of her dire distress in June 1940.

stalking horse: A candidate deliberately chosen in the interest of another candidate to divide the opposition, and to allow the second candidate thus to win.

Stalwarts: A title used to designate the regular faction of the Republican Party during Grant's administration as a contrast to the Liberal Republicans (q.v.). The Stalwarts were supposedly strongly in favor of their party as it was without any need for reform. *See* OLD GUARD.

standing committee: A committee appointed at the start of each new Congress, having jurisdiction over all bills which may be introduced concerning a specific subject matter. In the Senate the Legislative Reorganization Law of 1946 has reduced the number of standing committees from thirty-three to fifteen, and in the House from forty-eight to nineteen. Through the party caucus (q.v.) and the Committee on Committees every member of the House or Senate is assigned to some such committee. The individual committee membership varies from about twenty-five to thirty-three members. Some of the House Committees are: Ways and Means, Agriculture, Banking, Interstate Commerce, and Rules, with parallel committees established in the Senate making possible occasional joint action. The ratio of Democrats to Republicans for the committees is determined by the party ratio in the House or Senate. The seniority rule is rigidly applied in regard to the chairmanship of the committees. Though this rule, that the man or woman who has the longest period of uninterrupted service in the Congress gains the chairmanship, has been much criticized as rewarding the "stagnant" districts, and those least likely to follow a program that would bring defeat at the polls, no substitute proposal that would not have equally bad features has as yet been seriously considered.

standpatter: A term used to indicate the part of the Republican Party shortly after 1900 which was willing to "stand pat," that is, not agitate for reform. In opposition to this conservative position were the insurgents (q.v.) who as advocates of more progressive ideas were to lead later in the "Revolution of 1910," and later still to the creation of the Progressive Party (q.v.).

stare decisis: A Latin phrase meaning—adhere to the decisions. A principle of law establishing the importance of precedent, so that there is the presumption that the decision in the earlier case should govern the disposition of the later.

State aid: Subsidies or grants-in-aid apportioned by a State legislature to local subdivisions as a means of participating in the total state income. State aid for education is awarded to New York City on a special formula passed by the legislature and calculated on the attendance multiplied by a predetermined figure.

State Department: One of the four original cabinet positions, the department was created in 1789 to supervise foreign affairs; now some of its separate offices cover special areas such as the American republics, Europe, Far East and Africa, and the Near East, and special duties such as International Trade, Information, Intelligence and Research, Passport and Visa controls. The foreign service brings the long arms of the State Department to every capital and to every commercial center of every country recognized by the United States. Our chief representative is an ambassador or a minister, many of whom were formerly chosen as payment of a political debt, but in recent years there has been a tendency to appoint career diplomats (q.v.) who have worked their way up in the service.

state instrumentalities: The agencies or means of raising revenue by the states or federal government represents a jealously guarded prerogative. From the days of the famous decisions of the Supreme Court, such as McCulloch vs. Maryland (1819), the United States would not allow a state to tax one of its creations, the United States Bank, and the converse was also upheld. In the 1930's the federal government began to collect an income tax on those sources of state income which seemed to be remotely connected with the state's direct payments to individuals. Then came a general approval of the right of the federal government to collect taxes from the state-paid salaries. The long accepted dictum of John Marshall that "the power to tax was the power to destroy" seemed about to lapse if the federal government could tax the "instrumentalities" of the state. The interpretation became "might destroy but would not." Now federal employees pay a state income tax if their state collects one, and the employees of the state pay their federal income tax. Going still further in this direction it has been suggested that a federal tax be collected on privately owned state securities which have been held tax exempt, and that consistently the state be permitted to tax the yield on certain, as yet tax free, federal bonds.

"stateism": The practice of the federal government to legislate for the general welfare to such an extent that individual initiative is weakened through creating dependence on the government for providing many services, such as compulsory health insurance, or public works projects, or school lunches, is called by many "stateism" or state socialism. The issue usually follows political lines with the Republicans accusing the Democrats of advancing further and further into the danger zone leading toward socialism, and the Democrats countering with instances to show the "predatory" practices of big business which makes these regulatory efforts necessary. The debate usually ends on a note of inquiry from the Republicans as to what chance private enterprise is to have; and the Democratic plea as to what services, which the government is now providing, do they think they could dispense with?

statelessness: Those individuals, particularly displaced persons, who no longer owe loyalty to their mother country because of political changes which have occurred there, or whose birthplace has been distributed to another country to which they have no legal ties, and who have been unable to qualify for naturalization in the country in which they have sought asylum are literally "men without countries." Following World War I the League of Nations issued a special passport to such refugees called a Nansen passport; today the International Refugee Organization is struggling with the problem.

"State of the Union" message: The President is required by the Constitution to give to Congress information on the state of the Union, and recommend to its consideration such measures as he shall judge necessary and expedient. This is done formally by the President in his annual message to Congress and is usually related particularly to problems waiting to be solved. The famous Monroe Doctrine was such a message to Congress in 1823.

States' Rights (State Sovereignty): A policy held by those who felt that the states were supreme, and that when there was a conflict of interest, the states should be favored as closer to the people and more likely to look out for their interests. The followers of this policy became the Democratic-Republicans (q.v.) and were known as "strict interpreters" of the Constitution because they did not wish to have the "necessary and proper" clause (q.v.) referring to delegated powers of Congress enlarged in any sense so as to broaden the power of the federal government.

States' Rights Democrats: A group of dissatisfied Democrats bolted from the Democratic Convention in 1948 largely over the Civil Rights program that was being advocated, and met in Alabama where they proposed their own presidential candidate, Governor Strom Thurmond of South Carolina, who carried four states in the election. *See* DIXIECRATS.

statute of limitations: A law which fixes a time during which existing claims may be collected, judgments enforced or crimes prosecuted.

Statutes at Large of the United States: This series of volumes contains all the bills and resolutions passed by Congress which are published as soon as Congress has adjourned, at which date the Secretary of State officially declares the laws in effect. One volume contains public acts and resolutions, a second, private acts, concurrent resolutions, treaties and proclamations.

stealing the thunder: The action when one party or candidate takes over the program, or campaign issue of another party or candidate on the expectation that it will be equally good as a vote getter for them. When the Republicans copied some of the foreign policy proposals of Mr. Truman in the 1948 campaign a slight variation of this idea was repudiated by the Democrats as "Me tooism."

steam roller: An expression referring to the power of a political organization to put over its opinions very forcibly against any opposition, possibly ignoring the usual rules or principles. Theodore Roosevelt was under the steam roller at the 1912 Republican National Convention when his delegates were not seated, but he was on top of the steam roller in 1908 when he was dictating the nomination of Taft.

steering committee: Each political party in the House of Representatives has a steering committee. The Democratic Committee is composed of certain ex-officio members, such as the Speaker, majority leader and others plus fifteen members from various geographical areas of the country. It determines the order in which bills on the House calendar should be taken up and cooperates closely with the Rules Committee (q.v.). The Republican Steering Committee consists of the floor leader and seven other members of the House and has similar duties but from the opposition viewpoint (1952 Session).

Stimson Doctrine: A policy advanced by Secretary of State Stimson in 1932 following Japanese "penetration" into Manchuria, stating that the United States did not intend to recognize any situation, or agreement, which involved acquisition of territory by means outlawed in the Paris Peace Pact (q.v.).

straight-ticket voting: A practice by which a person votes for all the candidates of a particular party without any attempt to "split" his ticket, that is, make a selection on the basis of the individual but only on partisanship.

strict interpretation of the Constitution: Also called strict construction. In the early days of our history the Democratic-Republicans (q.v.) felt that the power of Congress should be limited to exactly what the eighteen powers listed called for. However, the Federalists (q.v.) believed they could, by implication, greatly extend the power of Congress. Strict construction was also intended to be a safeguard for the power of the states so that there would be no encroachment on their "sovereignty."

subpoena: A judicial writ requiring a person to appear at a specified time and place under penalty for default.

subsidiary coinage: Coins issued in units representing values less than one dollar, but redeemable in dollars. The commodity value, that is, the value the metals would represent if melted down and sold on the commercial market, is much less than their monetary value, that is, their value as money, except in unusual cases of shortages as in the case of copper in the pennies during the war.

subsidy: Any gift of financial aid given to a private enterprise by a government. This may be a direct grant as payment to those producing a certain amount of sugar, or indirectly for compliance with certain restrictions, as under the Agricultural Adjustment Act for not producing grain; or by paying a larger sum for services rendered than is normally charged, as the air mail subsidy, or to make up a higher cost of operation as in regard to the Merchant Marine (q.v.).

subsistence farming: This new, experimental program expects that there may in the future be a combination of farming and industry especially in the production of seasonal goods, whereby the worker may have a small piece of land on which he may grow vegetables or fruit just for his own use, or subsistence. Attempts at this have already started in some coal mining communities where the temporarily unemployed miner gives time to canning and preserving his own crops.

subsistence level: A plane of living in which the individual barely manages to eke out an existence with a minimum provision for the necessities of life as regards food, shelter, and clothing. The number of persons likely to exist at such a level has been somewhat reduced since 1930 with provisions for "relief" to be administered by welfare agencies of city, state or nation.

substantive law: This is the law that tells us what our rights and duties are. It is to be distinguished from adjective or procedural law which deals with the remedies provided by law.

subtreasury system: In many parts of the United States subtreasuries were constructed as repository for government funds. This system was authorized in 1840 and became necessary due to the situation occasioned by Jackson's opposition to the Second United States Bank and his removal of government funds from it in 1832. After the experiment of keeping the funds in certain state banks (pet banks) and the Panic of 1837 the new system of the subtreasuries became necessary and remained in use until replaced by the Federal Reserve System in 1913.

suburban: With the development of comfortable and high speed transportation, an outward shift of population from the cities has been a characteristic part of the development of the past quarter century. The boundaries of the city fill up and overflow into, and cause the growth of the contiguous suburban regions, which often become areas of residence, with the population commuting to the nearby city where industry is centered. Living standards are usually high and there is much awareness of servant problems. Country clubs, private schools and conspicuous consumption give considerable family prestige.

subversive activity: Support of a program aiming to overthrow the existing government constitutes subversive activity. The Internal Security Act of 1950 (McCarron Act) aims particularly at curbing such action on the part of communists or fascists.

suffrage: The privilege of voting. States set the qualifications for voting. All persons voting for the lower house of a state legislature may vote for Congressmen. Basic requirements usually include: citizenship, age 18-21, residence of one year. Some states have literacy tests (q.v.) and formerly many had a poll tax (q.v.).

summary action: Such action occurs where the usual judicial formalities are not observed. A police court or a court of no record may so perform.

supernumeraries: More than the number required. The party out of power is usually quick to accuse those in office of having the government pay rolls burdened with supernumeraries.

Supreme Court (United States): The highest court created by the Constitution in the federal system. The membership has varied from six to ten but remained nine since 1869. It has original and appellate jurisdiction (q.v.) and assumed early the function of judicial review (q.v.). Criticism of the four-five decisions as making for lack of stability due to the possible shift in opinion of one man has been frequently offered. A six-three requirement has been suggested as a reform but no action has been undertaken.

Supreme Court Reorganization Bill: Part of this bill included provisions for changing the Supreme Court which F. D. Roosevelt sent to Congress in 1937 following the rejection of so many of the New Deal laws. Discussion of the proposals made it one of the most controversial issues of that year. The provision for a court of fifteen members started up great public indignation over what was called "court packing" (q.v.), while others eagerly welcomed the provisions for getting rid of the "nine old men." The Senate held the bill for five months during which time lengthy hearings were held. The Judiciary Committee finally reported adversely on the bill. A compromise measure later in the year expedited appeals on constitutional questions and allowed the

Department of Justice to appear in the lower courts to defend congressional statutes.

surrogate: A local judicial office with jurisdiction over the probate of wills, disposition of estates, and the guardianship of orphaned minors.

surtax: A tax levied in addition to the normal tax in calculating individual income obligations and increasing to considerable amounts on higher incomes.

suspended sentence: After a person has been convicted, the court may under certain circumstances, as in the case of a first offender, decide not to carry out the terms of the sentence at that time but arrange for the release of the prisoner under terms of probation or similar arrangements for an indefinite period as long as there is no lapse in the individual's good conduct.

sweat shops: Places of employment in the middle Nineteenth Century where very low wages were paid under poor working conditions and usually on a piece basis. This sweated labor usually consisted of women and children and was particularly harmful to the health of the teen age youngsters.

swing around the circle: Usually an extensive speaking tour around the country during which a presidential candidate is stumping for office. Franklin D. Roosevelt attempted it in one month in 1936, and Willkie made a valiant attempt in 1940, but each had great assistance from radio. The tremendous undertaking like that of William Jennings Bryan in 1896 was a real test of a man's strength. McKinley, his opponent, resorted to the opposite tactics and used the "front porch" campaign where he spoke to the people who came to him.

sympathy strike: When a group strikes as a symbol of labor solidarity, merely out of sympathy for the group originally involved, but not because of some particular act of their own employer, the second strike would be called a sympathy strike.

Syndicalism: An economic system in which ownership and control of production is in the hands of the particular workers of that industry as carried out by the trade union involved. Such a group oppose the use of parliamentary procedure or any political controls. They favor the use of sabotage and direct action (q.v.) to attain these goals.

T

Taft-Hartley Act of 1947: *See* LABOR MANAGEMENT ACT.

talesman: The person summoned for jury duty.

Tammany Hall: Tammany Hall represents one of the oldest and most famous of the political clubs in America. It is the Democratic organization of the borough of Manhattan. It took the name of a famous Indian chief noted for his wisdom and diplomacy and was active in politics even in Jefferson's day. Though the Society of Tammany is well known for its social and benevolent work, it claims to be distinct from the political organization, despite the fact that the membership is practically the same.

tangible property: Such property is personalty; that is, property that has an actual existence, and therefore may be subject to taxation in the state where it is permanently located. Intangible property includes such objects as bonds, stocks, accounts receivable, and is usually taxed on the basis of the domicile of the owner.

Tariff Commission (United States): Tariff making by the Twentieth Century had become such an intricate and involved process that even the most conscientious Congressman could investigate only a small aspect of the controversial issue; therefore in 1916 a Tariff Commission was created to assist in obtaining comprehensive, exact and up-to-date information about comparable costs of production of goods in America and abroad. The Commission may not make changes in the schedules itself, but can recommend them to Congress. Its chief duty after the passage of the 1922 Tariff Law was to provide information for the President in connection with his right to raise or lower tariff duties fifty percent in accord with the flexible tariff (q.v.) provisions. The Commission was also to be busily concerned with assembling data for raising or lowering the duties under the reciprocal trade agreements (q.v.) which the President was empowered to negotiate under the 1934 Act.

tax dodging: Illegal efforts to avoid payment of a tax such as failure to report taxable income, or claims for non-existent dependents.

tax exemption: A policy of freeing an individual from the payment of the tax normally collected. This may be done in connection with a property tax in order to encourage building, being limited to a specified period, or in regard to religious, charitable, or educational institutions to encourage their activities.

tax offset: This is a device used by the Federal government to induce uniformity in regard to certain tax measures among the states. Federal credits are given for a payment of an equivalent tax to the state. For example, in connection with a Federal estate tax, the Treasury Department allowed 80% of the amount due the Federal government to be credited toward the payment of a state inheritance tax. Florida, which had been advertising freely that their state had no inheritance tax, quickly passed one in order to benefit from the "offset" features which promised to bring in additional revenue, more than their former bid to attract those who were going to retire.

tax power of the states: States may not interfere with the flow of interstate commerce, but aside from that they have practically unlimited power as to their means of raising income, including a real estate tax, a tax on gross income earned in the state, a sales tax, the opportunity to tax the entire income of an industry if located wholly within the state even if all the products it makes are shipped out of the state, and the right to tax corporations for their net worth as represented by their stock value, and, probably the most common of all, the tax on motor vehicles through the issuance of licenses.

technological unemployment: The discharge of workers due to the introduction of labor saving devices. This process greatly worried a group of "technocrats" who foresaw a serious threat to our economy with the vicious circle of unemployment reducing production and purchasing power. However, with the readjustments that have come about due to the re-employment of more people in the making of machines to make machines, and to sell such machines, and to advertise them and to service them and to transport and market the increased production resulting, little has been heard in the 40's of those fears of the 30's.

technology: The application of scientific knowledge for practically useful purposes represents the goal of technology that has brought incredible changes in American society. For a time there were those who feared the machines would throw men out of work and were greatly concerned about what they called technological unemployment (q.v.); however, still further inventions and application of technological improvements have been sufficient to redistribute the labor market.

"Teen Age Centers": Since World War II particularly young people have been found in need of supervised recreational activities. With both parents working, or with housing limitations, places for group play were felt to be essential. Satisfying such needs are the "Teen Age Centers." Under similar names, numbers of communities have provided meeting places with provision for games and entertainment, or with vocational or handicraft training for hobbies with volunteer or professional assistance to direct the program. The deterrent effect upon juvenile delinquency has been noticeable where such activities are provided adequately.

Teheran Conference: A meeting of President Roosevelt, Winston Churchill and Stalin in November and December of 1943. A declaration announced at the end of the Conference pledged the countries represented to work together in war and peace, and to push forward the destruction of Germany by encirclement from East, West and South.

temperance: Habitual moderation—especially in the indulgence of any appetite. The Women's Christian Temperance Union particularly advocates restraint in regard to the consumption of intoxicating liquor and was active in supporting the program for prohibition after World War I.

Temporary National Economic Committee: A special committee of Congress appointed in 1938 consisting of high government officials to study the business concentration and monopoly practices in the American economy. The two chief points in its study which Congress was recommended to remedy were 1) the full incorporation of all businesses in interstate commerce in order to establish national standards; 2) vigorous enforcement of all antitrust laws in areas not yet given over to government price control.

Tennessee Valley Authority: After World War I the Federal Government still had two plants at Muscle Shoals on the Tennessee River which had been used during the war to produce nitrates. Any attempts to extend their operation, especially the efforts of Senator George Norris to introduce bills in Congress for such a purpose, were blocked until the Tennessee Development Act of 1933 was signed by President Roosevelt. Within ten years, perhaps the most enduring of the New Deal projects was well under way. Hydroelectric plants were in operation, flood control to prevent soil erosion was worked out, and the manufacture of nitrogen products for explosives and fertilizer was going well. A whole geographic area had been regenerated through increased employment, better housing, cheap power, and improved soil. The legal attacks had been met by Supreme Court decisions finding the various activities constitutional. All that remained was to withstand the critics who attacked "government in business," and resented the implied "socialism" of the program. Six other regional "authorities" were being discussed by the 1950's including a "Missouri Valley" and a "Columbia Valley" Authority.

Tenth Amendment: Part of the first ten amendments added to the Constitution of the United States as the "Bill of Rights" in 1791. It stated: "the powers not delegated to the United States by the Constitution nor prohibited by it to the States, are reserved to the States respectively or to the people." These are the so-called reserve or residual powers which the states still jealously guard from possible Federal encroachment.

tenure: The interval during which an individual may continue in office. This may be established as during good behavior, or upon the discretion of the administration, or for a fixed period as in civil service appointments, with removal possible for only certain specific causes. A famous controversy arose between President Andrew Johnson and Congress over the passage of the Tenure of Office Act in 1867 which required that the Senate approve of the removal of a Presidential appointee. This led to Johnson's impeachment, but he was not convicted and the measure was later found unconstitutional.

"Territorial Integrity": The framers of the Constitution were fearful that territory of their states might be taken away by the national government, therefore they provided safeguards so that territorial integrity, that is, the "wholeness" of their states, would be maintained. Article four, section three of the Constitution states, "no new state shall be formed or erected within the jurisdiction of any other state, nor any state be formed by the junction of two or more states without the consent of the legislatures involved, as well as Congress." Though there has been much talk of creating certain metropolitan areas like New York or Chicago into separate states, with impressive arguments advanced for such action, that New York, or Illinois, or New Jersey or Indiana, or Connecticut or Wisconsin would agree is almost inconceivable. West Virginia was so separated, but chiefly as a war measure at a critical time.

territory: *See* UNINCORPORATED TERRITORY, INCORPORATED TERRITORY, NORTHWEST ORDINANCE.

Third Amendment: One of the first ten amendments added to the Constitution of the United States in 1791 as part of the Bill of Rights (q.v.). It states: "No soldier shall, in time of peace, be quartered in any house without the consent of the owner, nor in time of war, but in a manner to be prescribed by law."

Third Party Movement: This expression applies to a variety of political movements arising in addition to the two major parties. They usually appeal to a limited group, or geographical area, and do not sustain themselves very long, with the exception of the Socialist Party. However, they have served some valuable purposes in that they initiate many important reforms which seem radical at first and then are accepted by Republicans and Democrats; for example, women's suffrage, popular election of senators, initiative, referendum and postal savings banks. *See* POPULISTS, PROGRESSIVES.

Thirteenth Amendment: As a result of the Civil War this amendment was added to the Constitution of the United States in 1865. "Neither slavery nor involuntary servitude, except as a punishment for crime whereof the party shall have been duly convicted, shall exist in the United States, or in any place subject to their jurisdiction."

three-quarters vote: This vote is required only when the ratification of a proposed amendment to the United States Constitution is undertaken, when thirty-six of the state legislatures must approve.

tidelands oil controversy: A long and bitter dispute has been engendered over the conflicting claims to the resources of the tidelands, areas located between the low-water mark and the three mile limit, when oil was found obtainable from such coastal regions in California, Texas and Louisiana. Several bills in Congress have been proposed giving clear title to the states, but have been vetoed by the President (1946-1952). The Supreme Court has ruled against ownership by California in one suit, and has also confirmed specifically federal ownership. With estimates of billions of dollars involved the duel for control still goes on, full operation dependent upon a final decision in the matter. One group of politicians has offered a compromise based on having the federal government's case confirmed but with a promise that its share of the profits go to improve the schools of the United States.

torts: Any wrongful act which can be remedied by civil action exclusive of breach of promise.

town meeting (New England): A meeting convoked in the town hall once every year, usually in March, for which a prepared list of subjects to which discussion is limited is offered by the "selectmen," the governing board elected at the previous meeting. A tax rate is determined and by-laws passed regulating all aspects of the town's governmental activities. This type of meeting has for centuries symbolized in America the essence of pure democracy with all the townsmen meeting at one time to govern themselves.

Townsend Plan: A proposal originated in about 1934 by Dr. Francis Townsend in California in which he suggested that each person upon reaching the age of sixty would be paid a pension of $200 a month, if he refrained from competing in the labor market, and spent all his income within the month, thus leading to full employment of others and providing necessary purchasing power. He thought a two percent sales tax would provide a sufficient fund to meet the demands of the pensioners.

township: A unit of local government which may be a large or small portion of a county. It may resemble a New England town but is different from the town in its governing body, which usually consists of a board of commissioners or of a township supervisor. The functions of townships vary greatly though they usually include maintenance of local roads, administration of schools and poor relief. Government experts consider the township is on the wane. There is much duplication and overlapping with the county units that are not only confusing but expensive; though it is not expected that reduction in the number of townships will be speedily accomplished since there are many valuable functions that are taken care of.

trade association: About 1911 a proposal for "new competition" caused related enterprises, especially in the steel, lumber, and textile field to decide to formulate individual commercial policies with consideration for the entire industry by the interchange and dissemination of statistics on production, sales, prices, costs, and inventories. In 1949 over 8,000 such national groups existed. Though not held to be monopolistic, they have been carefully watched lest they offer any threat, especially in the field of price fixing.

trade barriers, state: One of the primary motives in calling the Constitutional Convention in 1787 (q.v.) was the elimination of state trade barriers. The writers of the Constitution hoped particularly to prevent any such recurrence by prohibiting state duties on imports and exports and assuming Federal control of interstate commerce. However, especially during the 1930's, state barriers have been created with some regularity through statutes or practices that unfairly tend to the disadvantage of persons or products coming from sister states and to the advantage of local residents. There are many examples possible—seemingly legitimate inspection and quarantine of plant and animal life have made it impossible to market certain goods in neighboring states; motor vehicles, especially trucks, are subjected to most diverse regulation which often cannot be met without excessive costs, not necessary for local licensees.

trademarks: An emblem, symbol or similar device used to distinguish the goods or services of a particular manufacturer, the exclusive use of which is granted by the Patent Office. Registration is for twenty years and it is possible to have an indefinite number of renewals.

"trade practice conferences": Joint conferences between industry representatives and the Federal Trade Commission representatives at which programs of fair competition are adopted as the standard of the industry. These voluntary conferences aid both the industry and the consumer and seem to serve the purpose of the Federal Trade Commission better than the older practices of waiting for complaints from competitors and consumers.

trade union: *See* LABOR UNION.

traditionalism: The habitual way of doing things because that is the way they have always been done, and the habitual way of thinking. This ultra-conservatism is likely to become encrusted with rationalization to justify its continuance in the good old way.

"transmission belts": This term was used to refer to the situation in the 1940's when it was suspected that all officials of the Soviet Union in the United States were gathering what information they could about conditions in America and sending these details back to Moscow under cover of diplomatic or business activities.

Transportation Act of 1920: This act provided for the return of the railroads to private ownership after the government operation during World War I. It also attempted to remedy the bad financial situation of some of the railroads by setting up a "pool," or reservoir, into which the efficient roads were to contribute half their excess profits over six percent (*see* RECAPTURE CLAUSE) to provide loans for the weak lines. Combination and consolidation of the railroad lines was to be permitted with the approval of the Interstate Commerce Commission in the interests of stockholders, workers, and the public.

treason: According to the Federal Constitution, consists only in levying war against the United States or adhering to their enemies, giving them aid and comfort. There must be two witnesses to the same overt act. Because of the narrow limits of this definition very few cases of treason have been prosecuted in the United States.

Treasury Department: This department was one of the original four cabinet positions filled by George Washington in 1789. All duties not concerned with foreign affairs (State Department), not military (War Department) and not of concern to the Attorney-General were handled by the Treasury staff until in time the other cabinet positions were created. Now, of course, the major task of this department is the collection of the nation's income, so that there are thousands of collectors of internal revenue, and others assigned to the collection of customs duties. Other financial matters are concerned with the supervision of National Banks, the activities of the Bureau of Engraving, and the Bureau of the Mint. Additional duties include the prevention of counterfeiting through the U. S. Secret Service, and some nonfiscal duties such as the work of the Coast Guard and the registering of ships.

"trial balloon": Politically to launch a trial balloon means to propose a candidate or an issue long before election time in order to gauge the public reaction after which the program or candidate may be accepted or repudiated.

trial by jury guaranteed: In criminal cases *see* SIXTH AMENDMENT. In civil cases *see* SEVENTH AMENDMENT.

"triple damage action": Under the federal antitrust laws any person whose business is injured by a monopolistic combination has the right to recover threefold the damages sustained including the cost of the suit. The purpose of this portion of the law was to encourage private individuals to take action themselves against monopolies and not wait for the rather lengthy process by the Federal Trade Commission or the Attorney-General.

truant officer: A local official responsible for preventing the breaking of the compulsory education law where children are illegally absent from school. The trend in many progressive cities today has been for these men and women to have a much better training in social welfare work so that they may exercise a real insight into the problem of the child's truancy. They cooperate closely with social agencies whose help may be needed and may recommend psychological or psychiatric care.

true bill: The term applied to the indictment (q.v.) issued by a grand jury when a person is accused of a crime and is to be held for a trial later.

Truman Doctrine: The policy announced in March 1947 when the President requested and obtained a four million dollar appropriation for aid to Turkey and Greece in economic and military assistance so that these countries would serve as a possible bulwark against Communist advance from the Near East.

trust: A form of business organization declared illegal by which the stock of several companies could be held by a group of "trustees" in exchange for trust certificates upon which dividends were paid. It was a device which allowed coordination of policies and could lead to monopolistic practices which the Federal government was trying to eliminate. A less formal organization "community of interest" (q.v.) was developed after the trust had been outlawed. *See* ANTITRUST LAWS.

trust busting: Because trusts (q.v.) had been found monopolistic an intensive program under Theodore Roosevelt was organized for attacking certain large business enterprises for actions that had led to high prices or limited output of the product involved. The Northern Securities Company in 1902 was the first trust to be "busted" when it was forced to separate its subsidiaries into the individual companies that had originally existed, so that these separate railroad lines would become competitive. Similar practices were continued under Taft, and a renewed effort was pushed during the "New Deal" period.

Trusteeship Council: One of the major divisions of the United Nations, this council was created to supervise the trust territories, the backward areas not yet ready for independence which were formerly either mandates taken from Germany after World War I or areas taken from Italy or Japan after World War II. Any nation may surrender a colonial possession to the protection of this council if it so desires. The membership includes the permanent members of the Security Council, nations administering the trust areas, and an equal number of nations not so engaged to act as "watchdogs" over the interests of the people of the trust territory. This Council is responsible to the Security Council for strategic areas that are also trust areas, but to the General Assembly for routine administrative functions.

trust territories: Areas administered by the Trusteeship Council of the United Nations.

turnpike: Originally this term referred to any road having a toll gate upon it. The meaning has been extended today to imply extensive highways with a staggered system of paying tolls according to the number of zones passed through. The New Jersey Turnpike opened in 1951 represents one of the most recent additions of this type of road.

Tweed Ring: In the period following the Civil War William Marcy Tweed was the absolute boss of New York City, and he and his gang by means of graft, padding of expense accounts and just plain stealing milked the government of millions of dollars. Samuel J. Tilden, a New York attorney, led the attack that disposed of this corruption and thus won a national reputation that also almost won him the Presidency of the United States in the election of 1876.

Twelfth Amendment: An Amendment added to the Constitution of the United States in 1804, which became necessary, because as originally provided in the Constitution, when the electors cast their votes the candidate with the greatest number of votes provided it was over one half became president and the next highest candidate became vice-president. This left a possibility that the two office holders might be of different parties, as did develop when Jefferson, a Democratic-Republican, was vice president, and John Adams, a Federalist, was president. Therefore in bringing about a remedy for this situation, the Twelfth Amendment states that separate ballots will be held in the electoral college, first for president, and then again for vice-president. With one party or other in the majority the two choices would reflect that majority. If no candidate obtains a majority, the election of president goes to the House, and of the vice-president to the Senate, where in each case the vote is by states and a majority vote is required.

Twentieth Amendment: The "Lame Duck" Amendment (q.v.) which eliminated the "holdover" Congressmen. Ratified February

1933. It sets the meeting of the Congress at the third of January every year and fixes the end of the Presidential and Vice-Presidential terms as January 20th after the November election day. Provision is also made for the replacement of the President-elect by the Vice-President-elect in case of death or inability to qualify before the new inauguration date. If both should have died Congress has the right to pass a law making appropriate arrangements for a successor.

Twenty-first Amendment: An amendment to the Constitution of the United States ratified in December 1933. It provided for the repeal of the Eighteenth Amendment (q.v.), the prohibition amendment, but continued to make it illegal to transport intoxicating liquor into a state which had a state law prohibiting the use therein.

"twilight zone": An area found to exist in the attempts to curb monopolies where the states could not operate because of the interstate character of many enterprises, and the federal government was restricted because of the "local" aspect of the business. This situation was later remedied by allowing the federal government to extend its influence into the intrastate field not just where there was a "direct effect," as at first interpreted by the Supreme Court, but where there was merely "a close and intimate effect." The tendency is to give the federal government every benefit of the doubt; therefore gradually closing up the gap between the two fields of regulation. For example, Consolidated Edison of New York with no sales beyond the state may still be subject to regulation by the Federal Power Commission (q.v.) because the power it produces is essential to so many interstate operations.

two-thirds vote: This vote is needed in both houses of Congress to propose an amendment to the United States Constitution, or to override a presidential veto, or in the Senate to ratify a treaty or to convict in impeachment proceedings.

tying leases: Arrangements made by a seller that if one commodity is sold to a purchaser he will agree to buy another kind of product from the vendor at the same time. This practice has been held illegal under the Robinson-Patman Act (q.v.).

U

ultimatum: A final demand made by one nation in a diplomatic negotiation. If rejected the next step has usually been the start of hostilities or at least the breaking off of diplomatic relations.

ultra vires: Literally the phrase means beyond the power. It is applied to acts done by a public or private corporation which may be found void because they are beyond the power conferred upon the corporation or agency by its charter.

Un-American Activities Committee (The Dies Committee): A committee organized by the House of Representatives in 1945 and made a permanent committee in 1945. It investigates subversive and un-American activities in the United States and makes suggestions for remedial legislation. There was much criticism of its program at different times, particularly of the methods employed at some of the hearings. Charges were made of attempts at sensationalism, and that there was insufficient investigation of material presented with some instances of "character assassination" leaving the individuals involved with no redress for false impressions created. Most frequently the attacks rested on the premise that the Federal Bureau of Investigation was the agency best equipped to really do the best job on specific individuals. On the other hand there were those who felt an excellent job had been done all along and that the subsequent indictment of Alger Hiss and other fellow-travelers (q.v.) proved its worth. Political overtones were also involved, Mr. Truman laying himself open to some criticism by his belittling references to "red herrings," and Mr. Nixon gaining a reputation that had much to do with his winning the vice-presidential nomination in July 1952.

unearned increment: Income acquired whose increase in value was enjoyed through no individual efforts of the person obtaining the benefits. It is a factor that worries the socialists considerably because they claim the increased values are due to the action

UNEMPLOYMENT COMPENSATION 270

of society itself, as for example when property once outside the city limits comes in time to gain value when the city has encircled it. The socialists feel this increased value should go to the "state" rather than to one lucky individual.

unemployment compensation: When this problem, after the crash of 1929, became too great for the local and state governments to handle, the national government had to come to the rescue, especially through the Social Security Act, which had immediate effect in regard to the provisions for unemployment payments. The states still continue to administer the program but the funds come from a federal pay-roll tax collected on the employee's income under $3,600 by a three percent levy paid by the employer only. Of this amount, 2.7% goes to those states maintaining an improved unemploymnt plan. The greatest variation between different state plans has been in the amounts per case paid out. The period for which payments would be made has generally been limited to 18 weeks but many states have extended it to 26 weeks. Average weekly amounts equal $20. Though about forty million employees are eligible now proposals are under way for an even broader coverage.

unicameralism: Though a few states had one-chambered legislatures in the early Eighteenth Century, none had adopted such a practice since until Nebraska did in 1937, changing from a two-chambered house of 133 to a single chamber of forty-three elected for two-year terms on ballots without party designations. In general this body has borne out the advantages claimed for a unicameral law-making body. There has been improved efficiency in that, since both houses usually represent the same people, same interests and same qualifications, and practically the same duties, one house is all that is needed. There are additional advantages in that the one-house idea prevents the shifting of responsibility, avoids unnecessary conference committees to reconcile variations in detail in similar measures introduced in both houses, and above all avoids delays and expenses of two houses. The National Municipal Council recommends this procedure in its Model State Constitution.

unincorporated territory: All territorial possessions of the United States bear this designation unless Congress provides otherwise by law or treaty. Technically the territory is not part of the United States and import duties may be levied. The inhabitants are "nationals" but not citizens. Reasonable attention must be paid to the general principles of the Constitution. The areas involved are Samoa, Panama Canal Zone, Midway and Wake, and formerly the Philippines.

union label: A method of identifying goods as made under favorable union conditions. A degree of labor solidarity has been obtained by the efforts of union organizers to educate workers to buy only goods carrying such tags or labels.

union-maintenance clause: A provision in a collctive agreement between an employer and a union by which all the employees who are at present or who may become members of the union, must remain members in good standing as a condition of remaining employed. This is permitted under the Taft-Hartley Law only if it is approved by a majority of the workmen involved.

union shop: An establishment where an employer has agreed to keep only union men on the payroll, but in which he may hire non-union workers who then must join the union. However, it has been made an unfair labor practice under the Taft-Hartley Act for a union to require an employer to deny employment under a union-shop agreement if such employer has reasonable grounds to believe that membership in a union is not available to a prospective employee (for example a Negro) on the same terms as others. It is also "unfair" for unions to charge "excessive" fees for joining the union. *See* CLOSED SHOP.

United Nations Charter: The constitution of the world organization replacing the League of Nations accepted at the United Nations Conference held from April to June 1945 and based upon the preliminary draft made at Dumbarton Oaks (q.v.) in 1944. Upon ratification by the original members the Charter became effective October 24, 1945. The first meeting of the General Assembly was held in London in January 1946.

United Nations Educational, Scientific, and Cultural Organization (UNESCO): A specialized agency of the United Nations, it was created to promote the appreciation of the social and cultural accomplishments of the members of the United Nations not only to bring about improved knowledge but on the assumption that wars begin in the minds of men and international understanding would be an important step toward world peace.

United Nations International Children's Emergency Fund (UNICEF): A specialized agency of the United Nations to aid refugee children and expectant mothers.

United States Employment Service: A service maintained by the states with funds provided by the Federal Government; it operates as a public placement service for the whole nation as part of Federal Security Administration.

United States Office of Education: An administrative agency in the Department of the Interior from 1867-1939, now in the Federal Security Agency. It collects statistics, makes available nation-wide information on schools, teaching requirements and related topics. It also supervises the administration of the federal grant-in-aid where educational matters are involved. Since control of education is a residual power (q.v.) still jealously guarded by the states, the work of this agency remains on the advisory level with no means of enforcing its recommendations but still a valuable clearing house of educational data.

unit rule: In the Democratic National Convention the practice was long carried out that the total vote of each state delegation was to be cast as a "unit" for the candidate for whom the majority of the delegation had voted. This procedure helped to maintain the Democratic policy of conforming to the importance of States' Rights (q.v.). It has since been allowed to lapse. The two-thirds rule was to serve the same purpose and has also been changed.

Universal Military Training: Congress has discussed many details in connection with their intention to carry through such a program of student preparation for military service of what was expected to be six months' basic training but with the competition of the draft and need for instructors for such a program coming first the implementing of the program has been more or less tacitly suspended until after the elections of 1952.

unofficial observer: In the late nineteen thirties though the United States had not yet joined the League of Nations we sent delegates unofficially to follow the sessions of many of the

League's organizations. The Council of the League gave the United States representation in their body in 1931 for the purpose of discussing Japanese aggression in Manchuria.

unregenerated slum: Unlivable dwellings given a patch of plaster and a dab of paint to comply with the local laws and thus be able to produce income. It is a practice tolerated because of the critical shortage of low-income housing.

unwritten constitution: The part of a constitution which sets forth in formal terms the provisions approved by a Constitutional Convention and ratified by the constituted authorities is the written constitution. By contrast the "unwritten" constitution refers to the "interpretation" of the actual terms of the constitution and to the customs and practices which have developed without having concrete provision made for them in the written document. *See* CUSTOM AND USAGE AS MEANS OF EFFECTING CONSTITUTIONAL EXPANSION.

unwritten law: A reference to a standard or precedent accepted by custom in some parts of the world by which a person may not be held fully responsible for a criminal act committed to defend or avenge the "honor" of an immediate relative.

Urban League: A nation-wide organization interested in improving employment and health conditions of Negroes, by attempting to increase the number placed in better jobs, and by stressing the need for better housing and recreational facilities. A series of offices in many key cities helps in this work by furthering research, gathering pertinent data, and helping to promote better interracial relations in all respects.

usury: The taking of a rate of interest beyond what is allowed by law. The amount fixed upon varies with the different states.

utopia: An imaginary island, the seat of an ideally perfect social life described by Sir Thomas More and given this title which literally means "no place." The adjective Utopian has been added to describe a certain group of Socialists of the middle nineteenth century because their program was concerned with proposals very idealistic and sometimes quite impractical such as those of St. Simon, Fourier or Robert Owen.

V

valuation: The determination of a fair estimate either of a rate as in regard to railroads or public ultilities, or in the calculation of profits in excess profit laws, or of the sum to be paid property owners in matters of eminent domain (q.v.).

vagrant: An individual who wanders about usually homeless and without adequate means of support. Some local communities enforce vagrancy laws, jailing such individuals or sending them on to the next town. Problems of peonage (q.v.) have sometimes arisen in this respect.

venal: Capable of being bought by underhanded means. In our early history votes might occasionally have been bought; but current investigations under Congressional auspices would seem to indicate that venality still exists in other corrupt fields.

venire: A writ issued by the judge of the court calling a citizen for jury duty. It is from the Latin "venire facias" meaning to cause to come.

venue: The locality in which a criminal trial or action is to be held. Occasionally requests for change of venue are entered before the court if popular feelings are running especially high over some aspect of the case and there is fear that the accused's case may be prejudiced.

verdict: The conclusion announced by a jury on the facts presented to it during a trial of a case in court, guilty or not guilty.

vertical integration: Following the great increase in "Big Business" in the 1880's some concerns saw the value of expansion so as to control production from the primary level of obtaining the raw materials to the final fabrication and marketing. This process was called vertical integration. Carnegie illustrated it well in combining ownership of coal deposits, coke ovens, iron mines and transportation facilities. By contrast, Standard Oil favored horizontal integration combining refineries and controlling pipe lines all the way across the United States.

vested interests: Those powerful persons or organizations who assumed special interests in certain situations and would exert considerable opposition to any attempt to take from them the privileges they had been accustomed to enjoying.

Veterans Administration: An independent agency created in 1930. Quite small originally, it mushroomed into great size after World War II, reaching expenditures of $7 billion a year. It has offices in every state and handles matters involving claims, construction, insurance, surgery, and vocational rehabilitation.

veterans' preference: From as far back as the Civil War honorably discharged or retired veterans and wives and widows of such have been eligible for civil service positions on easier terms than those applying to others. The Veteran Preference Act of 1945 sets aside certain jobs exclusively for veterans and arbitrarily adds ten points to earned examination ratings. In 1947 forty percent of the civil service jobs were filled through veteran preference. There has never been any question as to the responsibility of the government and of the public to see that the veteran received all the rights to which he was entitled, but there are those who feel that it is equally important that government positions be filled by the most capable person available. If the veteran is simply moved up the list more quickly they feel that is quite satisfactory for all concerned, but educational or performance standards should not be lowered according to some critics.

veto: The privilege resting with an executive to return a bill unsigned with his objections to it to the legislature which had passed it. The Congress in order to pass a bill over a presidential veto must obtain a two-thirds vote in each house. A bill may also fail to become a law if held by the president for ten days after Congress has adjourned.

Another form of veto is that which may be exercised in the Security Council of the United Nations if the measure under consideration fails to obtain the required seven votes for a procedural matter, or the seven votes including all the permanent members' approval for a substantive matter.

Vice-President: The officer who succeeds to the presidency in case of death or removal or resignation of the president. According to the Federal Constitution the vice-president must have the same qualifications as the president. As president of the Senate he must conduct himself as an impartial presiding officer. He votes only in case of a tie. When the position is vacated by the advancement of the vice-president to the presidency, a president pro tem is elected by the Senate after nomination by the majority party caucus. The vice-president may be invited to attend cabinet meetings. Some discussion has arisen from time to time that he be given a more responsible position in the government and be made a really effective "assistant president."

vigilantism: Vigilance groups were not uncommon in the West where they attempted to suppress crime where the processes of the law were either not available or neglected their duties. In a modern sense the program applies to the "witch hunts" of minor officials or private persons bent on assuming for themselves the prerogatives of trying, and convicting and punishing unpopular characters.

village: That concentration of population which does not exceed 2,500 and which usually is made up of a minimum of from two to five hundred depending on the states' provisions, which covers a limited amount of territory and may or may not be incorporated.

vindication: Justification or exoneration. A term often used after an election to indicate that the successful candidate's views have been widely accepted or his misconduct overlooked.

Virginia and Kentucky Resolutions: Measures passed by the state legislatures involved, about 1799, questioning the right of Congress to pass the so-called Alien and Sedition Laws since they claimed such powers were not specifically delegated to Congress and therefore should remain with the states. Primarily it was a case of the Democratic-Republicans (q.v.) resenting the program of the Federalists (q.v.) in passing such laws as would tend to restrict the right of the new immigrants, potential members of the Democratic-Republicans, as to freedom of expression and similar action. Several editors critical of the Federalists found themselves in jail convicted of sedition when all they were attempting to do was to overthrow the party in power, not the government. With the "Revolution of 1800," the election of Jefferson, the repeal advocated in the Kentucky and Virginia Resolutions was accomplished.

Virginia Plan: A plan also called the Randolph Plan proposed in the Constitutional Convention (1787) for a bicameral legislature with representatives selected on either the amount of money contributed by the states, or the number of free inhabitants resident in the states. This plan was favored by the large states and was opposed by the New Jersey Plan (q.v.) which favored the small states. A compromise was reached which provided for representation by population in the House of Representatives, and by equal representation from each state in the Senate; and for the Virginia Plan proposal for the complete revision of the Articles of Confederation (q.v.).

Virgin Islands: A group of three islands, St. Thomas, St. Croix and St. John, purchased from Denmark in 1917 by the United States, consisting of about 133 square miles, with a population of 26,000 (1950). They provide an important strategic link in the means of protection of the Panama Canal. The municipal councils of the three islands sit together as a legislature whose laws may be vetoed by Congress.

visit and search: The right which a belligerent nation has to stop and board an enemy ship to determine the disposal of the ship, or to investigate whether a neutral vessel is carrying contraband of war. American vessels were taken in to British control boards during World War I when the items that constituted "contraband" were undergoing many varying interpretations with the introduction of mechanized warfare.

vital statistics: These important records of both birth and death are often handled for cities by their Health Departments. They make indispensable sources for valuable information in the study of certain diseases. Issuance of burial permits is usually handled by the same authorities. In the counties, or small cities, the State Health Department may act for them.

viva voce vote: A vote during which the members respond orally, usually with no official recording of the individual record.

"Voice of America": A program of radio broadcasting undertaken by the Department of State for the dissemination of information in many languages in the form of newscasts, musical and other varied types of entertainment, to reach the foreign listener and obtain his sympathy for American institutions and aims in order to reduce the influence of Communist propaganda or expose activities behind the "Iron Curtain" (q.v.).

Volstead Act: An act of Congress that carried out the prohibition ordered by the Eighteenth Amendment (q.v.) Severe penalties were to be imposed for breaking any of the provisions of the law. An intoxicating liquor was defined as one containing one and one-half a percent of alcohol.

Vocational Education: An increased trend toward this type of education developed with the extension of the compulsory school period. It was felt that it was the responsibility of a democratic government to train properly for the jobs they were to hold the pupils up to sixteen who were forced to remain in school but were not concerned with college preparation. Now at all levels of the educational ladder vocational education is being presented including shop, industrial art and office work courses in amazing variety. Some schools have cooperated with industry to the extent that a student spends part of a term in the classroom and the remainder of the time in part time employment in the fields he has just been studying.

vocational guidance: Most commercial school courses today provide for some form of guidance to assist the student in his initial preparations for earning a living or in redirecting the dissatisfied. The content of specific courses available may be made clear or a sequel to a regular Civics course may be provided which provides a survey of the majority of vocations that may be followed describing their advantages and disadvantages. Some schools are also able to provide for a period of employment and of study in alternating intervals with conferences with teachers for self-evaluation.

W

"wadies": Because of the shallowness of the Rio Grande at certain points some individuals attempt to enter the United States illegally. These "wadies" are checked by the Border Patrol, which operates under the Bureau of Immigration and Naturalization of the Justice Department. *See* WETBACKS.

Wage and Hour Law of 1938 and 1949: *See* FAIR LABOR STANDARDS ACT.

Wage Stabilization Board: An agency of the federal government to provide for control of wages to prevent inflation in a period of national emergency.

Wagner-Connery Labor Relations Act of 1935: *See* NATIONAL LABOR RELATIONS BOARD.

waiver: To relinquish some legal privilege. A diplomat enjoying diplomatic immunity may "waive" or give up the privilege of freedom from a civil suit.

walking delegate: *See* BUSINESS AGENT.

ward: A political subdivision above the precinct in the urban areas. Wards vary in size from six to twenty precincts depending on the density of population. There are usually about 10,000 voters in one. Ward leaders are miniature political bosses gaining position through influence in the party and not responsible to the voters.

war debts: Probably the most discussed issue when the issue of more loans to Europe was under consideration by Congress was the reference to the money the United States had loaned to these same countries after and during World War I. Despite very generous refunding operations the major powers gradually failed to meet their obligations. When the "Crash of 1929" came they were still further financially handicapped so that President Hoover issued a Moratorium in 1931 to temporarily suspend repayment. At a conference at Lausanne the allies fixed on a lump sum they would accept as final payment from Germany—about $714 million, if the United States would cancel their war debts to her. The Senate rejected the proposal with the State Department reaffirming its continuously maintained position that there was no connection between reparations (q.v.) and war debts. Eventually Finland was the only nation to complete its payments.

War Department. Now Department of the Army: *See* DEFENSE, DEPARTMENT OF.

ward heeling: A practice by which a local politician looks after his particular ward or district, thus gaining the good will of the constituents. There may be some question at times of the propriety of the services performed but the material benefits are always very evident: food and coal for the indigent, jobs, finding of clients, fixing of tickets, and picnics. The "ward heeler" is the hanger-on who helps in these services.

war horse: An experienced party leader who can be relied upon to campaign strenuously for the support of the party.

warranty: Any material statement or assurance of fact made by a seller which induces a buyer to enter into a contract of purchase. These expressions may be expressed or implied and must rest on fact, not opinion.

Watch and Ward Society: An organization in Boston to exercise censorship. Although some obscenity has been curbed, it is felt by some that their efforts were directed more at certain books of high literary value and with little or no licentiousness involved, rather than toward the real purpose of the society.

watch dog committees: These represent groups of individuals who in any form of legislative body are appointed, or voluntarily constitute themselves a body, to check up on the activities of those they have had some reason to suspect are not performing their duties on the highest level, or whose organization seems to have been infiltrated by un-American interests, or either the extreme right or left.

watcher: At every polling place on election day each party provides an official watcher to see that no action occurs that would be contrary to the local election laws, or to the interest of the party.

waving the bloody shirt: A practice of the Republican Party candidates for many years after the Civil War in claiming credit for the Union victory, and in blaming the South for responsibility for the start of the War.

Ways and Means Committee: One of the most important committees in the House. The Democratic caucus (q.v.) chooses the party's representatives on the committee, and gives this group authority to select the Democratic members of all other committees subject to final caucus approval. The Senate has consolidated the work of this committee into the Appropriations Committee. However, the House which must originate all money bills has despite the Reorganization Act of 1946 maintained an Appropriations Committee of forty-five members, and a Ways and Means Committee of twenty-five.

Webb Export Act (Webb-Pomerene Act): This act states that there would be no antitrust restrictions levied against a corporation organized solely for the purpose of engaging in the export business.

welfare capitalism: A term somewhat in disfavor in liberal circles which indicates that business, of its own accord, has decided to hand over to the workers certain benefits, such as provisions for more generous pensions than under the Social Security provisions, hospitalization, arrangements to rent company homes or buy at lower rates through company stores. The resentment over these benefits which has arisen from organized labor is partly due to a suspicion that they are proposed to weaken the appeal of the unions, and partly due to the fact that there is no compulsion of law to force all kinds of businesses to carry out such a program. The program may or may not be accompanied by what unions consider the equally indispensable advantages of high wages and collective bargaining opportunities. For example, Ford provided many of these benefits for his workers and hoped to hold off their joining the newly organized Automobile Workers Union, but to no effect.

These welfare benefits are often classed as "paternalism" (q.v.), or as "state socialism," a mild program in which there is a compromise under which the workers make certain gains and there is the full retention of private capitalism. The Utopian Socialism of Robert Owen or of the French socialists like St.

Simon of over a century ago are close cousins of the movement.

welfare fund: A fund usually financed by employer contributions as provided for in union-employer contracts, to provide health, hospitalization and insurance benefits for workers, and often including their families. It may be a fixed monthly or weekly contribution, or be collected according to the workers' output as so much for each ton of coal mined.

"welfare state": The tendency of modern governments to extend more and more the activities that serve the public has led to a controversy as to how far these provisions for the general welfare may go. For those who feel that government has gone far enough in helping the individual the term "welfare state" is used in derision. The New Deal and the Fair Deal (q.v.) are thus criticized by this group as providing more for the common man than he really needs, and they will stress the need to return to the days of "rugged individualism." On the other hand the advocates of the welfare state proclaim the benefits of subsidized housing, praise the goal of socialized medicine, urge parity prices for farmers, and related projects, and see "Big Government" as a logical sequel to "Big Business" and "Big Labor." *See* STATEISM.

"wetbacks": Mexican workers who cross the border illegally by swimming the Rio Grande River. The Mexican and the United States governments have signed agreements for the legal entry of necessary Mexican agricultural workers into the United States. These now number some fifty thousand a year or more who are protected by wage guarantees, but the "wetbacks" as illegal entrants are exploited with wages as low as ten to twenty-five cents an hour. Authorities on both sides of the border are attempting to prevent this condition both for the advantage of the misguided and ignorant Mexicans thus taken advantage of, but also for the protection of Americans who must track down possibly diseased or otherwise unwanted immigrants. *See* WADIES.

Whig Party: The Whig Party was organized as a protest against President Jackson's program, especially his attack upon the monied interests in the Bank situation. As the President was derisively called "King Andrew the First" the Whigs played up their position as the "liberal" group in America duplicating the

Whig position in Britain as the opponents of "autocracy." The Whigs won in the election of Harrison in the 1840 election, but upon his death the Vice-President, Tyler, a Democrat, took office to their disgust. Their only other success was the election of Zachary Taylor in 1848. The platform they had favored, a national bank, internal improvements at national expense, and a protective tariff, became by 1852 vague platitudes and were soon replaced by the newly created Republican Party (q.v.).

whip: The House of Representatives has a majority whip and a minority whip and each may have many assistants. The whip is to see that the party members are at hand when significant votes are likely to be taken.

whispering campaign: A situation where criticism of a candidate or program is undertaken based on unfounded rumors, and never done in an official fashion so that the partial lies could be answered in any dignified manner.

White House Office: A staff of personal aids of the President, three personal secretaries, five administrative assistants, an executive clerk, and three attachés who form a portion of the Executive Office of the President (q.v.).

white paper: Report by a government on an important national or international problem intended for information and propaganda.

white primary: Primary elections are held for the purpose of making nominations by each party. Since a Texas Supreme Court found that a party was a voluntary private association, a party could therefore regulate its primaries as it pleased and exclude Negroes from the right of participating. Though a later United States Supreme Court decision denied the right to bar Negroes from the primaries since they are as important as the elections in many parts of the South with its single party system, the "white primary" still operates in many areas.

whitewash: If, upon investigation of a condition or of an official under some suspicion, the report of exoneration is issued without any criticism, it is often represented as a whitewash, a covering up of all faults or evils.

wildcat strike: An illegal strike not authorized by the union officials. Employers under the Taft-Hartley Law may sue the union for damages under such a situation. Employees who engage in wildcat strikes may be discharged.

wire-pulling: The exerting of influence upon government officials secretly so as to win their approval by unethical pressure or bribes not in the public's interest.

wire tapping: A practice of listening in on a private conversation. The question of the legality of such a performance has been before the Supreme Court on several occasions. In one case the evidence obtained was declared inadmissible in a federal criminal case against the person whose conversation had been tapped, but other evidence against another person was allowed to be used.

witch hunting: An investigation by a legislature or a committee created by it that tends to accept as facts evidence based on hearsay and innuendo that reflects on the character and integrity of those being investigated, affording them no opportunity for defense or explanation. Related to "guilt by association" (q.v.).

withholding tax: A method of taking a portion of a person's salary regularly and in advance, and then allowing credit for such deductions toward the final amount of the tax owed to the government when the individual files his full return. Allowances are made for dependents in the amount of the deductions so that there is some approximation to the ultimate amount due. If the individual has overpaid a refund is provided for.

women's suffrage: The right of women to vote in the United States was advocated by the suffragettes for years before it was obtained. The Western states were the leaders in this advance, Wyoming allowing the women in its state to vote as early as 1868, and Colorado and Idaho in 1890. It was granted to all the women of the country by the Nineteenth Amendment in 1920. World War II provided a great stimulus for the extension of women's suffrage to the rest of the world, Italy, France, and Japan permitting their women to vote in 1945.

workmen's compensation: Provision for payment to a worker in certain industries if he is hurt while on the job. The details as to amounts to be paid, usually scaled in accordance with the seriousness of his incapacity, and the length of time during which he is to receive payments, vary with the laws of the different states, practically every one of which has some provision for this purpose. There is no Federal legislation on this matter since control of intrastate labor conditions is a residual or state power. It is usual to have the employer carry insurance as a means of providing payments to the workers entitled to them. This may be done through a government fund, or by insurance with a private company, or by self-insurance.

writ: A formal written order issued by a court or other constituted authority commanding a person to perform or cease from doing a specific act. *See* WRIT OF HABEAS CORPUS.

writ of certiorari: *See* CERTIORARI.

writ of error: An order issued by an appellate court to a lower court to send the full record of the proceedings for examination. If error is discovered, especially if called attention to by the exceptions taken during the trial by the lawyers concerned, the decision rendered by the lower court may be reversed.

Y

Yalta Conference: A meeting of F. D. Roosevelt, Winston Churchill, and Stalin as heads of government in the Crimea, February 11, 1945. Besides agreeing on the continued military action against Germany they arranged for the post-war occupation of Germany in four zones, the payment of German reparations, governments for the liberated states of Poland and Yugoslavia, and the calling of a United Nations Conference at San Francisco the following April.

"Yankee Imperialism": A term used to denote disapproval with the foreign policy of the United States in applying the Roosevelt Corollary of the Monroe Doctrine in the early decades of the twentieth century toward our "little brothers" in Latin America. Our intervention in the internal affairs of our "veiled protectorates" of Haiti, Nicaragua, and Santo Domingo with the sending of marines on numerous occasions, and the official protectorate we established over Cuba by the Platt Amendment were felt by many Latin Americans to have been undertaken by the United States for the interest of its citizens rather than for them. This program was also belittled by the term "dollar diplomacy." Improvement in the tense situation started with the sending of Dwight D. Morrow to Mexico where with great tact and personal charm he helped to heal a serious breach in American-Mexican relations. The introduction of the "Good Neighbor Policy" improved the situation greatly after 1934. *See* INTER-AMERICAN COOPERATION.

"yardstick": A unit of measurement in which an attempt is made to compare the cost of certain services, such as the price of electricity as produced under one system, such as the Tennessee Valley Authority, with the price charged by a municipal power company, or a privately owned power company. Much controversy has arisen over using such comparisons because the units compared are not felt to be equal. The T.V.A. might write off some operational expenses as chargeable to navigation or flood control, and private concerns must include state and federal taxes, which T.V.A. does not have to meet, but which the consumer must make up indirectly.

"yellow-dog contract": An agreement between employer and employee by which the latter promises he will not join a union. The Norris-LaGuardia Act of 1932 held such an agreement unenforceable under the due process clause of the Fifth Amendment.

yellow journalism: The conspicuously playing up of the news in a sensational fashion to attract readers by appealing to their basest interests.

Young Plan: A committee under the chairmanship of Owen D. Young which proposed that Germany's reparation payments be radically reduced in 1929. However, the world depression caused all German payments to cease so the official program lapsed.

"Young Turks": An ambitious group of young Congressmen attempting to better fit themselves for their legislative job by meeting for discussion, pooling of research activities and listening to speeches. They were active in the middle thirties; the term, however, was revived for a similar group in the period before and after World War II who were feeling out their political strength. Though largely Democrats they stressed their independence of thought.

Z

zoning laws: With the great increase in the size and complexity of the modern city it became necessary to district the city into certain areas or zones for certain definite purposes. A residential zone would exclude industrial plants and mercantile establishments. Some zones were based on area or size, that is, restrictions were based upon how much of the actual building lot was covered, or restricted as to the height of the building. This latter requirement led to the development in our skyscrapers of some interesting patterns in "setbacks" after the minimum height for that zone had been reached.

BIBLIOGRAPHY CONSULTED

Anderson, William, and Weidner, E. *State and Local Government*. Henry Holt and Co., 1951, New York.
Bagley, William C., and Perdew, Richard. *Understanding Economics*. The Macmillan Co., New York, 1951.
Bailey, H. M., and Lazare, E. L., and Hawkins, C. H. *Your American Government*. Longmans, Green and Co., 1951.
Binkley, Wilfred, and Moos, Malcolm C. *A Grammar of American Politics*. Alfred A. Knopf, New York, 1949.
Blaich, Theodore P., and Baumgartner. *Challenge of Democracy*. Harper and Brothers, 1947.
Bliven, Bruce, and Mezerik, A. G., editors. *What the Informed Citizen Needs to Know*. Duell, Sloan and Pearce, New York, 1945.
Book of the States. 1950-1951. Vol. VIII. Council of State Governments.
Bowman, Mary, and Bach, George. *Economic Analysis and Public Policy*. Prentice-Hall, 1949.
Bryson, Lyman. *The Next America—Prophecy and Faith*. Harper and Brothers, New York, 1952.
Burns, James M. *Congress on Trial*. Harper and Brothers, 1949.
Carr, R. K., Morison, O. H., Bernstein, M. H., Synder, R. C. *American Democracy in Theory and Practice*. Rinehart and Co. Inc., New York, 1951.
Casselman, P. H. *Labor Dictionary*. Philosophical Library, 1949.
Cochran, Thomas C., and Miller, William. *The Age of Enterprise*. The Macmillan Company, New York, 1947.
Cook, Franklin. *Principles of Business and Law*. The Macmillan Company, 1951.
Daugherty, Carral R. *Labor Problems in American Industry*. Houghton Mifflin Co., 1949.
Dimock, Marshall E., and Dimock, Gladys O. *American Government in Action*. Rinehart and Company, New York, 1951.
Dulles, Foster Rhea. *Labor in America*. Thomas Y. Crowell Co., New York, 1949.
Fainsod, Merle, and Gordon, Lincoln. *Government and the American Economy*. W. W. Norton and Co., 1948.

BIBLIOGRAPHY CONSULTED

Faulkner, H. U. *American Economic History*, sixth edition. Harper and Brothers, New York, 1949.

Ferguson, John H., and McHenry, Dean E. *American Federal Government*. McGraw-Hill Book Co., 1950.

Gosnell, Cullen B., and Holland, Lynwood M. *State and Local Government in the United States*. Prentice-Hall, New York, 1951.

Griffith, Ernest. *Congress—Its Contemporary Role*. New York University Press, 1951.

Gunther, John. *Inside U.S.A*. Harper and Brothers, New York, 1947.

Harbison, Fred, and Coleman, John. *Goals and Strategy in Collective Bargaining*. Harper and Brothers, 1951.

Horton, Byrne, with Ripley, Julian, and Schnapper, M. B. *Dictionary of Modern Economics*. Public Affairs Press, Washington, D. C., 1948.

Huberman, Leo. *We, the People*. Harper and Brothers, Revised edition, 1947.

Johnson, Claudius O. *American National Government*. Thomas Y. Crowell Co., 1951.

Key, V. O. *Politics, Parties and Pressure Groups*. Thomas Y. Crowell Co., 1950.

Kinneman, John A. *The Community in American Society*. Appleton-Century-Crofts, Inc., New York, 1947.

Lavine, A. L., and Mandel, M. *Business Law for Everyday Use*. John C. Winston Co., 1947.

Magruder, Frank. *American Government*. Allyn and Bacon, 1950.

McLaughlin, Andrew G., and Hart, A. B., editors. *Cyclopedia of American Government*. Peter Smith, New York, 1949.

Millis, Harry, and Brown, Emily. *From Wagner Act to Taft-Hartley*. University of Chicago Press, 1950.

Mund, Vernon A. *Government and Business*. Harper and Brothers, New York, 1950.

Nash, B. D., and Lynde, C. *A Hook in Leviathan*. Macmillan Co., 1950.

Nevins, Allan, and Krout, John A., editors. *The Greater City—New York 1898-1948*. Columbia University Press, 1948.

Ogg, Frederic A., and Ray, P. Orman. *Essentials of American Government*. Appleton-Century-Crofts Inc., 1950.

Penniman, Howard. *Sait's American Parties and Elections*. Appleton-Century-Crofts, Inc., New York, 1948.

Riddick, Floyd. *United States Congress and Procedure*. National Capital Publishers Inc., 1949.

Schlesinger, Arthur. *The Vital Center—Politics of Freedom*. Houghton, Mifflin Co., Boston, 1949.

Schriftgiesser, Karl. *This Was Normalcy*. Little, Brown and Company, Boston, 1948.

Theimer, Walter. *An Encyclopedia of Modern World Politics*. Rinehart and Co., New York, 1950.

Tourtellot, Arthur B. *An Anatomy of American Politics*. Bobbs-Merrill Company, New York, 1950.

Voorhis, Jerry. *Confessions of a Congressman*. Doubleday and Company, New York, 1947.

Walker, Harvey. *The Legislative Process*. Ronald Press Company, New York, 1948.

White, Wilbur. *White's Political Dictionary*. The World Publishing Co., 1947.

Wilson, H. H. *Congress: Corruption and Compromise*. Rinehart and Company, Inc., New York, 1951.

Young, Louise. *Understanding Politics*. Pellegrini and Cudahy, 1950.

Zink, Harold. *Government and Politics in the United States*. Macmillan Co., 1951.

Zink, Howard. *Government of Cities in the United States*. Macmillan Co., 1939.